JAPANESE IN MANGALAND

LEARNING THE BASICS

Marc Bernabe

Prefaces:

Yoshito Usui
Shigeko Suzuki
James W. Heisig

Cover illustration:
Núria Peris

Inside illustrations:
Ken Niimura
Mary Molina
Guillermo March
Studio Kōsen

Japanese in MangaLand
Learning The Basics
By Marc Bernabe

Published and distributed: Japan Publications Trading Co.,Ltd.
                              1-2-1 Sarugaku-cho, Chiyoda-ku, Tokyo 101-0064, Japan.

First printing: *February* 2004
Second printing: February 2005

Overseas Distributors:
UNITED STATES:
  Kodansha America, Inc. through Oxford University Press,
  198 Madison Avenue, New York, NY 10016.
CANADA:
  Fitzhenry & Whiteside Ltd., 195 Allstate Parkway, Markham,
  Ontario L3R 4T8.
AUSTRALIA and NEW ZEALAND:
  Bookwise International Pty Ltd.,
  174 Cormack Road, Wingfield, South Australia 5013, Australia.
ASIA, EUROPE and JAPAN:
  Japan Publications Trading Co., Ltd., 1-2-1 Sarugaku-cho,
  Chiyoda-ku, Tokyo 101-0064, Japan.

ISBN 13:9-784889-961157
ISBN 10:4-88996-115-1

Printed in Spain

For Vero

臼井儀人からの挨拶

　近年、日本のマンガとアニメはアジア諸国だけでなく、欧米にも大きく普及しつつあるという現象は徐々に確かになっています。恐縮ですが、自分の作品を例として挙げましょう。「クレヨンしんちゃん」はマンガの形で既にカタロニア語・スペイン語・ドイツ語・英語など、色々な言語に翻訳されています。そして、自分のマンガを基に作られたテレビアニメの方はそれ以上に世界中のテレビ局で放送され、そのお陰で世界中の人たちに親しまれているということがなんとなく分かるようになりました。例えば、最近スペインのカタロニア州からこの日本に来たコンテストに当選された3人の読者に会え、わりと長く話をしました。そのお陰で、私の作品を本当によく読んでくださっているということがはっきりと理解できたと思います。彼らは「クレヨンしんちゃん」とその他の日本の作品をマンガで読んで、テレビで見てから私の生まれ育ちの国、この日本に「どうしても行きたいな、もっと日本の文化と言語について知りたいな」と考えるようになったらしいのです。やっと、コンテストに当選し、夢が叶ったようですね。彼らに会うことは私にとっても非常に勉強になりました。彼らの笑顔は一生忘れることはないと思います。

　しかし、もっと深く彼らに話を伺ったら、彼らだけでなく、そして「クレヨンしんちゃん」だけでなく、多くの欧米の若者が色々な日本マンガとアニメに刺激され、それを通じて日本についてもっと知りたくなるという日本人にとって信じがたいかもしれない現象が存在するそうです。このような小さな「マンガ革命」の中で、せっかく多くの若者がマンガとアニメの影響でもっと日本について知りたいのに日本のことを紹介している殆どの本は若者にとって硬くてつまらないと聞いています。しかし、最近は私の友達、マルク・ベルナベが書いた「Japanese in MangaLand」のような本が出たお陰で、やっとこのギャップを埋め始めているらしいです。誰でも「楽しみながら学べる」という概念を基に作られたこの一冊の日本語講座の挨拶をさせていただきました。マルクみたいな面白くて楽しい人が書いたので、きっと誰でも楽しめる本です。是非、この本を読んで、日本語を学んで、楽しんで、自分の夢を叶えてください。

臼井儀人

【漫画家・主な作品は「クレヨンしんちゃん（双葉社）」他】

Greetings from Yoshito Usui

In recent years, Japanese manga and anime are no doubt becoming increasingly popular not only in Asian countries but in Europe and America as well. Please excuse me for giving my own work as an example. "Shin-chan," in its manga form, has already been translated into several languages, such as Catalan, Spanish, German, and English. And now, the TV anime based on my work is being shown on TV channels worldwide, therefore allowing me to fraternize with people from all over the world. For instance, I recently met three of my readers who had won a contest in Catalonia, Spain, and come to Japan, and we had a quite long conversation. Through this conversation, I came to clearly understand how my works are actually being read. Apparently, having read "Shin-chan" and other Japanese manga, as well as having watched the anime on TV, they had been "willing to learn more about Japanese culture and language, and been dying to come to Japan," the country were I was born and grew up. At last, they won the contest and their dream came true. Meeting them was a great experience for me too. I don't think I will ever forget their smiling faces.

However, following a deeper conversation with them, it became clear that not only them, and not only "Shin-chan," but many young people from Europe and America are thrilled by manga and anime of different kinds, so thrilled in fact that they want to learn more about Japan, a phenomenon which may be hard to believe for the Japanese. In this small "manga revolution," even though many young people, influenced by manga and anime, want to learn about Japan, I have heard most books introducing Japan are hard and boring for the young. Nevertheless, owing to the recent publication of books like my friend Marc Bernabe's "Japanese in MangaLand," it seems this gap is finally being filled up. I have been asked to introduce this Japanese course, a book based on the idea that anybody "can learn while having fun." Since it has been written by such an interesting and fun person as Marc, I am sure it will be a book anybody can enjoy. Please read this book, learn and enjoy Japanese, and fulfill your dreams to the end.

Yoshito Usui
(Mangaka, his main work is "Shin-chan.")

Introducing the book and its author
By Shigeko Suzuki

Shigeko Suzuki has presented us with a wonderful introduction for this book, which all students and would-be students of Japanese should read extremely carefully. Shigeko Suzuki, apart from having been the first Japanese teacher the author of this book had is a renowned translator and interpreter, both from Spanish into Japanese and vice versa, as well as being a wonderful person. Thank you, Shige!

When the subject of Japanese language arises, the first thing you hear are remarks such as: Oh, it's really difficult and complicated!... not to mention ideograms, you must learn them all by heart!

Traditionally, Japanese was learned memorizing both grammar and writing, making use in that task of all the patience of Job. Then, about twenty years ago, audiovisual teaching methods were introduced, trying to help achieve the understanding of the global Japanese language, written as well as spoken, through the use of tapes and videotapes. Nowadays, the approach to Japanese has been given another turn with the development of the computer world and all its derivatives, such as CD-ROM, the Internet, and so on.

And now, Marc Bernabe has written a book devoted to the teaching of Japanese, dealing with it in a completely new way: through "manga." Now, this really is an innovation! It brings fresh air to the area of Japanese language teaching! About time a book like this came out! Considering the popularity of this genre, specially among young people, the publishing of something of this sort has come as a natural and necessary thing.

Using manga as a basis, this book makes the access to Japanese language easier, and the course of its learning more enjoyable. The visualization of its content with the already familiar figures permits its quick understanding, thus overcoming the legend: "Japanese language = difficult."

Moreover, when choosing his educational material, the author has taken a very flexible approach, a true reflection of himself, keeping those key elements in the traditional method. Which means the book doesn't fall to the level of a superficial handbook, seeking only to entertain, but carries weight in itself.

I love to see the progress made by those boys and girls who not so long ago moved restlessly in the classrooms. Apart from having a great gift for Japanese, Marc was "crazy about manga." That seed has now become a young plant breathing with all its might, and it will keep on growing until it becomes a strong and solid tree. I am convinced he will manage to make all those dreams come true, as twelfth-century Kenko Hoshi said in his essay *Tsurezuregusa* "When someone is good at something, it's because he loves it."

Shigeko Suzuki
Interpreter and Professor of Japanese Language and Culture
Faculty of Translation and Interpreting
UNIVERSITAT AUTÒNOMA DE BARCELONA

Preface, by Marc Bernabe

It is possible that some readers of this book, not acquainted with the manga and anime world (Japanese comic books and animation), will wonder why panels from Japanese comic-books have been chosen to illustrate the lessons.

The first reason is that the lessons that make up this course were originally published in a well known Japanese comic book and animation magazine in Spain. When Mary Molina, the magazine's editor-in-chief at the time, asked me to produce a monthly Japanese course, I thought a Japanese course in a manga and anime magazine should somehow be in line with the general subject matter of the magazine. Following the example of the famous lessons in the no longer existing American magazine *Mangajin*, where every month a linguistic subject was explained using manga panels as examples, I managed to find the formula, which consisted in developing a course in Japanese with a clear structure: a page of theory, which always had vocabulary and grammar tables so as to make it more visual and convenient for the reader, and a second page with examples taken directly from Japanese manga, which would illustrate and expand what had just been explained in the theory. In fact, the idea worked perfectly well, and the course became the longest-lived among those published in manga magazines (it lasted more than two years, appearing in every issue of the monthly magazine), and it received many demonstrations of support from the readers.

The second reason is that manga is a real phenomenon, not only in Japan, its country of origin, but also in the rest of the world, where it has gradually been spreading and becoming increasingly popular and accessible.

The word "manga" literally means "spontaneous and meaningless drawings", and is used in Japan when referring to comic books. By extension, the West has adopted this word with the meaning of "Japanese comic book." However, the popularity of manga in Japan cannot be compared with anything similar in Western countries. There, the manga phenomenon could just as easily find its equivalent in films or some popular sport. A manga author can charge a remarkable amount of money per page drawn. Here are a few illustrative data:

a) In 2001, 38.2% of all books and magazines published in Japan were manga, producing 22.9% of the total benefits of the publishing industry of Japan, according to the 2002 Shuppan Shihyō Nenpō (Annual Publishing Index).

b) Weekly manga magazines have amazing print-runs. It is not rare in the Japanese market to have weekly manga magazines selling over a million copies every week. For instance, in 2001, *Shōnen Magazine* and *Shōnen Jump* sold an average of 3.5 million copies weekly… Nothing compared to the 6.5 million weekly attained by *Shōnen Jump* in its golden age of the end of the 80s and the beginning of the 90s.

c) The industry manga has given rise to cannot be ignored: cartoons or anime, now a great success throughout the world, are a clear example.

There are manga of all kind of interests, plots, artistic styles, and for all ages and social strata. There are manga for young people, teenagers, housewives, laborers, office workers, even erotic and pornographic manga, and so on. In Japan, manga is not only for children… In fact, everybody in Japan reads or has read manga, and their culture is obviously influenced by it.

Manga is not only science fiction, violence and blood shedding, in fact there is ALL kind of manga, but those that reach the West are mostly the violent type, which has contributed to create a distorted view of what manga really is. Personally, I recommend reading Osamu Tezuka's works, for instance, to understand manga can be an authentic art.

From my point of view, the idea that "all manga are the same," speaking in terms of graphics, is another mistake. In the West, when we talk about manga, the image we immediately have is that of slender people with huge and shiny eyes. Many manga certainly have that kind of aesthetic, but all you need to do is take a look at authors like Naoki Urasawa, with his realistic style, or at a series like *Crayon Shin-chan*, in which characters appear completely deformed. And there are countless other examples.

Manga are originally published in thick, cheap weekly magazines, at around 20 pages per week; *Shōnen Magazine*, *Shōnen Jump*, *Big Comics*, *Shōnen Sunday*, and a long list of other magazines are among the most wellknown. When a series is successful, it's usually compiled into a volume of about 200 pages (compiled of about 10 or 11 chapters previously published in a weekly magazine) called *tankōbon*, which is how it usually reaches Western readers who get hold of manga in Japanese.

All in all, manga is a very important phenomenon in Japan. Through these comic books we can learn Japanese and, as important or even more so, we can learn a lot about Japanese culture and idiosyncrasy. I can tell you it is most interesting...

I truly hope this book will help you learn both the Japanese language and about the culture. It is a great honor for me to be your *sensei*.

Thank you very much!

Marc Bernabe

How to use this book and its structure

This book is directed at the study of the Japanese used in manga, so that the reader can, after its intensive study, get to understand a children's Japanese comic-book in Japanese, with the obvious help of a good dictionary.

The understanding of Japanese in manga being the aim of the course, the reader will find there are many aspects of the Japanese language that are not usually explained in "normal" courses. We will study distinctive features in the informal oral language, like, for instance, the different personal pronouns (Lesson 7), emphatic particles at the end of sentences (Lesson 17), or verbs in their simple form, which are not usually studied until a more advanced level in the "orthodox" study of the language (Lesson 20).

The main body of the book consists of thirty lessons, clearly structured in three parts:

A) **Theory.** This part deals with a written explanation of the lesson's subject. There are usually one or two grammar or vocabulary tables which help summarize and comprehend what has been explained.

B) **Manga-examples.** Examples originally taken from Japanese manga, which have been specially redesigned for this book, without changing the text. They are used to illustrate and expand what has been previously explained in the theory pages. In this part, a system inspired by the lessons from the now defunct American magazine *Mangajin* has been used to better illustrate the language structure. The following is an example:

> この本はとても面白いですね。
> *kono hon wa totemo omoshiroi desu ne*
> this book SP very interesting EP
> **This book is very interesting, isn't it?**

First line. Exact transcription of the bubble's original Japanese.
Second line. Text's transcription into the Western alphabet (*rōmaji*).
Third line. Literal translation, word for word. The meaning of the different abbreviations can be found in the glossary.
Fourth line. Recommended translation into English.

C) **Exercises.** These are always related to the lesson's subject, and the answers can always be obtained or deduced from the content of the lesson to which they refer. The right answers to the exercises can be found at the end of the book.

A small dictionary of one hundred and sixty basic Japanese characters (kanji), with five compound words each, has been added after the thirty lessons. The study of these characters can provide a very solid basis for the subsequent in-depth study of the language.

Likewise, a glossary with all the words which have appeared throughout the lessons is given at the end of the book.

We also offer the reader a web page with information on the project "Japanese in MangaLand," as well as information on the misprints that may arise. This is the address:

http://www.nipoweb.com/eng

Glossary

Common expressions:	Groups of words with a more cultural meaning rather than a lexical one.
Counters:	They are used to indicate number, because Japanese nouns are invariable (Lesson 25).
Furigana:	Small hiragana characters which tell you how to read kanji, and which are placed next to the corresponding kanji.
Gion:	Sound imitating words, similar to our onomatopoeias.
Gitaigo:	Words which describe physical states or moods.
Hiragana:	One of two Japanese syllabaries, together with katakana. It's used to write strictly Japanese words (Lesson 1).
"i" adjective:	One of two kinds of Japanese adjectives, together with the "na" adjective. This adjective always ends in *i* (Lesson 13).
Imperative:	Conjugation used to give orders.
Kanji:	Ideograms originally taken from Chinese, with which most common words and proper nouns are written (Lesson 3).
Katakana:	Together with hiragana, the second Japanese syllabary. It's used to write foreign words and onomatopoeias (Lesson 2).
–*masu* form:	Formal verb conjugation. This form always ends in *masu* (Lesson 19).
"na" adjective:	The second kind of adjective, together with the "i" adjective. It always ends in *na* (Lesson 14).
Particles:	Hiragana characters which either indicate the function of the word they follow (subject, direct object, adverbial of time/place…) (Lesson 16), or add a certain nuance at the end of the sentence (Lesson 17).
Rōmaji:	Western characters (our alphabet).
Simple or dictionary form:	Informal verb conjugation. It is used in dictionaries (Lesson 20).
–*suru* verb:	Kind of verb which consists of *noun+suru* (Lesson 24).
Topic:	Indicates "what is important in a sentence," "what the sentence is about."

ABBREVIATIONS USED IN MANGA-EXAMPLES

Emph.:	Emphatic.	**CP:**	Company Particle. Ex.: *to.*
Excl.:	Exclamation.	**DOP:**	Direct Object Particle. Shows the previous word
Fem. Emph.:	Feminine emphatic.		is a DO. Ex: *o* (Lesson 16).
Imp.:	Imperative.	**DP:**	Direction Particle. Ex.: *e* (Lesson 16).
Masc. Emph.:	Masculine emphatic.	**EP:**	Emphatic Particle. Most end-of-sentence
Neg.:	Negation, negative.		particles state emphasis or add a certain nuance.
Past:	Past tense.		Ex.: *ne, yo, zo…* (Lesson 16).
Q?:	Interrogative particle. Shows the previous	**ID:**	Indirect Object Particle. Ex.: *ni.*
	sentence is a question. Ex.: *ka* (Lesson 16).	**PoP:**	Possessive Particle. Ex.: *no* (Lesson 16).
Ques.:	Question.	**PP:**	Place Particle. Ex.: *de, ni* (Lesson 16).
Rel.:	Relative.	**SP:**	Subject Particle. Ex.: *ga*
Suf.:	Suffix.	**ToP:**	Topic Particle. Shows the previous word is the
Noun Suf.:	Suffix for proper names (people), (Lesson 15).		topic in the sentence. Ex.: *wa* (Lesson 16).
Vulg.:	Vulgarism.	**TP:**	Time Particle. Ex.: *ni.*

Marc Bernabe was born in L'Ametlla del Vallès, Barcelona, in 1976, and is a Universitat Autònoma de Barcelona graduate in Translation and Interpreting, which he studied at the same time as Japanese Language and Culture at the Kyoto University of Foreign Studies. He is presently working as a Japanese-Spanish translator. He is behind the Spanish adaptation of the Japanese kanji course *Kanji para recordar* (Herder, 2001), together with **James W. Heisig** and **Verònica Calafell**. He is also the author of *Apuntes de Japón* (Glénat, 2002), and creator of www.nipoweb.com.

JAPANESE IN MANGALAND

LEARNING THE BASICS

Marc Bernabe

Lesson 1: Hiragana

We are going to start this Japanese course with the writing system. We are obviously talking about those "scribblings" which many of you wonder about. Japanese writing is fundamental for the correct learning of the language, because textbooks in rōmaji —that is, written in the Western alphabet— are useful, but eventually inadequate.

The syllabaries

In Japanese there is no such thing as a real alphabet as we know it. Instead, there are two syllabaries called hiragana and katakana. A Japanese character usually equals a two-letter syllable in English. Thus, the character か is read ka. Both hiragana and katakana have 46 syllabic symbols — each symbol in one syllabary has an exact equivalent in pronunciation (but not, of course, in writing) in the other. For instance, the hiragana character ち and the katakana character チ are both read *chi*. This may seem very strange, but is less so when you think that we have a very similar system too: upper-case and lower-case letters. Try thinking about the purely formal similarity between "a" and "A," or between "g" and "G." Do they look the same?

Japanese also has kanji — ideograms taken from Chinese about 1,600 years ago, which represent concepts rather than sounds. There are many kanji (an estimated number of more than 50,000) but "only" 3,000, more or less, are actually used.

The subject in this first lesson is the hiragana syllabary, undoubtedly the most basic and essential for learning the basis of the Japanese language.

Writing

First, we must point out that Japanese can be written in Western style, that is, horizontally and from left to right, as well as traditionally, that is vertically and from right to left. Most of the time, manga tend to use the traditional style. However, both methods are generally used in Japan nowadays, with perhaps a slight predominance of the Western style.

But, in almost all printed material, books, magazines, and manga, is read "backwards." Therefore, in Japanese books, the front cover is placed where we would usually find the back cover, and that is why they are read right to left, just the opposite to Western books. If you think about it, that is not so odd. Arabic books, for that matter, are also opened Japanese style. Japanese punctuation marks are different from Western ones. A period is written with a small circle (。) and the coma is written upside down (、). The reason for this is that punctuation marks didn't exist in Japanese before Western influence. All these marks were imported from Western languages to make reading easier. We mentioned earlier that there is no alphabet strictly speaking, but rather signs that represent syllables, that is, combinations of consonant and vowel, with one exception: the letter "n" is the only consonant to go on its own.

Both syllabaries have the same number of signs, and they are equivalent – there are two different signs for each syllabic combination. For instance, the syllable *ko* can be written either こ (in hiragana) or コ (in katakana.)

Hiragana

After that brief but illustrative general introduction to Japanese, we will go fully into the subject we are dealing with in this first lesson: the hiragana syllabary.

日本語ひらがな五十音表												
Full list of hiragana characters												
あ a	い i	う u	え e	お o								
か ka	き ki	く ku	け ke	こ ko	が ga	ぎ gi	ぐ gu	げ ge	ご go	きゃ kya	きゅ kyu	きょ kyo
										ぎゃ gya	ぎゅ gyu	ぎょ gyo
さ sa	し shi	す su	せ se	そ so	ざ za	じ ji	ず zu	ぜ ze	ぞ zo	しゃ sha	しゅ shu	しょ sho
										じゃ ja	じゅ ju	じょ jo
た ta	ち chi	つ tsu	て te	と to	だ da	ぢ ji	づ zu	で de	ど do	ちゃ cha	ちゅ chu	ちょ cho
な na	に ni	ぬ nu	ね ne	の no						にゃ nya	にゅ nyu	にょ nyo
は ha	ひ hi	ふ fu	へ he	ほ ho	ば ba	び bi	ぶ bu	べ be	ぼ bo	ひゃ hya	ひゅ hyu	ひょ hyo
										びゃ bya	びゅ byu	びょ byo
					ぱ pa	ぴ pi	ぷ pu	ぺ pe	ぽ po	ぴゃ pya	ぴゅ pyu	ぴょ pyo
ま ma	み mi	む mu	め me	も mo						みゃ mya	みゅ myu	みょ myo
や ya		ゆ yu		よ yo								
ら ra	り ri	る ru	れ re	ろ ro						りゃ rya	りゅ ryu	りょ ryo
わ wa				を wo								
ん n												

The hiragana syllabary is the most important and most used of the two, because it is used to write strictly Japanese words. When a word has no kanji or if the author doesn't remember the corresponding kanji, hiragana is used. Likewise, particles (Lesson 16) and verb endings are written in hiragana.

Hiragana is what Japanese children learn first, therefore, all children's reading books are entirely written in that syllabary. Later, as children increase their knowledge, katakana and kanji are introduced.

Syllabary description

There are 46 basic sounds, which are placed in the first column of the above syllabary. In the second column we see the list of impure sounds –derived from other sounds. Note that the *ka* か syllable is the same as *ga* が, but *ga* has two small lines on the top right-hand corner of the sign; the same applies when we go from the *s* line to the *z* one, from *t* to *d*, and from *h* to *b*.

To go from *h* to *p* we must place a small circle on top of the character. は (ha) → ぱ (pa).

In the third column, we see the combinations of the characters in the *i* column (*ki* き, *gi* ぎ, *shi* し, etc.) with those in the *y* line (*ya* や, *yu* ゆ, *yo* よ), the later ones written in a smaller size. These combinations are used to represent more complex sounds, such as *cha* ちゃ, *hyo* ひょ, or *gyu* ぎゅ.

You have probably noticed that there are two *ji* sounds (じ and ぢ) and two *zu* sounds (ず and づ). There are no differences in pronunciation, but their usage is different. For the time being, let's say that, overwhelmingly, most of the time we will use ず and じ, hardly ever the other two.

There is no letter "l" in Japanese. Whenever we need to write a foreign word with the letter "l" in it, we will have to replace it with an "r." Lance, for example, would be pronounced Ransu. It is a completely different aspect from Chinese, and its causes very serious misunderstandings. How often have we heard someone trying to be funny and using the "l" to talk like a Japanese?

But don't worry about it for the moment, because we will never use hiragana to transcribe our names into Japanese. We will see more about this in Lessons 2 and 8.

Pronunciation

Japanese is pronounced with really few sounds, all of them very simple and basic. Thus, it can pose a problem for English speakers because sounds in English are rather "complicated" or "twisted." Let's have a look. In Japanese we pronounce:

The "a" as in "cat."
The "i" as in "bin" or "deer."
The "u" as in "juice."
The "e" as in "Henry."
The "o" as in "lot."
The "g" is always pronounced as in "get" and never as in "gentle."
The "r" is always pronounced the Spanish fashion (not the rolling one, don't worry). It's somewhat between the "l" and the "r" and can be the most difficult sound to get right. Examples in Spanish: "Sonora," "Merida."
The "ch" as in "church."
The "tsu" as the tz-u part of "Ritz Uruguay."

Hiragana

a	一	さ	あ		*su*	一	す	
i	し	い			*se*	一	せ	
u	ニ	う			*so*	そ		
e	ニ	ゑ			*ta*	一	ナ	た	た
o	二	お	お		*chi*	一	ち	
ka	ラ	カ	が		*tsu*	つ		
ki	二	二	き	き	*te*	て		
ku	く				*to*	と		
ke	レ	に	け		*na*	一	ナ	が	な
ko	ラ	こ			*ni*	レ	に	に
sa	一	さ	さ		*nu*	し	ぬ	
shi	し				*ne*	ー	ね	

no	の				yu	ゆ	ゆ	
ha	㇏	に	は		yo	㇈	よ	
hi	ひ				ra	㇉	ら	り
fu	㇉	ふ	ふ	ふ	ri	㇑	り	
he	へ				ru	る		
ho	㇑	に	に	ほ	re	㇑	れ	
ma	㇐	ㇸ	ま		ro	ろ		
mi	み	み			wa	㇑	わ	
mu	㇐	む	む		wo	㇈	を	を
me	㇏	め			n	ん		
mo	し	も	も					
ya	㇈	㇅	や					

漫画例：*Manga-examples*

We are now going to see some examples of hiragana in use. We will always see examples inspired by real Japanese manga to illustrate what has been explained in the theory pages.

a) Yawn

Katsuko:	ふわあっ。
	fuwaa...
	(Onomatopoeia for yawn)

This first example shows us Katsuko saying: *fuwaa...* This onomatopoeia's meaning is obvious, isn't it? The small *tsu* character at the end of the exclamation means the sound stops abruptly, that is, it ends sharply.

You can practice your skill reading hiragana in any manga. There are plenty of onomatopoeias written in hiragana, and recognizing them is already a very satisfactory first step.

b) Laughing

Mifumi: あはははははははははははは。
Ehahahahahahahahahaha...
(Onomatopoeia for laugh)

Tatsuhiko: ヘヘヘヘヘヘヘヘヘヘヘ。
Ehehehehehehehehehe...
(Onomatopoeia for laugh)

Here we see Tatsuhiko and Mifumi the instant they meet. Their reaction is most curious. Onomatopoeias for sounds issued by manga characters (laughs, doubts, screams...) are usually written in hiragana, unlike sounds caused by human acts, things and animals (barks, explosions, blows...), which are usually written in katakana, as we will see in Lesson 2.

c) Mix of hiragana, katakana and kanji

Tarō: わしよりハンサムなのは杉本明だけだ。
washi yori hansamu na no wa
sugimoto akira dake da
I more handsome than sugimoto
akira only be
Only Akira Sugimoto is more handsome than me.

Sugimoto: わーい　ありがと。ヘヘヘ…。
waai arigato he he he...
cool! thanks he he he
Well, thanks! He, he, he.

(*Washi* = I (for older people) / *yori* = more than / *hansamu-na* = handsome (from the English word) / *dake* = only / *da* = verb "to be", simple form / *arigato* = thanks)

This last example scarcely bears any relation to the rest of this first lesson. It shows us one of the most curious characteristics of the Japanese language. We are talking about the use in the same sentence of the three Japanese writing forms: the hiragana and katakana syllabaries and kanji. Note that the whole text is written in hiragana, apart from *hansamu* (ハンサム) —which comes from English and is, therefore, written in katakana (L. 2)— and *Sugimoto Akira* (杉本明), written in kanji —with the corresponding kanji reading above in *furigana*.

Note: Sugimoto's T-shirt says aho, which means "stupid" (Lesson 23).

1 Does the Japanese language use an alphabet, strictly speaking? How many Western letters is a hiragana sign usually equivalent to when transcribed?

2 What kind of signs do we use to write Japanese (3 kinds)?

3 How are manga's text usually written, horizontally and from left to right (Western style) or vertically and from right to left (traditional style)?

4 What do we use the hiragana syllabary for?

5 Write in Japanese the following syllables: *te*, *mu*, *i* and *sa*.

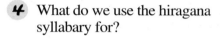

6 Transcribe into English the following hiragana signs: に, る, き and え.

7 Write in Japanese the impure syllables *de*, *pi*, *da* and *za*.

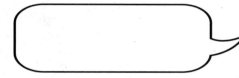

8 Transcribe into English the following hiragana: ぶ, ず, ぱ and じ.

9 How do we form complex sounds such as *cha*, *hyo*, *jo*? Write them in Japanese.

10 How do we pronounce in Japanese the "g" in "Sugimoto"? Like the "g" in "get" or like the "g" in "gentle?"

第②課：カタカナ

Lesson 2: Katakana

In Lesson 1 we saw how hiragana is used to write strictly Japanese native words. So, what do we use katakana for? Katakana has a rather limited use, and in fact Japanese children learn hiragana first, and then, in good time, they learn katakana. But learning this syllabary is essential to read Japanese. Especially if you like Japanese comics, because this syllabary is very often used there.

Foreign words

Basically, katakana is used to write foreign words which have been previously adapted to the rather poor Japanese phonetics. Thus, "computer" becomes *konpyūtā* コンピューター, "part-time work" becomes *arubaito* アルバイト, and "prêt-à-porter" becomes *puretaporute* プレタポルテ. The previous examples come from English (computer), German (Arbeit), and French (prêt-à-porter), although there are also examples from Portuguese (パン, from *pan*, "bread") and Spanish (カッパ, from *capa*, "cloak"). It is important to state 11% of Japanese words are foreign expressions, and most of them come from English, so speaking English is a great advantage. Such an enormous proportion of foreign expressions cannot be found in any other language in the world. Besides, katakana is often used for onomatopoeias in manga, so finding words written in katakana on the pages of any comic-book is extremely frequent.

People's names

All non-Japanese people's and place names —names of cities or geographic places— must be written in katakana. First of all, the sounds of the word we want to write in Japanese must be transcribed into Japanese phonetics. The main problem is Japanese has no individual consonant sounds —apart from the *n*. Therefore, for each consonant on its own, we will add a "u", except in the case of "t" and "d", where we will add an *o*. Thus, yours truly's name (Marc) would become *Maruku* マルク, Sandra would become *Sandora* サンドラ, and Alfred would become *Arufureddo* アルフレッド (remember "l" doesn't exist and must be replaced with an "r"). We will expand on the subject of foreign name conversion into katakana in Lesson 8.

Short and long vowels

Now we'll explain some particularities of the two syllabaries. In the previous lesson, we left some hiragana characteristics aside —most of which can be applied to katakana as well— which we will now explain. We are talking about long vowels and double sounds. Long vowels, as their name suggests, are pronounced for a little longer. This subtle difference is very important in such a phonetically poor language as Japanese, since the difference between *kūso* (empty, vain) and *kuso* (literally, "shit") is based on this distinction.

So you need to be very careful with your pronunciation if you go to Japan and try to speak some Japanese. To indicate vowel lengthening we will write a hiragana "u" after "o" and "u." Ex.: *kūso*, くうそ, *gakkō* がっこう, which is not pronounced "gakkow" but "gakkoh." Throughout this course we will use a dash on top of "u" and "o" to indicate this lengthening. In katakana we will use a dash. Ex: New York, *Nyūyōku* ニューヨーク, Madrid, *Madorīdo* マドリード.

Double sounds

Double sounds are consonants that have a longer and more abrupt sound than normal ones. This effect is indicated by a small *tsu* っ character before the consonant to be doubled, both in hiragana and katakana. Ex.: しゅっぱつ *shuppatsu* (starting, departure) / きっさてん *kissaten* (coffee shop) / ラケット *raketto* (from English "racket") / マッサージ *massāji* (from English "massage".)

Some basic vocabulary

Yes (*hai*) はい
No (*iie*) いいえ
Good morning (*ohayō gozaimasu*)
おはようございます
Good afternoon (*konnichi wa*) こんにちは
Good evening (*konban wa*) こんばんは
Thank you (*arigatō*) ありがとう
You're welcome (*dō itashimashite*) どういたしまして

Goodbye (*sayōnara*) さようなら
Please (*dōzo*) どうぞ
That's right (*sō desu*) そうです
I understand (*wakarimashita*)
わかりました
I don't understand (*wakarimasen*)
わかりません
Excuse me (*sumimasen*) すみません

日本語カタカナ五十音表
Full list of katakana characters

ア a	イ i	ウ u	エ e	オ o						キャ kya	キュ kyu	キョ kyo
カ ka	キ ki	ク ku	ケ ke	コ ko	ガ ga	ギ gi	グ gu	ゲ ge	ゴ go	ギャ gya	ギュ gyu	ギョ gyo
サ sa	シ shi	ス su	セ se	ソ so	ザ za	ジ ji	ズ zu	ゼ ze	ゾ zo	シャ sha	シュ shu	ショ sho
										ジャ ja	ジュ ju	ジョ jo
タ ta	チ chi	ツ tsu	テ te	ト to	ダ da	ヂ ji	ヅ zu	デ de	ド do	チャ cha	チュ chu	チョ cho
ナ na	ニ ni	ヌ nu	ネ ne	ノ no						ニャ nya	ニュ nyu	ニョ nyo
ハ ha	ヒ hi	フ fu	ヘ he	ホ ho	バ ba	ビ bi	ブ bu	ベ be	ボ bo	ヒャ hya	ヒュ hyu	ヒョ hyo
										ビャ bya	ビュ byu	ビョ byo
					パ pa	ピ pi	プ pu	ペ pe	ポ po	ピャ pya	ピュ pyu	ピョ pyo
マ ma	ミ mi	ム mu	メ me	モ mo						ミャ mya	ミュ myu	ミョ myo
ヤ ya		ユ yu		ヨ yo								
ラ ra	リ ri	ル ru	レ re	ロ ro						リャ rya	リュ ryu	リョ ryo
ワ wa				ヲ wo								
ン n												

Characters only found in katakana						
ヴァ va	ヴィ vi	ヴ vu	ヴェ ve		ピャ pya	ピュ pyu	ピョ pyo
ファ fa	フィ fi	フォ fo	フェ fe		シェ she	ジェ je	チェ che

Katakana

a	ァ	ア			*su*	ヲ	ス		
i	ノ	イ			*se*	ヲ	セ		
u	゛	゛	ウ		*so*	゛	ソ		
e	ニ	ヱ	エ		*ta*	ク	ク	タ	
o	一	ナ	オ		*chi*	ニ	二	チ	
ka	ヲ	カ			*tsu*	゛	゛	ツ	
ki	ニ	二	キ		*te*	二	二	テ	
ku	ヮ	ク			*to*	┤	ト		
ke	ノ	ヒ	ケ		*na*	一	ナ		
ko	ヲ	コ			*ni*	二	二		
sa	一	十	サ		*nu*	ヲ	ヌ		
shi	゛	゛	シ		*ne*	゛	ヲ	ネ	ネ

no	ノ				yu	ユ	ユ		
ha	ノ	バ			yo	ヨ	ヨ	ヨ	
hi	ニ	ヒ			ra	ニ	ラ		
fu	フ				ri	リ	リ		
he	ヘ				ru	ノ	ル		
ho	ニ	ナ	オ	ホ	re	レ			
ma	マ	マ			ro	ロ	ロ	ロ	
mi	ミ	ミ	ミ		wa	ウ	ウ		
mu	ム	ム			wo	ヲ	ヲ		
me	ノ	メ			n	ン	ン		
mo	ニ	ニ	モ						
ya	ヤ	ヤ							

漫画例：*Manga-examples*

We are now going to see some examples of the widespread use of the katakana syllabary in Japanese. In the first two examples we will see how katakana is used in onomatopoeias, and its spectacular effect. In the second group of examples we will see some manga titles written in katakana, where we will notice that most non-onomatopoeic words written in this syllabary come from English. However, these words are hardly recognizable due to the phonetic transformation they have undergone in their adaptation to Japanese.

Glancing through a manga and starting to be able to identify katakana onomatopoeias and words is very useful and rewarding, give it a try!

a) Explosion

> Onomatopoeia: ドカン
> *dokan*
> **(Sound of explosion)**

Sound onomatopoeias which are not voices or screams are almost always written in katakana. For instance, blows, explosions, motor noises, etc... are very often written in this syllabary.

b) Blow

Onomatopoeia: ズガッ
zuga!
(Sound of blow)

Katakana in this example is almost unreadable to someone who is not familiar with it. However, with some practice you will identify katakana quite effortlessly.

c) Manga title (1)

Title: ファン
fan
Phan

Fan (here transcribed as "Phan") is a proper name, but it isn't a Japanese name. That is why it is written in katakana. (Japanese names are almost always written in kanji.)

d) Name of weekly manga magazine

Name: イーブニング
iibuningu
Evening

This word comes from English too. Here we have a very clear example of how to spell and pronounce many foreign words in Japanese way.

e) Manga title (2)

Title: ロストユース
rosuto yūsu
Lost Youth

Like the previous example, this title comes from English too and has been adapted to Japanese. With all these examples you must already have noticed the way the Japanese tend to "twist" English words to adapt them to their particular phonetic system. Don't worry for the moment if you don't even recognize the original English word when you read a katakana transcription. Getting used to "katakanization" is only a matter of time, and you will eventually find you are able to recognize the "hidden" English words in katakana, and vice-versa —that is, you will be able to transcribe English words into katakana.

1 What is the katakana syllabary used for?

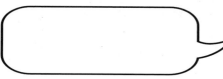

2 What percentage of Japanese words are foreign expressions, and which syllabary are they written in?

3 To write an English name, which syllabary should we use?

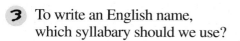

4 Try to write your name in katakana.

5 The letter "l" doesn't exist in Japanese. What letter do we use to represent it instead?

6 What are long vowels, and how do we represent them in the hiragana syllabary?

7 What are double sounds, and how do we represent them in both syllabaries?

8 Write the following letters in katakana: *ho*, *ku*, *wa* and *no*.

9 Transcribe the following katakana characters into English: ド, エ, ヨ and ペ.

10 How do we say "yes" and "no" in Japanese?

Lesson 3: Kanji

In this lesson we are going to deal with one of the most complex as well as essential subjects in the Japanese language. We are talking about kanji, or ideograms.

A little bit of history

In China, 5,000 years ago, a type of writing based on drawings was invented. That represents different material or abstract concepts. This is not unusual in human history, you just need to look at the Egyptian hieroglyphics to understand that the Chinese is not an isolated case. The unusual fact about Chinese characters is that their writing didn't become progressively simpler, forming in the end an alphabet which merely represented sounds, as was the case with Roman writing, which had its origin in Phoenician, filtering through Greek. In China, the function of ideograms was to express at once sound and meaning, unlike Western writing, which simply expresses sound.

Obviously, the form of these characters is different now from the original one. They started off with more or less realistic drawings of things, and with use, they became stylized and simpler, developing into their actual forms.

Relationship with Japanese

In the fourth century of our era, the inhabitants of the Japanese archipelago didn't have a writing system; then, Chinese writing was introduced in to Japan through the Korean peninsula. In the beginning, only a few educated people could read Chinese and all they read were treatises on Buddhism and philosophy. But Chinese ideograms were gradually used to write Japanese. There was however a problem here. The Japanese language already existed, but it had no writing system, and Chinese characters were imported along with their pronunciation —with substantial changes due to the poor Japanese phonetics. So there were two or more different ways to read one same character.

For example, the character representing mountain 山 can be pronounced "the Japanese way," that is *yama*, or Chinese style, *san*. And this is where we find one of the most typical interpretation mistakes in Japanese, as the word 富士山, which means "Mount Fuji," is pronounced *Fuji-san* and not *Fuji-yama* as we have always been made to believe!!

On'yomi and kun'yomi

These different ways of pronouncing a character are called *on'yomi* (reading which comes from Chinese) and *kun'yomi* (original Japanese reading.) How can we tell that the word 富士山 is pronounced *Fuji-san* and not, for instance, *Fuji-yama* or *Tomishi-san* or *Tomishi-sen* or *Fuuji-yama*, or any other perfectly possible combinations for these kanji?

The answer is, we can't. But we have clues. When a character is on its own in a sentence, it is usually read the *kun'yomi* way; if it comes with other kanji, it is usually read the *on'yomi* way. This rule works 90% of the time (but careful with the remaining 10%!).

Example: the character 新 (new)

その新しい新聞はおもしろいです。
Sono atarashii shinbun wa omoshiroi desu
That new newspaper is interesting.

Sono = that / *atarashii* = new / *shinbun* = newspaper / *wa* = subject particle /
omoshiroi = interesting / *desu* = verb *to be*

We see that the same character appears twice in the sentence but it has two different pronunciations. The first time it is pronounced the *kun'yomi* way, *atara (shii)*. The word *atarashii* means "new." Notice that this character is on its own in the sentence, so it is logical to pronounce it the *kun'yomi* way.

The second time it is read *shin*, that is, the *on'yomi* way, and it comes with another kanji, 聞, which means "to hear." *Shin* = new, *bun* = to hear, together they form the word "newspaper" 新聞, which is something that gathers "new reported things" (things that have been heard). These two characters are not on their own, they are together, therefore, we will pronounce them the *on'yomi* way.

Japanese and *nihongo*

Let's first analyze the word *nihongo*, which is the name given to the Japanese language. Its written form is 日本語.

The first kanji, *ni* 日, means "day, sun;" the second kanji, *hon* 本, means "origin, root;" and the third one, *go* 語, "language." Japan's name is *Nihon,* but it can also be read *Nippon,* and we write it like this: 日本. And what have "sun and origin" got to do with Japan? Doesn't the expression "the country of the rising sun" ring a bell? So this is where it comes from. Therefore, *nihongo* means "the language of the country of the rising sun," that is, "Japanese."

By the way, English in Japanese is 英語 (*ei-go*) *Ei* = kanji for England. (There is also a katakana word for England, *igirisu* イギリス, but in kanji combinations, the kanji word is used.)

Kanji are complex

Mastering kanji writing represents an important challenge, since there are many similar characters, there is a stroke order to follow to write kanji correctly, and, also, we must bear in mind *on'yomi* and *kun'yomi* readings. There are quite easy kanji, like "person" 人 (*hito, nin,* or *jin,* with 2 strokes), but there are also complicated ones, like "machine" 機 (*ki,* with 16 strokes.) At the end of this book you will find a small glossary with 160 of the most basic kanji with their stroke order, *on'yomi* and *kun'yomi* readings, and several examples of compound words.

How many kanji are there?

There are technically over 45,000 kanji, but don't worry, "only" about 3,000 are normally used. There is a list of 1,945 kanji called *Jōyō kanji* or "common use kanji," which are those that can be used in published works. If a kanji not included in the list is used, its reading must be given in hiragana in small characters above each kanji (these hiragana readings on top of the kanji are called *furigana*).

Some easy kanji: numerals and interesting words

一	いち	*ichi*	1	人	ひと	*hito*	person
二	に	*ni*	2	男	おとこ	*otoko*	man
三	さん	*san*	3	女	おんな	*onna*	woman
四	よん／し	*yon/shi*	4	月	つき	*tsuki*	moon, month
五	ご	*go*	5	火	ひ	*hi*	fire
六	ろく	*roku*	6	水	みず	*mizu*	water
七	なな／しち	*nana/shichi*	7	木	き	*ki*	tree
八	はち	*hachi*	8	金	かね	*kane*	money, gold
九	きゅう／く	*kyū/ku*	9	土	つち	*tsuchi*	earth
十	じゅう	*jū*	10	日	ひ	*hi*	day
百	ひゃく	*hyaku*	100	山	やま	*yama*	mountain
千	せん	*sen*	1000	川	かわ	*kawa*	river
万	まん	*man*	10000	田	た	*ta*	field

How some characters were formed

Original forms	Modern Character	Meaning
	木	tree
	林	wood
	森	forest
	日	sun, day
	月	moon, month
	明	bright
	山	mountain
	鳥	bird
	島	island

漫画例：Manga-examples

We will now see some examples of the use of kanji. The last two examples show us, specifically, the most common difficulties we will find when studying kanji. In them we see the almost illiterate King Slime, who can't read or write kanji very well (not even hiragana!).

a) Kanji in manga

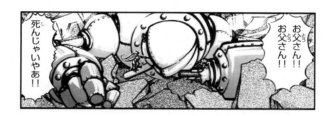

> Rinrin: お父さん!! お父さん!! 死んじゃいやあ!!
> *otōsan!! otōsan!!shinja iyaa!!*
> **Father! Father! Don't die!**

This panel has two easy kanji, one is "father" 父, and the other is "to die" 死. In addition, we are given the *furigana* reading, something very frequent in *shōnen manga,* or manga aimed at teenagers, who still haven't completely mastered the reading of the most difficult kanji. Reading *shōnen manga* is a good exercise to learn kanji readings, as long as we have mastered the hiragana syllabary.

b) The error of writing an extra stroke

> Autograph: しげおゝんえ　　宇宙の玉者スライム大玉
> *Shigeo-kun e*　　*uchuu no tamaja suraimu ōtama*
> Shigeo (suf.) for　space PoP ball person slime big ball
> **For Shigeo**　　**Big ball Slime, the space ball.**

Note: The hiragana *ku* in *Shigeo-kun* is written the other way around. The correct way to write it is く. Hiragana *e*, which means "for" should be へ and not え.

Shigeo: みんなみんな!!このひと『宇宙のタマジャ』だって!『スライムオオタマ』だって!!
minna minna ! kono hito "uchuu no tamaja" da tte! "suraimu ōtama" da tte!!
Everybody everybody! this person "space PoP ball person" be say! "slime great ball" be say!!
Hey, look! This guy's name is "Space Ball"! He's "Great Ball Slime!"

What is Shigeo laughing at? He's laughing at Slime's mistake. Instead of writing the kanji for "king," 王, he has written the kanji for "ball," 玉. Notice how the only difference between "king" and "ball" is one sole stroke. What Slime really wanted to write on the autograph was "Great King Slime, space king." The kanji for "king" is read *ō* and the kanji for "ball" is read *tama*.

Moral of the story: Be very careful with your strokes, you can't write too many and you can't leave any out, as you run the same risks as Slime!

c) Errors when reading kanji: on'yomi and kun'yomi readings

Planet: 火星 (火 (fire) + 星 (star)) = fire star = Mars)
kasei
Mars

Kumiko: なに?
nani?
What?

What mistake has Slime made? He has misread the kanji on the planet. Instead of using the *on'yomi* reading (Chinese reading), which would be the most logical one, he has used the *kun'yomi* reading. His vassal has realized and has corrected him. Remember the clue: if a kanji is on its own, it is usually read the *kun'yomi* way, and if it comes with other kanji, it is read the *on'yomi* way. "Fire" 火 is read *hi* on its own, and *ka* when it comes with other kanji. "Star" 星 is read *hoshi* on its own, and *sei* with other kanji. Why are the readings written in katakana? So that they stand out in the sentence. Katakana here has the same function as our italics.

Moral of the story: Be careful with the kanji *on'yomi* and *kun'yomi* readings. Reading well is very important!

Slime: あのヒボシをよくみとれよ!
ano hiboshi o yoku mitore yo!
That "hiboshi" DOP well see EP
Take a good look at that "Hiboshi!"

Vassal: カセイとよむのです大王様。
kasei to yomu no desu daiō-sama...
kasei read be great king (suf.)
It says "Kasei", your Highness...

1 What are kanji and where do they come from?

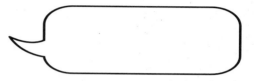

2 Write the corresponding kanji for "tree," "river," "money," and "woman."

3 What do the following kanji mean, and how do you read them in Japanese:水, 男, 山, and 火?

4 What are *on'yomi* and *kun'yomi*?

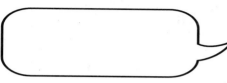

5 When a kanji character comes with another kanji, what is its usual reading (*on'yomi* or *kun'yomi*)?

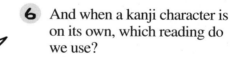

6 And when a kanji character is on its own, which reading do we use?

7 Is the word "Fuji-yama" a Japanese word, strictly speaking?

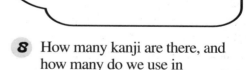

8 How many kanji are there, and how many do we use in everyday life?

9 What is the difference between the kanji for "ball" and the kanji for "king?"

10 What is *furigana* and what do we use it for? (See glossary for clues.)

第 3 課

練習

Exercises

第 4 課：日常会話集

Lesson 4: Basic expressions

In this lesson we will offer a short list of basic expressions so you begin to feel that you are studying Japanese. We have already given you a very basic list in Lesson 2, and some of those expressions will be repeated here to further clarify concepts. But, of course, in this lesson we will learn many more new expressions.

Greetings

おはようございます。 (*ohayō gozaimasu*)	Good morning (until 11 am)
こんにちは。 (*konnichi wa*)	Good afternoon (from 11 am to 6 pm)
こんばんは。 (*konban wa*)	Good evening (from 6 pm on)
お休みなさい。 (*oyasumi nasai*)	Good night (when going to bed)

After the corresponding greeting, you can say:
お元気ですか。 (*o-genki desu ka?*)　　　　How are you?

And you answer to that expression with:
はい、元気です。 (*hai, genki desu*)　　　　I'm fine.

Introducing oneself

Using the following conversation as a model, we can introduce ourselves in Japanese.

Person A: はじめまして。 (*hajimemashite*)　　　How do you do?
私の名前は＿＿＿＿＿＿＿です。　　　　My name is ＿＿＿＿ .
(*watashi no namae wa ＿＿＿＿ desu*)

よろしくお願いします。　　　　Pleased to meet you.
(*yoroshiku o-negai shimasu*)

あなたの名前はなんですか。　　　　What's your name?
(*anata no namae wa nan desu ka*)

Person B: 私の名前は＿＿＿＿＿＿。　　　My name is ＿＿＿＿＿ .
(*watashi no namae wa ＿＿＿＿ desu*)

こちらこそよろしく。　　　　Pleased to meet you (too).
(*kochira koso yoroshiku*)

So all you need to do is to put your name in the corresponding place, and you can introduce yourself in Japanese. If you live close to a tourist site which is popular among the Japanese, you can practice there.

Thank you

The most basic way of saying thank you is:

ありがとう。(*arigatō*)

But there are more combinations, such as this very formal one:

どうもありがとうございます。 Thank you very much.

(*dōmo arigatō gozaimasu*)

The next one is a little less formal than the previous one:

ありがとうございます。 Thank you.

(*arigatō gozaimasu*)

Or there this very informal and simple one:

どうも。(*dōmo*) Thanks.

The answer usually is:

どういたしまして。(*dō itashimashite*) You're welcome.

Or a simpler one:

いいえ。(*iie*) It's okay.

Asking for prices

Knowing how to ask for prices is very important if we want to go to Japan and buy lots of manga!

The first thing the shop assistant will say when the client comes into the shop is:

いらっしゃいませ。(*irasshaimase*) Welcome. / Can I help you?

Then, not being able to speak Japanese, we must point at the thing we want and say:

これはいくらですか。 How much is this?

(*kore wa ikura desu ka?*)

And the shop assistant replies:

これは＿＿＿円です。(*kore wa __ en desu*) This is _____ yen.

Don't worry, we know you can't count in Japanese yet. This will be solved in the next lesson, where we will talk about numbers.

If we want to buy something, we will say:

これをください。(*kore o kudasai*) I want this, please.

Or:

これをお願いします。 I would like this, please.

(*kore o o-negai shimasu*)

Then, the shop assistant will give you the object, and all you need to do is pay for it!

Other expressions

はい (*hai*)	Yes.
いいえ (*iie*)	No.
そうです (*sō desu*)	That's right.
すみません (*sumimasen*)	Sorry, excuse me.
ごめんなさい (*gomen nasai*)	Excuse me.
やった！(*yatta*)	Yes! I did it!
おめでとうございます (*omedetō gozaimasu*)	Congratulations!
わかりました (*wakarimashita*)	I understand.
わかりません (*wakarimasen*)	I don't understand.
何？ (*nani*)	What?

Farewells

Now we will say goodbye to this lesson's theory section, listing the different ways of saying "goodbye."

The best known way of saying goodbye is:

さようなら。(*sayōnara*)   Goodbye.

But it is not the most usual. Combinations with ja-mata are more common in colloquial Japanese:

それじゃまた明日会いましょう。
(*sore ja mata ashita aimashō*)

This is the complete form and it means "Well, let's meet again tomorrow."

じゃ、また明日。(*ja mata ashita*)
This is a shorter form and it means "Well, see you tomorrow."

Even shorter forms can be:
じゃね、また。(*ja ne, mata*)   Well, see you later.

Or an even shorter one:
またね。(*mata ne*)   See you later.

There are English imported farewells too:
バイバイ。(*bai bai*)   Bye bye.

			Short list of useful kanji				
学生	がくせい	*gakusei*	student	目	め	*me*	eye
先生	せんせい	*sensei*	teacher	口	くち	*kuchi*	mouth
学校	がっこう	*gakkō*	school	手	て	*te*	hand
大学	だいがく	*daigaku*	university	耳	みみ	*mimi*	ear
何	なに	*nani*	what?	鼻	はな	*hana*	nose
男	おとこ	*otoko*	man	春	はる	*haru*	spring
女	おんな	*onna*	woman	夏	なつ	*natsu*	summer
子	こ	*ko*	child	秋	あき	*aki*	autumn
円	えん	*en*	yen	冬	ふゆ	*fuyu*	winter
右	みぎ	*migi*	right	東	ひがし	*higashi*	east
左	ひだり	*hidari*	left	西	にし	*nishi*	west
上	うえ	*ue*	up	南	みなみ	*minami*	south
下	した	*shita*	down	北	きた	*kita*	north

This kanji list complements the one in Lesson 3. Between the two of them we have given you a total of 52 basic kanji which you should learn. You may have noticed that the first four words are formed by 2 kanji... Hey, you've made great progress!

漫画例：*Manga-examples*

a) Morning greeting

Yui: おはよう。 *(ohayō)*
Tetsuya: おはよ。 *(ohayo)*
Good morning.

This is the morning greeting, usually said until noon, when it is replaced by *konnichi wa* (good afternoon). It is a simplification of *ohayō gozaimasu*. *Tetsuya* is more concise and doesn't pronounce the long *o* —it sounds more masculine.

b) Afternoon greeting

Professor Shinobu: こんにちは。
(konnichi wa)
Good afternoon.

This greeting is usually said from noon until late in the afternoon (around 6 or 7).
Note: The syllable は is pronounced *wa* here, and not ha, which is how it should be read according to the hiragana table in Lesson 1. The reason for this is that this syllable works here as a grammatical particle, and whenever this happens it is pronounced *wa*. You will gain an insight into this in Lesson 16.

c) Evening greeting

Cinderella: こんばんは　王子様。
konban wa ōji-sama
Good evening, my prince.

This is the evening greeting, used from around 6 or 7 pm; *ōji* means "prince", and *–sama* is a honorific suffix for people's names (Lesson 15).

c) Expression of gratitude

Takashi: どうもありがとう。
dōmo arigatō
Thank you very much.

Tokiko: 博士によろしく。
hakase ni yoroshiku
doctor IP regards
Give the doctor my regards.

Here we see a very common way of saying "thank you": *dōmo arigatō*. It is a very useful expression and it always sounds good. You will never make a mistake if you use this.

e) Exclamation / Question

Kumiko: なに！！
nani!!
What? / Sorry?

This is a very common exclamation, and we see it very often in manga, both in hiragana —as in this example—, and in kanji. The kanji for *nani* is 何.

f) Farewell

Musashimaru: 気をつけろな。
ki o tsukero na
mind DOP take care EP
Take care!

In its literal translation, this expression means something like "take care of your spirit." It is actually used to say goodbye to someone, asking them to take care. Therefore, "take care" is a more exact translation. The more informal and usual farewell greeting is 気をつけて (*ki o tsukete*).

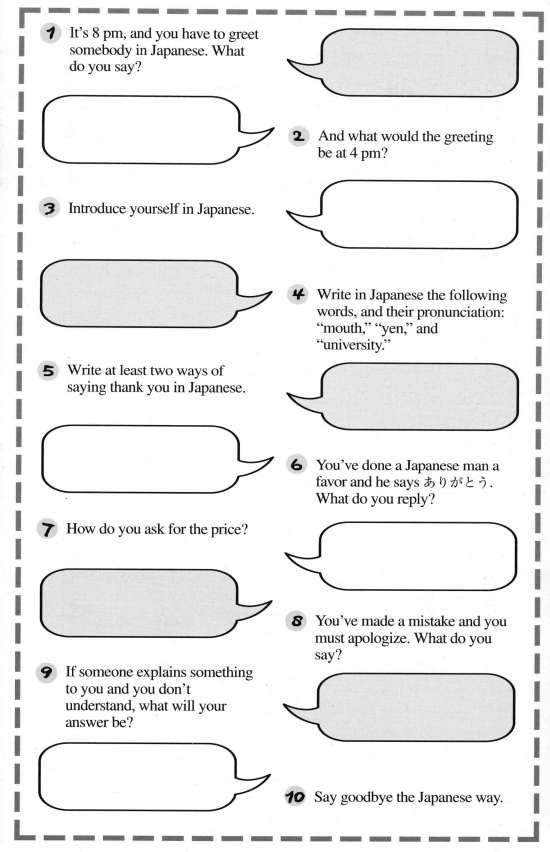

We are going to study numbers in this lesson, very important for going in to Japanese bookshops and filling your bags with comics! (among many other very useful things, of course).

Do the Japanese use "our" numbers?

First of all, we must point out that, even though Japanese has a series of kanji which correspond to each number, and that numbers can be written in kanji, nowadays this way of representing them is not used very often. To our relief, they basically use Arabic numerals, just like us. But they are pronounced the Japanese way!

We are going to study the numbers with the help of three different tables. The first two tables show the number in Arabic first, then in kanji, and finally in hiragana. We will also give the rōmaji pronunciation.

Table 1

Here are the numbers from 1 to 20. We see that 11, 12, 13, etc., are pronounced *jū* + number. That is, number 15 is called *jū go* (ten-five). Notice that numbers 4, 7, and 9 have two different pronunciations.

1	一	いち	ichi	11	十一	じゅういち	jū ichi
2	二	に	ni	12	十二	じゅうに	jū ni
3	三	さん	san	13	十三	じゅうさん	jū san
4	四	し、よん	shi / yon	14	十四	じゅうし、じゅうよん	jū shi / jū yon
5	五	ご	go	15	十五	じゅうご	jū go
6	六	ろく	roku	16	十六	じゅうろく	jū roku
7	七	しち、なな	shichi / nana	17	十七	じゅうしち、じゅうなな	jū shichi / jū nana
8	八	はち	hachi	18	十八	じゅうはち	jū hachi
9	九	く、きゅう	ku / kyū	19	十九	じゅうく、じゅうきゅう	jū ku / jū kyū
10	十	じゅう	jū	20	二十	にじゅう	ni jū

Table 2

Now numbers start getting a bit more complicated. In this table, we have tens, hundreds, thousands, and in the mini-table below it, the "ten-thousands." Tens have no secret, they consist of "number + 10." That is, 60 is *roku jū*, "six ten" in its literal translation, and 30 is *san jū*, "three ten." Pay attention to the two pronunciations of 70.

Hundreds and thousands are just like in English. 500 is *go hyaku*, "five hundred," 900 is *kyū hyaku*, "nine hundred," and 2,000 is *ni sen*, "two thousand." Pay attention to the special reading of 300, 600, 800, 3,000, and 8,000.

What are the "ten-thousands"? They are an expression we have made up to define number *man*. The Japanese don't have the same concept we have for 10,000, a number we interpret as "ten thousand." They say this number is *ichi man*, "one man" and

0	○	れい、ゼロ	rei/zero	100	百	ひゃく	hyaku	1000	千	せん	sen			
20	二十	にじゅう	ni jū	200	二百	にひゃく	ni hyaku	2000	二千	にせん	ni sen			
30	三十	さんじゅう	san jū	300	三百	さんびゃく	san byaku	3000	三千	さんぜん	san zen			
40	四十	よんじゅう	yon jū	400	四百	よんひゃく	yon hyaku	4000	四千	よんせん	yon sen			
50	五十	ごじゅう	go jū	200	五百	ごひゃく	go hyaku	5000	五千	ごせん	go sen			
60	六十	ろくじゅう	roku jū	600	六百	ろっぴゃく	roppyaku	6000	六千	ろくせん	roku sen			
70	七十	しちじゅう ななじゅう	shichi jū nana jū	700	七百	ななひゃく	nana hyaku	7000	七千	ななせん	nana sen			
80	八十	はちじゅう	hachi jū	800	八百	はっぴゃく	happyaku	8000	八千	はっせん	hassen			
90	九十	きゅうじゅう	kyū jū	900	九百	きゅうひゃく	kyū hyaku	9000	九千	きゅうせん	kyū sen			

10000	一万	いちまん	ichi man	1000000	百万	ひゃくまん	hyaku man
100000	十万	じゅうまん	jū man	10000000	千万	せんまん	sen man

not *jū sen*, "ten thousand" —this latter expression being totally wrong in Japanese. Look out, this *man* can easily confuse you! A million in Japan is interpreted as *hyaku man*, "one hundred *man*," and ten million as *sen man*, "one thousand *man*."

Table 3

								一	1
							十	一	11
						二	十	一	21
					百	二	十	一	121
				三	百	二	十	一	321
			千	三	百	二	十	一	1321
		四	千	三	百	二	十	一	4321
	一	万	四	千	三	百	二	十	一	14321
五	万	四	千	三	百	二	十	一	54321
							百		一	101
						百		十	110
				四	千			一	4001
			四	千		二	十		4020
五	万			三	百			一	50301

いち
ichi

じゅういち
jū ichi

にじゅういち
ni jū ichi

ひゃく にじゅういち
hyaku ni jū ichi

さんびゃく にじゅういち
san byaku ni jū ichi

せん さんびゃく にじゅういち
sen san byaku ni jū ichi

よんせん さんびゃく にじゅういち
yon sen san byaku ni jū ichi

いちまん よんせん さんびゃく にじゅういち
ichi man yon sen san byaku ni jū ichi

ごまん よんせん さんびゃく にじゅういち
go man yon sen san byaku ni jū ichi

ひゃく いち
hyaku ichi

ひゃく じゅう
hyaku jū

よんせん いち
yon sen ichi

よんせん にじゅう
yon sen ni jū

ごまん さんびゃくいち
go man san byaku ichi

In this table, we can see the composition process of a much more complex number. To exercise your mind, we are going to give a similar example. How do you say 34,267 in Japanese? First, let's see how many *man* there are. Since there are three, let's start from *san man*, 30,000; then we have 4 thousand (*yon sen*, 4,000). At the moment we have *san man yon sen*, 34,000. Then, there are 2 hundreds (*ni hyaku*, 200), 6 tens (*roku jū*, 60), and one 7 (*nana.*) If we put it all together, we find 34,267 is pronounced *san man yon sen ni hyaku roku jū nana*. Now, the other way around. How would we write the following words in numbers: *go man san zen roppyaku ni jū hachi*? Let's see, *go man* = 50,000, *san zen* = 3,000, *roppyaku* = 600, *ni jū* = 20, and *hachi* = 8. Therefore, the answer is 53,628. Written in kanji it would be even easier. That is: *go man* = 五万, *san zen* = 三千, *roppyaku* = 六百, *ni jū* = 二十, and *hachi* = 八. If we put all the kanji together, we will have 五万三千六百二十八, which is the equivalent in Japanese writing to the number 53,628.

Be careful, because Western numbers are very often combined with kanji, especially when dealing with round numbers. For example, this number 3万, *san man*, that is, 30,000.

To find out about the price for something, we will always find the kanji 円 after a number. This kanji means "yen," the Japanese currency. If an object is marked 4千円, then we will know its price is 4,000 yen.

漫画例: *Manga-examples*

In the manga-examples in this lesson we have chosen somewhat difficult panels, as the Japanese level required to understand them is quite high. The recommended strategy is to look carefully at the numerals and leave aside the rest of the text. After all, we need to practice numerals.

a) 20 million

Hashizaki: 二千万ある。
ni sen man aru
two thousand *man* there are
Here is 20 million.

Here we see how an executive tries to obtain Mei's contract cancellation by bribing her. What we want to look at in this example is the number, *ni sen man*, that is, literally translated, "two thousand ten-thousands," or 20 million.

Hashizaki 契約破棄の違約金だ。
keiyaku haki no iyakukin da
contract cancellation compensation is
It's a compensation for the cancellation of your contract.

Hashizaki 受け取りたまえ。
uketori tamae
accept (imp.)
You must take it.

b) 8 millions

> Princess Rage: 帝国第六機甲軍が…。
> *teikoku dai roku kikōgun ga...*
> Empire sixth division armoured
> **The Empire's sixth armoured division...**

> Princess Rage: 八百万の艦隊が…。
> *happyaku man no kantai ga...*
> eight hundred *man* squadrons
> **It has eight million squadrons!**

In this example, we see Princess Rage surprised at the power of the enemy fleet. In reference to the text, we see once more a very large number in which the kanji of *man* 万 appears again. In this case, the number is 800 times 10,000, which is literally equivalent to 8 million, but it is used to convey that the number is a very large one, non countable, or infinite —8 *man* is like saying "millions." We don't really want to say a specific figure, but a very very large number. We must point out Princess Rage doesn't finish her sentences, she uses no verb and it must be deduced. This is another problem with Japanese in manga that we have to deal with: its ambiguity.

About ordinal numbers

Forming ordinals in Japanese is very simple. All you have to do is place the prefix *dai* 第 before the number. We see Princess Rage talking about the sixth division and she says *dai roku kikōgun*. We can find another example in the Japanese titles of all the lessons in this book, for example, the title of this lesson: 第五課：数字, that is, *dai go ka: sūji*. Breaking it down, we have: *dai go* = fifth, *ka* = lesson, *sūji* = numeral, that is, "fifth lesson: numerals."

c) A strange watch

This rather beautiful watch was part of a magazine draw for its readers. It is interesting how the numbers are written the Japanese way and not the Western way.
Let's see the numbers:

Watch: 十二　　　三　　　六　　　九
jū ni　　*san*　　*roku*　　*kyū*
Twelve　**Three**　**Six**　**Nine**

Circle: 100人
hyaku nin
One hundred people

The small circle in the bottom right corner shows an inscription with another number.

The number 100 (*hyaku*) is next to the kanji for "person." This means there were one hundred watches for one hundred lucky people. Another way of writing it using Japanese numbers would be 百人.

1 In everyday life in Japan, how do you usually write numbers: in kanji or in Arabic numbers?

2 How do you pronounce the following numbers: 十, 八, 三 and 七?

3 How do you say the following numbers: 50, 800 and 2,000?

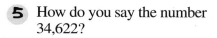

4 What does the concept *man* stand for in Japanese? How do you pronounce these numbers in Japanese: 20,000 and 400,000?

5 How do you say the number 34,622?

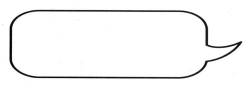

6 Write the number 45,853 in kanji, and give its pronunciation.

7 Write in Arabic numbers the following number: 一万二千六百八十一. How do you say it in Japanese?

8 Write the figure 2,000,000 (two million) in Japanese.

9 To what Arabic number does the following Japanese number correspond: 4千万?

10 How do you form ordinal numbers? Give the ordinal numbers for 4 and 25.

第5課

練習

Exercises

第 6 課：年・月・日・曜日

Lesson 6: Days of the week, days of the month and months

We looked at numbers in Lesson 5, and now we are going to study the days of the week, the days of the month, and the months. You may find it hard to believe, but Lessons 5 and 6 have a lot in common, so you should review the previous lesson thoroughly before you carry on.

Days of the week

The first table shows how to say the days in Japanese. First, we have the kanji translation, then we have the hiragana one, and, for those who still haven't learnt hiragana, we have the *rōmaji* transcription. Note that all days have the *yōbi* 曜日 part in common. The reason for this is that *yōbi* means "day of the week." The kanji before *yōbi* shows the meaning, as the small table indicates. Therefore, Monday would be the "moon day," Tuesday the "fire day," and so on…

週の曜日 Days of the week			
Monday	月曜日	げつようび	(getsuyōbi)
Tuesday	火曜日	かようび	(kayōbi)
Wednesday	水曜日	すいようび	(suiyōbi)
Thursday	木曜日	もくようび	(mokuyōbi)
Friday	金曜日	きんようび	(kin'yōbi)
Saturday	土曜日	どようび	(doyōbi)
Sunday	日曜日	にちようび	(nichiyōbi)

月 moon / 火 fire / 水 water / 木 tree
金 metal / 土 earth / 日 sun

A brief remark

Remember how in Lesson 3 we talked about kanji and their different readings according to the kanji position and its meaning? Do you see something odd in the table? That's right, Sunday is pronounced *nichiyōbi*, and the same kanji 日 is read *nichi* and *bi* in the same word. The reason for this is that the same character means sun and day. The first time it appears (*nichi*) it refers to sun, and the second time (*bi*), to day. Therefore, Sunday = sun day (hey, like in English!)

The same happens with 月, as it has two meanings, "moon" and "month" and it is read differently according to its meaning.

Days of the month

There are no specific names for the days of the month in English, we simply say "today is the first" or "today is the twenty-fifth," that is, we use numbers alone.

In Japanese, names for the days of the month do exist, at least from one to ten. From the eleventh on, the corresponding number is used and all you need to do is add the word *nichi* (day). Therefore, if we are on the 26th, we will say *kyō wa ni jū roku nichi desu* (today is the 26th) (*kyō* = today / *wa* = subject particle / *ni jū roku* = 26 / *nichi* = day / *desu* = verb *to be*). However, the problem lies in days 1 to 10, with their special pronunciations which you can see on the second table, left column.

Notice how the kanji are those which correspond to the numbers plus the kanji for "day" 日, but, for example, the reading for the 4th 四日 is not *yon nichi* (*yon* = 4 / *nichi* = day) but *yokka*... There are some words with special readings and you have no choice but to learn them by heart.

From the 11th on, as we mentioned before, there is no problem, except with the 14th, which is not *jū yon nichi* but *jū yokka*. And again with the 24th, which is pronounced *ni jū yokka*, and not *ni jū yon nichi*. Pay attention to the 17th and the 19th, which are pronounced *jū shichi nichi* and *jū ku nichi*, respectively, and not *jū nana nichi* nor *jū kyū nichi*, which would be the other options. Oh, and the 20th has a special pronunciation too!

	Days of the month	日 hi	Months	月 tsuki
1	ついたち tsuitachi	(一日)	いちがつ ichigatsu	(一月)
2	ふつか futsuka	(二日)	にがつ nigatsu	(二月)
3	みっか mikka	(三日)	さんがつ sangatsu	(三月)
4	よっか yokka	(四日)	しがつ shigatsu	(四月)
5	いつか itsuka	(五日)	ごがつ gogatsu	(五月)
6	むいか muika	(六日)	ろくがつ rokugatsu	(六月)
7	なのか nanoka	(七日)	しちがつ shichigatsu	(七月)
8	ようか yōka	(八日)	はちがつ hachigatsu	(八月)
9	ここのか kokonoka	(九日)	くがつ kugatsu	(九月)
10	とおか tooka	(十日)	じゅうがつ jūgatsu	(十月)
11	じゅういちにち jūichinichi	(十一日)	じゅういちがつ jūichigatsu	(十一月)
12	じゅうににち jūninichi	(十二日)	じゅうにがつ jūnigatsu	(十二月)
14	じゅうよっか jūyokka	(十四日)		
17	じゅうしちにち jūshichinichi	(十七日)		
19	じゅうくにち jūkunichi	(十九日)		
20	はつか hatsuka	(二十日)		
?	なんにち nannichi?	(なん日)	なんがつ nangatsu?	(なん月)

Months

At last something easy in Japanese! Indeed, the Japanese don't have month names like we do (March, July...), they use numbers to name them instead, followed by the word *gatsu*, which means "month." Therefore, July is *shichi gatsu* in Japanese, that is, "seventh month."

And to make things even easier, you can have a look at the second table, above column, where you'll find all the names of the months.

Pay attention to the pronunciation of April, July, and September. They are pronounced *shigatsu*, *shichigatsu,* and *kugatsu*, respectively, and not *yongatsu*, *nanagatsu*, or *kyūgatsu*, which would be the other options, since these numbers have two different pronunciations (remember the previous lesson).

On years

The Japanese, not being Christians, don't follow our calendar, which started in remembrance of the birth of Christ. Year 2004 A.D., for instance, is equivalent to year 16 of the Heisei Era.

This doesn't mean they don't use our calendar in everyday life. Western influence has overcome tradition and nowadays, year 2004 is used as often as year 16 of the Heisei Era, if not more.

What is the basis for the Japanese way of counting years? It is the reigns of the emperors. 1989 was the first year of the Heisei Era because it was then that the present emperor, Akihito, came to the throne. To end this lesson, we will see some of the most recent eras and their emperors.

Meiji Era　明治　(1868–1912)　Emperor Mutsuhito
Taishō Era　大正　(1912–1926)　Emperor Yoshihito
Shōwa Era　昭和　(1926–1989)　Emperor Hirohito
Heisei Era　平成　(1989–　　)　Emperor Akihito

漫画例：Manga-examples

What better way to give examples for the days of the week and the months than by having a look at a Japanese calendar? In the first part of this section of manga-examples, we will see a page from a Japanese calendar and we will break down its characteristics. Then, as usual, we will see some examples "in panels."

a) Calendar

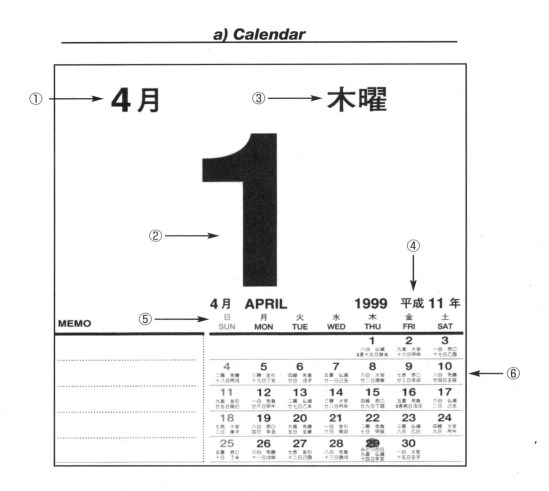

Notice how we are going to look at the 1st of April. Why have we chosen this day? Because in Japan this day is also called "April Fools' Day" (エイプリルフール, ēpuriru fūru), or "All Fools's Day," having adopted the American tradition (like many other things). So, be careful if you go to Japan on April 1st!

①4月

shigatsu

This is April's name (its literal translation would be "fourth month"). Under the number 1 we see the same character once more, but this time it comes with the English translation, "April."

②1日

tsuitachi

This is how we read number 1 when we are talking about the day of the month (look out, it is a special reading). It also is an abbreviated form, as it would usually be written with the kanji for "day" next to it, 1日.

③木曜

mokuyō

This word means "Thursday." Its literal translation would be "tree day." Here we find an abbreviated form, the complete form being 木曜日 (*mokuyōbi*).

④平成11年

heisei jūichi nen

Literally translated as "year eleven of Heisei." Heisei is the present era's name, which started when Emperor Akihito came to the throne in 1989 —pay attention to the fact that 1989 is year number 1 of the Heisei Era and not year number 0.
To avoid confusions, they also write 1999 next to it.

⑤日　月　火　水　木　金　土

These are the most abbreviated forms for the names of the days of the week. You simply write the first kanji and forget about the rest, 曜日 (*yōbi*). To avoid confusion, the English abbreviations are underneath. Oh, it is an English style week, starting with Sunday, and not Monday like in other countries.

⑥八白　先勝

The characters under each day show details such as "lucky number and color for that day," "good or bad day, following Buddhism beliefs," and other typical aspects of the Chinese zodiac (often used in Japan).

b) December 28th

12月
28日
東京立川競輪場
競輪GP'97 S級シリーズ

The bicycle race in the Tachigawa cycle track is about to begin and bets are sky-high…

Overprint: 12月28日
jū ni gatsu ni jū hachi nichi
twelve month twenty-eighth day
December, twenty-eighth

東京立川競輪場
Tōkyō Tachigawa keirinjō
Tokyo Tachigawa bicycle race place
Tachigawa cycle track, Tokyo

競輪GP'97　S級シリーズ
Keirin Guran Puri kyūjū nana Esu-kyū shiriizu
Bicycle race GP'97 S class series
Grand Prix in cycling '97, S series

c) June 26th

The eagerly awaited basketball game between universities *Gaidai* and *Jōchi* is here!

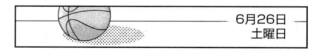

6月26日
土曜日

Overprint: 6月26日
rokugatsu ni jū roku nichi
six month twenty-six day
June twenty-sixth

土曜日
doyōbi
Saturday

1 Translate into English the words 金曜日, 月曜日, and 木曜日.

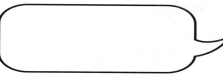

2 Write in Japanese the seven days of the week and indicate their readings.

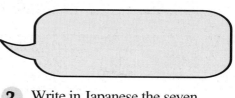

3 What do the kanji 土, 火, and 木 mean?

4 Why can the kanji 日 have two different readings, even in the same word, 日曜日, (*nichiyōbi*, "Sunday")?

5 Write in Japanese the following date: May 15th, and indicate its reading.

6 Translate into English the following date: 三月三日. How do you read these kanji?

7 Write in Japanese the twelve months of the year and indicate their readings.

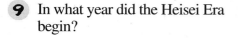

8 How do you say "the 6th (day)" in Japanese? And how about "the 11th (day)?"

9 In what year did the Heisei Era begin?

10 To what Christian year does the year 20 of the Shōwa Era correspond?

第6課

練習

Exercises

第 (7) 課：人称代名詞

Lesson 7: Personal pronouns

Konnichi wa! O-genki desu ka? **In this lesson we will study personal pronouns in Japanese. For those who are a bit lost, personal pronouns in English are,** *I, you, he, we,* **etc.**

Before we start...

Before we start, a few important things need clarifying so this lesson can be understood.

Japanese is a very hierarchical language, that is, according to the social position of the person talking and the one listening, the talker will use certain words which he would never use in other situations. Further on, we will give some examples so you can get a clear idea.

Moreover, Japanese spoken by men is quite different from that spoken by women. There are expressions, words, and constructions which a man would never use for fear of sounding effeminate, and vice versa.

Isn't there a single word for "I" ?

In Indo-European languages there is only one first person singular personal pronoun. It's the *I* in English, *yo* in Spanish, *ich* in German, *jo* in Catalan, *eu* in Portuguese… The same doesn't happen in Japanese, far from it. There's a huge variety of pronouns, both in first and second persons. The third person is an exception, we will see why later.

Depending on whether you are a man or a woman, and depending on who you are talking to, you will use a different personal pronoun. In the first vocabulary table we have the most common and important ones.

Here are a few examples of which pronoun certain persons would use in certain situations:

a) A 40-year-old Osaka-born employee in an important company

  1 If he is talking to his boss: *watashi*

  2 If he is talking to his wife: *washi*

b) A 20-year-old girl

  1 If she is talking to her boyfriend: *atashi*

  2 If she is talking to a teacher: *watashi*

c) A 25-year-old male student

  1 If he is talking to another student: *ore*

  2 If he is talking with the father of a friend: *boku*

Personal Pronouns / Formality Levels	First Person	
	Singular (I)	**Plural (we)**
Very formal	わたくし watakushi	わたくしども watakushidomo
Formal	私(わたし)　あたくし(fem.) watashi　atakushi(fem.)	わたくしたち　わたしたち watakushitachi　watashitachi
Informal	僕(ぼく)　あたし boku(masc.)　atashi(fem.)	ぼくたち　あたしたち(fem.) bokutachi(masc.)　atashitachi(fem.) ぼくら　あたしら bokura(masc.)　atashira(fem.)
Very informal	俺(おれ) ore(masc.)	おれたち oretachi(masc.)

Second person

The second person singular (you in English) is very similar in use to the first person. There are also respectful and informal terms.

As before, we will give some examples:

Someone you don't know: *anata*

Personal Pronouns / Formality Levels	Second Person	
	Singular (you)	Plural (you)
Formal	あなた anata	あなたがた anatagata
Informal	君 (きみ) kimi (masc.)	きみたち　　　あなたたち kimitachi(masc.)　anatatachi (fem.) きみら kimira (masc.)
Very informal	お前 (おまえ)　あんた omae　　　　　　anta	おまえたち　　　あんたたち omaetachi (masc.)　antatachi おまえら　　　　あんたら omaera (masc.)　　antara

A girl to a close female friend: *anta*

A boy to his girlfriend: *kimi*

A boy to a male friend: *omae*

But very often, instead of the corresponding pronoun, we use the person's name, title, or profession, even though we are talking directly to them.
Examples:

"You are intelligent".

Talking to a teacher:

先生は頭がいいです。

Sensei wa atama ga ii desu

(*sensei* = teacher / *atama ga ii* = intelligent / *desu* = verb *to be*)

Talking to Tanaka:

田中さんは頭がいいです。

Tanaka-san wa atama ga ii desu

It may seem we are talking about a third person, but it's in fact a face-to-face conversation.

Third person

The third person (*he, she* in English) is a special case. Traditionally, the Japanese don't use the "he" or "she" pronouns much. They simply use the name or title of the person they want to talk about.

We could use the same examples we used in the second person (*sensei wa atama ga ii desu*). Thus, the same sentence could be translated in two different ways:

    1 You are intelligent.

    2 The teacher is intelligent.

The difference lies in the fact that, in the first case, we are talking *with* the teacher, and in the second case we are talking *about* the teacher. We can only tell whether we must use second or third person through the context.

Still, Japanese does have third person pronouns, these being:

彼 *(kare)* he

彼女 *(kanojo)* she

Be careful with these pronouns, as they also mean, respectively, "boyfriend" and "girlfriend," depending on the context. When you say the sentence:

彼女は頭がいいです。 (*kanojo wa atama ga ii desu*)

People might understand *My girlfriend is intelligent* instead of *She is intelligent*, which is really what you want to say...

How about the plural?

The plural is very similar to the singular as far as use is concerned. You already have the tables as a guide, and the examples we used in the singular can also be used in the plural: all you need to do is change the pronoun.
The third person plural is 彼ら (*karera*, they, talking about men), and
彼女たち (*kanojotachi*, they, talking about women).

Other pronouns

However, apart from the list in this lesson, there are more pronouns.
Other examples are:

washi (I) — Men over 40 (often dialectal)
asshi (I) — Women in informal situations
kisama (you) — Used threateningly (masc.)
temee (you) — Used by angry men

And many more... A piece of advice a *gaijin* (foreigner) might find very useful is to use *watashi* in all situations. It is easy to remember and you will never make a mistake. Besides, the person you are talking to will think you are most polite.

漫画例：*Manga-examples*

As usual, theory is supplemented with the manga-examples section. This time we will see the use of personal pronouns in manga, which is common and very varied...

a) I

In this first section we will see two ways of saying *I*. One is *boku*, used by young men (and not that young, actually). The second one is *ore*, also used by men, but with a more rough and informal nuance than *boku* (it makes you sound more "macho").

Keita: やだよ　オレあんなカオになりたくないもん。
ya da yo! ore anna kao ni naritakunai mon
unpleasant! I that kind of face don't want to become
No way! I don't want to look like that.

Suzuki: オレもだよ !!!
ore mo da yo!!!
me too be EP!!!
Me neither!

Blade: 俺は…ちがう…。
ore wa... chigau...
I wrong
I'm wrong...

Dong-Lee: こいつは僕が殺す…。
koitsu wa boku ga korosu...
this guy I kill
I'll kill him!

b) You

In this second section we will see two ways of saying *you*. The first one is *omae*, exclusively used by men, since it is a rather rough and informal word which women would never use. The second way is *kimi*, quite informal, but very common.

Hagiwara: さ…さつき　お前たばこを吸うのか…？
sa... satsuki　omae tabako o suu no ka...
sa...satsuki　you tobacco smoke Q?
D... do you smoke, Satsuki?

Kishiwada: 誰かね君は？
dare ka ne kimi wa?
who you?
And who are you?

Amaterasu: 女神のアマテラスと申します !!
megami no amaterasu to mōshimasu!!
Goddess Amaterasu I am called!!
I am Amaterasu, the goddess.

c) We

A final example. This time we will learn how to say *we*. It is a girl who says it, and the sentence is a serious one. Therefore she uses the pronoun *watashitachi* (formal), which is better in this kind of circumstances.

Girl: 私たちっ別れましょう。
watashitachi wakaremashō
we are going to split
I want to split up.

Chico: ええっ何故だ !?
ee! naze da!?
eh? why!?
What? Why?

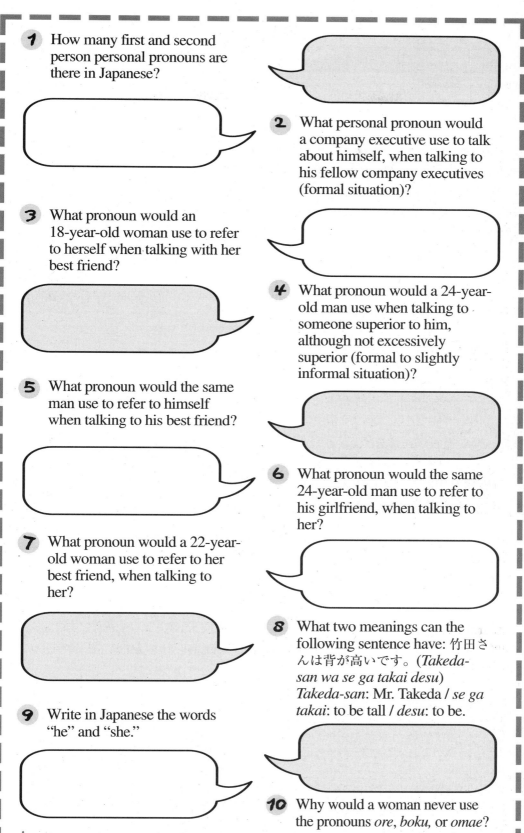

1. How many first and second person personal pronouns are there in Japanese?

2. What personal pronoun would a company executive use to talk about himself, when talking to his fellow company executives (formal situation)?

3. What pronoun would an 18-year-old woman use to refer to herself when talking with her best friend?

4. What pronoun would a 24-year-old man use when talking to someone superior to him, although not excessively superior (formal to slightly informal situation)?

5. What pronoun would the same man use to refer to himself when talking to his best friend?

6. What pronoun would the same 24-year-old man use to refer to his girlfriend, when talking to her?

7. What pronoun would a 22-year-old woman use to refer to her best friend, when talking to her?

8. What two meanings can the following sentence have: 竹田さんは背が高いです。(*Takeda-san wa se ga takai desu*) *Takeda-san*: Mr. Takeda / *se ga takai*: to be tall / *desu*: to be.

9. Write in Japanese the words "he" and "she."

10. Why would a woman never use the pronouns *ore*, *boku*, or *omae*?

第 8 課：カタカナ特集

Lesson 8: Katakana special

We saw in Lesson 2 how the katakana syllabary worked. However, in this lesson we are going to go into this topic in greater depth, because it is rather complex and one lesson is not enough. We recommend you to review Lesson 2 as a reminder of what katakana is and how to use it.

The lack of phonetics in Japanese

You'll need to be very familiar with the characteristics of Japanese pronunciation (see Lesson 1) to be able to make good transcriptions into katakana, and to interpret words written in that syllabary. Japanese has certain characteristics which make the transcription of foreign words very difficult.

a) The main characteristic is that, having a syllabic system, there are no consonants on their own, except for one. A consonant is always followed by a vowel. The only consonant on its own is ン (*n*).

b) The sounds *l*, and *v* don't exist.

c) The following combinations don't exist in "pure" Japanese: *ti*, *tu*, *fa*, *fe*, *fi*, *fo*, *she*, *che*, *je*, *zi*, *di*, and *du*.

Strategies to overcome phonetic limitations

Due to the phonetic poverty of Japanese, there is a transcription system for foreign words every Japanese knows and has never learnt anywhere.

1) *What is the basis for this transcription? Is it pronunciation or the way the original word is written?*
It is the original pronunciation.
Examples: コンピューター (*konpyūtā*) comes from *computer*. Since it comes from English, it is transcribed according to the English pronunciation.
オランダ (*Oranda*) comes from Portuguese *Olanda* (Holland). Since it comes from Portuguese, it is transcribed according to its original pronunciation.

2) *How can we transcribe a consonant on its own, if there is not such thing, except for the* n*?*
The solution lies in choosing the column from the katakana table which most resembles the original pronunciation, and then choosing the character which stands for that consonant + *u*. The reason for this is *u* in Japanese has a very weak pronunciation, it goes almost unnoticed.
For example, how do we transcribe the word *crack*? We see we have two *k* sounds on their own (they come with no vowels), and they must be transcribed. We go to the *k* column in the syllabary and choose *k* + *u* (ク). Thus, the word *crack* would become クラック (*kurakku*). In another example, when transcribing the final *s* sound in *service*, we need to choose the katakana *su* (ス), and we would get サービス (*sābisu*). There is only one exception: as the *tu* and *du* combinations don't exist (we find the *tsu* ツ and *zu* ヅ sounds instead), we need to use katakana *to* and *do* to transcribe the *t* sound.
Examples: ヒント (*hinto*, from hint), ベッド (*beddo*, from bed).

3) *How do we represent long sounds?*
With a dash. A dash means the previous vowel is pronounced for a little bit longer than a single one.
Examples: バレーボール (*barēbōru*, volleyball), カレー (*karē*, curry), ドライバー (*doraibā*, screwdriver).

4) *What about the l sound?*
Since the *l* sound doesn't exist in Japanese, it has to be replaced with the sound that most resembles the original pronunciation, that is, the *r*.
Examples: ボール (*bōru*, ball), レンズ (*renzu*, lens).

5) *And the v sound?*
Traditionally, the *v* sound was transcribed the same way as the *b* sound. Thus, we had バイオリン (*baiorin*, violin). In recent years, though, there is a tendency to use the katakana *u* with two little slashes ヴ to represent more faithfully this sound that doesn't exist in Japanese. We add a smaller *a, e, i, o* to it to represent *va, ve, vi* and *vo* (ヴァ, ヴェ, ヴィ, and ヴォ). For example, "violin" is now written this way: ヴァイオリン *vaiorin*. Other examples are エヴァンゲリオン (*evangerion*, evangelion), ヴェロニカ (Veronica).

6) *How are double consonants represented?*
We have many words in English where a consonant is pronounced more abruptly than usual. This is called a double consonant. To represent this effect, a small *tsu* ッ character is used before the consonant to be doubled.
Examples: カーペット (*cāpetto*, carpet), スリッパ (*surippa*, slipper), ポケット (*poketto*, pocket).

7) *If combinations* ti, tu, fa, fe, fi, fo, she, che, je, zi, di, du, hu, *don't exist, how do we transcribe words containing these sounds?*
There is a series of rules, which we will now explain. The most common strategy is using a katakana character plus a smaller size vowel next to it.
a) *Sounds with f.*
The only character with *f* pronunciation is *fu*. To transcribe *f* + vowel syllables (except for *u*, since we already have *fu*), we will use katakana *fu* + the corresponding vowel next to it, written in a smaller size.
Examples: *fa* = ファ (*fu* + small *a*), *fi* = フィ (*fu* + small *i*).
Examples in real words are ファン (*fan*, fan), フォント (*fonto*, font.).
b) She, che *and* je.
To make *she* we use katakana *shi* + small *e* (シェ), to make *che* we use katakana *chi* + small *e* (チェ), and to make *je* we use katakana *ji* + small *e* (ジェ).
Examples: チェス (*chesu*, chess), ジェット (*jetto*, jet).
c) Ti, di.
Transcription: *te, de* + small *i* (ティ、ディ).
Examples: スパゲッティ (*supagetti*, spaguetti), ディスク (*disuku*, disk).
d) Tu, du.
These are rather special sounds because they can be transcribed in several ways. The most common way of transcribing *tu* is using katakana *tsu*, as in ツアー (*tsuā*, tour). The *du* sound is seldom used, but should we need to transcribe it, we would use the ドゥ (*do* + *u* combination).

漫画例：*Manga-examples*

In the manga-examples section we will look at some uses of katakana, and how foreign words become transformed in Japanese; most of the time extravagant pronunciations, far from the original one, are adopted.

a) Foreign expressions (1)

> Keiko: 一郎ォスタジアムの中に入るんだ。
> *Ichirō sutajiamu no naka ni hairu n da*
> Ichiro stadium in enter
> **Ichirō, let's go into the stadium!**

> Ichirō: いま手が離せねェんだよォ。
> *ima te ga hanase-e n da yo-o*
> now hand release (neg)
> **I can't now, I'm busy!**

In this example we see the word *sutajiamu* (from the English *stadium*) is used. Notice how the Japanese word is transcribed according to the English pronunciation and not to its written equivalent.

b) Foreign place names

Cindy: なにをしにブロードウエーまでいったのだろう…。
nani wo shi ni burōdouē made itta no darō...
what do Broadway to go I wonder…
I wonder why he went to Broadway…

Here we see how the Japanese write place (or people's) names. In this example, Broadway has been transformed into *burōdouē*…

c) Onomatopoeia and foreign expressions

Ryōko: ヒック
hikku
(hiccups sound)
Hic!

Tetsu: アルコールの臭い…？
arukōru no nioi...?
Alcohol smell?
I can smell alcohol…

In this example we have two words in katakana. The first is *hikku*, the sound someone makes when having the hiccups. This is an onomatopoeia, and katakana is normally used to represent them (see Lesson 2). The other word is *arukōru*, which comes from the word "alcohol."

d) Foreign proper names

Captain George: キャプテン　ジョージ！！
Kyaputen Jōji!!
Captain George!!
I'm Captain George!

キャプテン
ジョージ
！！

Another example of foreign name transcription into Japanese. "Captain George" is obviously not a Japanese name. Being a foreign name, the katakana syllabary must be used when writing it, and the full name has to be adapted to the Japanese pronunciation. Thus, Captain George is transcribed as *Kyaputen Jōji*. Try writing your own name in Japanese, it's really good practice!

e) Foreign expressions (2)

目標をセンターに入れてー

Kurō: 目標をセンターに入れてー。
mokuhyō o sentā ni irete...
target centre put in...
Center the target and then...

Here we have Kurō fighting against an enemy. He uses the word *sentā*, from the English word *center*. Japanese has a word for *center*, but it sounds more "interesting" and "modern" if you use an English word instead.

1. What is the katakana syllabary used for?

2. Japanese is based on syllable combinations, but which is the only consonant that can go on its own, without the support of any vowel?

3. How do we transcribe isolated consonants into Japanese? For example, when we have to write the consonant "s" in Japanese, what do we do?

4. If we want to transcribe the consonants "t" and "d", what do we do?

5. What are double consonants, and how do we represent them in katakana? Give an example.

6. Since "f" doesn't exist, how do we transcribe the syllable "fi" into Japanese?

7. How do we transcribe the syllable "ti" into Japanese?

8. Transcribe into Japanese the English word "American."

9. Transcribe into Japanese the English word "family."

10. Write your own name in Japanese.

第 9 課：基礎文法

In this lesson we will get right into the Japanese grammar, starting with the use of the most common verb in any language: the verb "to be."

The verb "to be"

The verb "to be" is です (*desu*) in Japanese. Let's try making a few very short and simple sentences with this verb:

> これはりんごです。
> *kore wa ringo desu*
> **This is an apple.**
> それはテーブルです。
> *sore wa tēburu desu*
> **That is a table.**
> あれはとりです。
> *are wa tori desu*
> **That is a bird.**
> どれがボールペンですか。
> *dore ga bōrupen desu ka?*
> **Which is the ballpoint pen?**

Verb to be です		
	Formal	**Informal**
Present	です desu	だ da
Past	でした deshita	だった datta
Negative	ではありません de wa arimasen	ではない de wa nai
		じゃない ja nai

You can tell from the examples that the verb *desu* always goes at the end of the sentence. This is always the same in Japanese, the verb always goes at the end, and there are no exceptions. In addition, there is an advantage over English: you don't conjugate it. That is, the verb is always *desu*, and it doesn't change, not when you are talking about yourself (僕はジョンです / *boku wa John desu* / I am John), nor when you are talking about your interlocutor (君はばかです / *kimi wa baka desu* / you are an idiot), nor when you are talking about a thing (これはテレビです / *kore wa terebi desu* / this is a television). The verb is always *desu*. Note on pronunciation: the *u* in desu is hardly pronounced. Thus, the sentence 僕はジョンです is actually pronounced *boku wa John des*.

Kosoado

You must have noticed there are very similar words in the examples. They are これ, それ, あれ, どれ (*kore, sore, are, dore*). These words respectively mean "this," "that' (close), "that" (far), and "which." You'll notice they all have the same root (*re*) and before this *re* we find the syllables *ko, so, a, do*.

There are many more words like these in Japanese, where the syllables *ko* (very close), *so* (close), *a* (far) and *do* (question) go before the root. For example: ここ, そこ, あそこ, どこ (*koko, soko, asoko, doko*), which mean "here, there, over there, where." This is the so called *kosoado* system, which is worth mastering.

Wa

You have probably noticed as well how, after a noun, we always find the particle は (ha). This particle comes after a noun to indicate topic (Lesson 16.) It is a very important particle in Japanese, and there are many more, but we will explain them in another lesson, because they are more complicated than you would think. Moreover, in this case, when the は (ha) particle indicates topic —we will see more about this in Lesson 16, but let's say that the topic is "what we are talking about in a sentence"— we pronouncd it *wa*, although we write it *ha*.

Past

However, the verb "to be" is not that simple. It can also be conjugated in the past, negative, and interrogative forms. We will use the same previous examples, this time in the past tense.

> これはりんごでした。
> *kore wa ringo deshita*
> **This was an apple.**
> それはテーブルでした。
> *sore wa tēburu deshita*
> **That was a table.**

As you can see, the past tense of the verb "to be" is *deshita*, and it also goes at the end of the sentence and there is nothing more to it.

Note on pronunciation: the "i" in "deshita" is hardly pronounced. Thus, でした *is pronounced* "deshta" *rather than* "deshita."

Negative

Let's look now at the negative, which is not complicated either. It is just a question of replacing *desu* with *de wa arimasen*.

> これはりんごではありません。
> *kore wa ringo de wa arimasen*
> **This is not an apple.**
> それはテーブルではありません。
> *sore wa tēburu de wa arimasen*
> **That is not a table.**

Interrogative

The interrogative in Japanese is not difficult. All you need to do is make a sentence in the affirmative and add the hiragana か (ka) at the end, giving the sentence an interrogative intonation when you say it. The *ka* particle serves as question mark in Japanese, that is why question marks are not used that much (although it is quite often used in manga, because of its visual effect).

Let's look at the same previous sentences, this time in the interrogative form.

> これはりんごですか。
> *kore wa ringo desu ka?*
> **Is this an apple?**
> それはテーブルですか。
> *sore wa tēburu desuka?*
> **Is that a table?**

As you can see, it is most simple: you just place *ka* at the end.

And now we are going to introduce the word *nan* or *nani*, the kanji for which is 何. This word means "what" and it is basic when asking questions. For example:

これは何ですか。

kore wa nan desu ka?

What is this?

これはりんごです。

kore wa ringo desu

This is an apple.

Simple form

To finish, we will introduce the simple form of the verb "to be", which is used very often in conversation. It is a shortened form, and it is used in informal situations.

です＝だ

desu = da

でした＝だった

deshita = datta

ではありません＝ではない／じゃない

de wa arimasen = de wa nai / ja nai

Therefore, *desu* becomes *da*, *deshita* becomes *datta* and *de wa arimasen* has two options, *de wa nai* and, more informal, *ja nai*.

We will give you the usual example, for a better understanding.

これはりんごじゃない。

kore wa ringo ja nai

This sentence means exactly the same as "*kore wa ringo de wa arimasen*," but it is much more colloquial.

Some vocabulary		
Kana	**Rōmaji**	**Meaning**
りんご	*Ringo*	Apple
テーブル	*Tēburu*	Table
とり	*Tori*	Bird
ボールペン	*Bōrupen*	Ballpoint pen
ばか	*Baka*	Idiot
テレビ	*Terebi*	Television
いす	*Isu*	Chair
ねこ	*Neko*	Cat
いぬ	*Inu*	Dog
ふで	*Fude*	Writing brush
コンピュータ	*Konpyūtā*	Computer
レモン	*Remon*	Lemon
本 (ほん)	*Hon*	Book
うた	*Uta*	Song
しゃしん	*Shashin*	Photo
アニメ	*Anime*	Animation film
漫画 (まんが)	*Manga*	Manga
おかね	*Okane*	Money

漫画例： *Manga-examples*

And, as usual, in the manga-examples section, we will illustrate the theory with manga panels. This time we will look at examples with the verb "to be" (です), in its different conjugations (present, past, and future tenses, and so on), and in its simple and formal forms.

a) Formal present form

Fabriō: そして私がアナタ達のコーチです。
Soshite watashi ga anatatachi no kōchi desu
Then I you PoP coach be
I am your coach, then.

We see here the simplest form of the verb "to be", that is the present form, which is です (*desu*). Remember, we hardly pronounce the *u*, and we will usually say something like *des*.

b) Informal present form

Kenji: あった！これだ！！！
atta! kore da!!!
Found! this be!
I found it! This is it!

We can see here two things we have learnt in this lesson. First, we have the verb "to be" in its simple form だ (*da*), much more informal, but with exactly the same meaning as です (*desu*). On the other hand, we have これ (*kore*), which means *this*.

c) Informal present form

> Irumi: 世の中正しいことばかりではありません。お気をつけて。
> *yo no naka tadashii koto bakari de wa arimasen O-ki o tsukete*
> World inside correct thing only not be Careful
> **Not everything in the world is good. Be careful.**

Here we see the negative form ではありません (*de wa arimasen*), which means "not be". The simple negative form of *desu* is *de wa nai* ではない, or *ja nai* じゃない We see this last form in most manga, since the conversations in them are usually colloquial. Going back to our example, we can also see the farewell expression (お気をつけて, *o-ki o tsukete*) (see Lesson 4).

d) Formal interrogative form

> Kurō: これも父の仕事ですか。
> *kore mo chichi no shigoto desu ka*
> This also   father job (Ques.)
> **Is this. . . my father's job as well?**

In this example we have the verb *desu* again, but now in the interrogative form. All we need to do is add the hiragana か (*ka*), which serves more or less as a question mark (?).

e) Informal past form

> Anne: 総理大臣ってどんな顔の人だった？
> *Sōri daijin tte donna kao no hito datta?*
> Prime Minister what kind of face person was?
> **What kind of person was the Prime Minister?**

Here we see the past form of the verb "to be" in its simple form, pronounced だった (*datta*). The formal form of the same verb is でした (*deshita*). The formal and simple forms of the same verb are used depending on the situation. In a conversation with friends we will use the simple form, and in more formal conversations we will use the formal one.

1 In a Japanese sentence, where does the verb always go?

2 Conjugate the past of the formal form of です (*desu*).

3 Conjugate the negative of the simple form of です (*desu*).

4 Write the following words in Japanese: "television," "song," "cat," and "bird."

5 How do you form the interrogative in a Japanese sentence?

6 Translate into English the following sentence: これはしゃしんではありません (*kore wa shashin de wa arimasen*).

7 Translate into English the following sentence: あれはとりじゃなかった (*are wa tori ja nakatta*).

8 Translate into Japanese the following sentence: "This was a manga" in both, simple and formal forms.

9 What is the meaning of the following words: *kore*, *sore*, *are*, and *dore*?

10 Which form will we use in a conversation with our best friend, the formal or the simple one?

This lesson deals with the four seasons, and the different meteo-rological phenomena. We will also give lots of words, for you to increase your Japanese vocabulary. However, don't forget you have a full glossary of all the vocabulary in the book in the appendixes.

Meteorological situation in Japan

As an introduction, we are going to explain the meteorological situation in Japan, so you can get a general idea. Japan, pronounced 日本 (*nihon or nippon*) in Japanese, is situated in the planet's northern hemisphere, and that means the seasons follow the same order as in United States or England, that is, in July and August it is summer, in January and February it is winter, etc.

Japan is situated in an area of great meteorological turbulence, and it has very changeable weather depending on the month of the year. In addition, Japan is in one of the areas with most tectonic activity, and this means there's a great risk of earthquakes (地震 *jishin*).

With regard to temperatures (温度 *ondo*), Japan, being a group of islands covering a long distance from the north (北 *kita*) to south (南 *minami*), has many meteorological changes. For example, Hokkaido (北海道 *hokkaidō*), the northernmost island, has an almost Siberian climate, extremely cold in winter and very cool summers, whereas the Okinawa archipelago (沖縄 *okinawa*), the group of islands in the southern end of Japan, has a tropical climate.

Climate

The other three large main islands in Japan, Honshu (本州 *honshū*), Shikoku (四国 *shikoku*), and Kyushu (九州 *kyūshū*), have a varied climate, depending on the latitude, but, generally speaking, they have not very cold winters (冬 *fuyu*), and quite hot summers (夏 *natsu*). For example, in Kyoto (京都 *kyōto*), a city placed more or less in the center of Japan, in the south of the largest island, Honshu, summer is very hot, the temperature easily reaching 97–98 °F (36℃), and very sultry (蒸し暑い *mushi atsui*), due to high humidity. Winters are quite cold, and temperatures below freezing point are not unusual. By the way, in Japan they use degrees centigrade, or Celsius, not Fahrenheit, as in the USA.

冬	春	夏	秋	寒い	涼しい	暑い	暖かい
Fuyu	*Haru*	*Natsu*	*Aki*	*Samui*	*Suzushii*	*Atsui*	*Atatakai*
Winter	Spring	Summer	Fall	Cold	Cool	Hot	Warm

風	台風	雨	雪	日	星	梅雨	嵐
Kaze	*Taifū*	*Ame*	*Yuki*	*Hi*	*Hoshi*	*Tsuyu*	*Arashi*
Wind	Typhoon	Rain	Snow	Sun	Star	Rainy season	Storm

月	雲	晴れ	曇り	きり	ひょう	紅葉	桜
Tsuki	*Kumo*	*Hare*	*Kumori*	*Kiri*	*Hyō*	*Momiji*	*Sakura*
Moon	Cloud	Sunny	Cloud	Fog	Hail	Autumn leaves	Cherry blossoms

Meteorological peculiarities

In Japan, the four seasons —spring 春 (*haru*), summer 夏 (*natsu*), fall 秋 (*aki*), winter 冬 (*fuyu*)— are very different, that is, there is a very clear division between the seasons, and each has its own peculiarity. It is very cold (寒い *samui*) in winter, the beautiful *sakura* (桜 cherry tree) blossoms in spring, it is very hot (暑い *atsui*) in summer, and the leaves in autumn take on red and brown tonalities, and are called *momiji* 紅葉.

Rain 雨 (ame) and snow 雪 (yuki)

It rains quite often in Japan, which is why they hardly have water restrictions, even though the Japanese take an *ofuro* お風呂 everyday—their daily bath with a lot of water, because a very deep bathtub must be filled. There are two months when it rains very often, they are June and September. In June, they have the rainy season (梅雨 *tsuyu*), so all through this month it rains almost every day. September is the typhoon (台風 *taifū*) season, with heavy storms and torrential rains. By the way, to say "It's raining today," you say 今日は雨が降ります。(*kyō wa ame ga furimasu*).

With regard to snow (雪 *yuki*), we will just mention it doesn't snow much in Japan, except in Hokkaido, where it snows heavily, but it is unusual on the other islands. To say "It's snowing today," we say 今日は雪が降ります。 (*kyō wa yuki ga furimasu*).

Some geography

To end the lesson, we will talk about Japanese geography. Japan (日本) has over 2,000 islands, but the four main ones are: Honshu 本州, Shikoku 四国, Kyushu 九州, and Hokkaido 北海道. Honshu is the largest island and that is where we find the main cities in Japan: Tokyo (東京 *Tōkyō*), Osaka (大阪 *Ōsaka*), Kobe (神戸 *Kōbe*), Nagoya 名古屋, Yokohama 横浜, Hiroshima 広島. Then, there is an archipelago called Okinawa 沖縄 in the south, and many, many small islands around the four large ones.

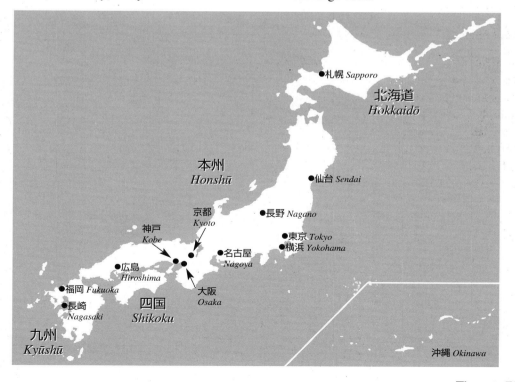

漫画例: *Manga-examples*

Here we have the usual manga-examples. The topic in this lesson is the four seasons, meteorology, and Japanese geography. The examples are in keeping with the topic, and they will illustrate everything we have said in the theory pages.

a) Wind and typhoon

Captain: 風が静まったわよ　台風はどうしたんだ!?
Kaze ga shizumatta wa yo　taifū wa dōshita n da!?
Wind died down typhoon what happened!?
The wind has died down.
What happened to the typhoon?

We see here two words related to the weather: wind 風 (*kaze*) and typhoon 台風 (*taifū*). Typhoons are very common in Japan around the month of September.

b) Snow

Conan: その年最初の雪が降り始めた…。
sono toshi saisho no yuki ga furi hajimeta...
That year first snowfalls start...
The first snowfalls of the year started...

In this example we have the word 雪 (*yuki*) which means snow. We can also see the verb used with this word to form the verb "to snow." 雪が降る (*yuki ga furu*) means "it's snowing." We see here a somewhat different form, 雪が降り始めた (*yuki ga furihajimeta*). If we use the suffix *hajimeru* after a verb, we give that verb the meaning of "it's starting to..." Therefore, this example, 雪が降り始めた (*yuki ga furihajimeta*) means "it started snowing." We find here as well the word 年 (*toshi*), year, which appeared in Lesson 6.

c) I'm cold

John: どうしたジェシカ？
Dōshita Jeshika?
What is the matter Jessica?
What's the matter, Jessica?

Jessica: う ううんなんだか寒いだけ。
u uun nanda ka samui dake
n nothing a little bit cold just
N... nothing, I'm just a little bit cold.

We have here the word 寒い (*samui*), very often used in Japan. It is a very important word, together with its opposite, 暑い (*atsui*), with means "hot." Incidentally, this word can be used to start any conversation. You only need to say 寒いですね (*samui desu ne*), "It's cold, isn't it?" to start a conversation with someone you don't know.

d) Some geography

Keita: サッポロラーメン食べたい。できれば家族そろって北海道へ…。
Sapporo rāmen tabetai   dekireba kazoku sorotte Hokkaidō e...
Sapporo *ramen* eat want if I could family gather Hokkaido to...
I'd like to eat Sapporo *ramen*. If I could, I'd go with my family to Hokkaido...

In this final example we will review Japanese geography. Here Keita is talking about Sapporo *ramen* (*ramen* are very popular Chinese noodles in Japan. Apparently, Sapporo ramen are specially good.) Then, Keita talks about going to Hokkaido (北海道.) If you take a look at the map in the theory section, you'll notice Hokkaido is the northernmost island in Japan, and that the main city in this island is Sapporo, with a population of over a million. An interesting fact we will point out is that Sapporo is where the winter Olympics were held in 1972.

1 In which hemisphere is the Japanese archipelago?

2 List the four seasons in Japanese.

3 What is peculiar about June in Japan, meteorologically speaking?

4 Write the following words in Japanese: "wind," "cold," "moon," and "star."

5 Write the pronunciation of the following words and their translation into English: 雪, 嵐, 暑い, and 桜.

6 How many islands form the Japanese archipelago?

7 Which are the 4 main islands in the Japanese archipelago?

8 Write at least 3 names of main Japanese cities.

9 What is the climate like in Hokkaido? And in the Okinawa archipelago?

10 What is a wise strategy to start a conversation with someone you don't know?

Lesson 11: Nouns

We are going to deal some more with grammar in this lesson, although it will not be very difficult, since nouns in Japanese are quite simple. We will take the opportunity to give some more vocabulary, which you will be needing from now on!

Japanese nouns

What is so special about Japanese nouns for us to devote a whole lesson to them? Well, there are two reasons: first, talking about nouns we can give a great deal of vocabulary in Japanese, something absolutely necessary, and very useful, of course, when studying a language; second, nouns don't work the same way in Japanese and English.

Differences

The main difference between English and Japanese nouns is that the latter have neither gender nor number. That is, the English words *boy*, *boys*, *girl*, and *girls* in Japanese are all *ko*, without distinction between one or more, male or female. This may seem surprising, but once you get used to it, it is very simple, because you don't need to think which is the correct way when there is one or several, or when it is male or female.

Let's have a look at an example:

これは子です。

kore wa ko desu

This sentence can have up to four different meanings:

a This is a boy.
b This is a girl.
c These are boys.
d These are girls.

Don't people get confused?

Well, yes, people can get mixed-up. If we want to specify whether something or someone is male or female, or whether there is one or several, we will have to make a more complex sentence. Thus, the following sentences correspond to a, b, c, and d.

A これは男の子が一人です。
kore wa otoko no ko ga hitori desu
This is a boy.

B これは女の子が一人です。
kore wa onna no ko ga hitori desu
This is a girl.

C これは男の子が五人です。
kore wa otoko no ko ga go nin desu
These are five boys.

D　これは女の子が五人です。

kore wa onna no ko ga go nin desu

These are five girls.

But this is very complicated, if you just say これは子です (*kore wa ko desu*) you'll be understood, you don't need to specify that much, unless the situation is a very extreme one where determining gender or number is absolutely necessary.

Counters

This leads us to how to count things in Japanese. In the previous sentences we see the word 人 (*nin*, with the exceptions of *hitori*—1 person, and *futari*—2 people) is used. That is what we call a counter. The use of counters is as follows: *thing that must be counted + ga + number + counter + verb*. For example:

これは紙が三枚です。

kore wa kami ga san mai desu

These are three sheets of paper.

kami = paper, *san* = 3, *mai* = counter

There are many counters, and they change depending on what we wish to count, therefore, there will be a lesson devoted to counters further on (Lesson 25). We give you some of them here:

人 *nin* for people　　　　本 *hon* for long things
枚 *mai* for flat things　　台 *dai* for machines
匹 *hiki* for small animals　さつ *satsu* for books, magazines...

Now you will study some new vocabulary so you can start forming your own sentences.

車	じてんしゃ	カメラ	しんぶん	たばこ	きって	えんぴつ	きょうしつ
kuruma	*jitensha*	*kamera*	*shinbun*	*tabako*	*kitte*	*enpitsu*	*kyōshitsu*
car	bicycle	camera	newspaper	tobacco	stamp	pencil	class

パン	にわ	たてもの	びょういん	トイレ	うち	さかな	にく
pan	*niwa*	*tatemono*	*byōin*	*toire*	*uchi*	*sakana*	*niku*
bread	garden	building	hospital	toilet	home	fish	meat

スープ	レストラン	かみ	おかし	バナナ	コーヒー	ごはん	やすみ
sūpu	*resutoran*	*kami*	*okashi*	*banana*	*kōhī*	*gohan*	*yasumi*
soup	restaurant	paper	sweet	banana	coffee	rice	rest

ギター	パーティー	うた	ざっし	えいが	てがみ	ビデオ
gitā	*pātī*	*uta*	*zasshi*	*eiga*	*tegami*	*bideo*
guitar	party	song	magazine	film	letter	video

きょう	あした	きのう	あさ	ひる	ゆうがた	よる
kyō	*ashita*	*kinō*	*asa*	*hiru*	*yūgata*	*yoru*
today	tomorrow	yesterday	morning	noon	evening	night

漫画例：Manga-examples

In this lesson's manga-examples we will see some nouns which are different to the ones we have given before. Nouns are usually written in kanji in manga, and they are the easiest words to look up in a dictionary, since their form never changes (there are neither plurals, nor male or female forms, etc.)

a) Tear / blood

Yūsuke: 血の…涙
chi no... namida
Blood PoP tear
Tears of... blood.

In this example we find two nouns, 血 *chi* (blood) and 涙 *namida* (tear). As we can see, it doesn't say whether there is one tear or there are several, but we could almost tell for certain there are more than one, hence the translation in the plural form. We also find the particle の (*no*), used to show possessive. We will explain the particles in a lesson further on (Lesson 16).

b) Heart / Review of lesson 7

おまえの心臓よ！！

Kamada: おまえの心臓よ！！
omae no shinzō yo!!
you PoP heart (emph.) !!
It's your heart!

We will use this example to review Lesson 7, where we talked about personal pronouns. We have here the word おまえ (*omae*), which means "you," but *omae* has a superiority connotation, where the person talking feels superior to the person he or she is talking to. Therefore, it is quite rough and used in very informal conversations…
On the other hand, we have the particle の (*no*) again, indicating possessive, and the noun 心臓 (*shinzō*), which means "heart." The ending particle よ (*yo*) is used to emphasize the sentence. We will give more information on this particle further on.

c) Several nouns (1)

Ujihira: 歯向かうヤツはブチころす！！　酒と女と悦楽の日々！
Hamukau yatsu wa buchi korosu!!　sake to onna to etsuraku no hibi!
Defy person (vulg.) kill!!　alcohol and woman and pleasure PoP day after day!
I'll kill whoever defies me!　A life of drink, women, and pleasure!

We have here some more nouns, like ヤツ –*yatsu*, person, in a vulgar sense, more or less equivalent to "guy"–, 酒 –*sake*, alcohol, in the broad sense of the word, or Japanese *sake* in the limited sense–, 女 –*onna*, woman–, 悦楽 –*etsuraku*, pleasure–, and 日々 –*hibi*, day after day.– We have translated the word 女 (*onna*) as "women," in plural, for an English speaker would talk about women, and not about one only woman in this case.

d) Several nouns (2)

Inaho: やった！やったわ！！
Yatta! yatta wa!!
Done! (past) done (past) (fem. emph.)!!
Yes! I made it!

血の契約完了よ！！
chi no keiyaku kanryō yo!!
Blood PoP contract completion (emph)!!
I made a blood pact!

More nouns: 血 (*chi*, blood), 契約 (*keiyaku*, contract), 完了 (*kanryō*, completion). We see here the word やった (*yatta*), used in the sense of "Yes!," or "I made it!" We've given both translations, to avoid repetition. We also have the end-of-sentence particles, わ (*wa*, used by women) and よ (*yo*). We will see more about this kind of particle in Lesson 17.

e) People counter

Seiichiro: おそらく… 『七人の御使い』。
...osoraku... "shichinin no mitsukai"
...maybe... "seven people PoP use (rel.)"
Maybe… "A user of seven people."

In this example we have several interesting things. First of all, the counter *nin*, which, together with 七 (*shichi*, seven), means "seven people." This is a very common example of the use of counters.

On the other hand, we see the Japanese quotation marks, written in a totally different way from English. In Japanese, the symbols 『 and 』 are used to indicate quotation marks. The prefix 御 (*mi*) from 御使い (*mitsukai*) gives the word 使い (*tsukai*, use) a "mystical" or "religious meaning."

1 What are the main features of Japanese nouns?

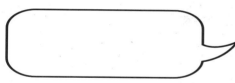

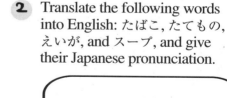

2 Translate the following words into English: たばこ, たてもの, えいが, and スープ, and give their Japanese pronunciation.

3 Translate the following words into Japanese: fish, rice, noon, and restaurant.

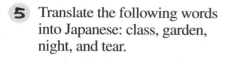

4 Translate the following words into English: 車, 血, ギター, and 酒, and give their Japanese pronunciation.

5 Translate the following words into Japanese: class, garden, night, and tear.

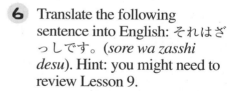

6 Translate the following sentence into English: それはざっしです。(*sore wa zasshi desu*). Hint: you might need to review Lesson 9.

7 Translate the following sentence into Japanese: That is a letter. Hint: review Lesson 9.

8 Translate the following sentence into English: これはバナナでした。(*kore wa banana deshita*). Hint: review Lesson 9.

9 If Japanese nouns have neither gender nor number, how can we tell we are talking about one or more, feminine or masculine?

10 What are counters and what do we use them for?

第⑫課：何時ですか？

In this lesson, we will learn how to tell the time. As you might have deduced, this lesson will have a lot to do with numbers, so we highly recommend you to thoroughly review Lesson 5 before beginning this one.

Some special readings

First and foremost, you must focus on the vocabulary. You have probably noticed there are words in bold type in the adjunctive table. They stand for special kanji readings. For example, the kanji 四時 is pronounced *yo ji* and not *yon ji* or *shi ji*, which would be the other options (see Lesson 5). Likewise, 六分 is pronounced *roppun* and not *roku fun*.

We will mention as well the case of the kanji 分, usually read as *fun*, except in certain cases when, due to phonetical reasons, it is pronounced *pun*. This is the case with 1, 3, 4, 6, 8, and 10, *ippun, san pun, yon pun, roppun, happun,* and *juppun,* respectively. The kanji 十分 has two valid readings, *juppun* and *jippun*.

The correct pronunciations of the kanji for hours and minutes are actually quite difficult, since there are many exceptions and you need to learn the different pronunciations by heart.

Telling the time

Telling the time in Japanese is really very easy, there are only three points to be explained, and they aren't essential, anyway. We will explain why further on.

When someone asks for the time, the first word you say is 今は (*ima wa*), which means "now." Then you tell the time, and finish with the verb です (*desu*, to be—see Lesson 9).

We will now look at the first clock in the next page to tell the o'clock times, a very simple expression. You only have to follow the pattern 今はX時です。(*ima wa X ji desu*), replacing X with a number. For example, 今は九時です。(*ima wa ku ji desu*) means "it is now nine o'clock."

Other constructions

There are three other basic constructions in Japanese: half past, a quarter past, and a quarter to. Once more, let's look at the clocks. To say "It's half past X," all we need to do is add 半 (*han*) after 時 (*ji*): 今はX時半です。(*ima wa X ji han desu*)

To say "It's a quarter past X," we add 十五分すぎ (*jū go fun sugi*): 今はX時十五分すぎです。(*ima wa X ji jū go fun sugi desu*)

And finally, "It's a quarter to X" is constructed by adding 十五分まえ (*jū go fun mae*): 今はX時十五分まえです。(*ima wa X ji jū go fun mae desu*)

A hint to better understand these constructions: 半 (*han*) means "half," すぎ (*sugi*) means "to exceed," and まえ (*mae*) means "before." This way it is easier to understand, isn't it?

Still simpler

Actually, none of this is essential, since you can always say "it's X Y (minutes)." For example, at 6:30 you can either say 今は六時半です。 (*ima wa roku ji han desu*), "It's half past six," or 今は六時三十分です。 (*ima wa roku ji san juppun desu*) "It's six thirty."

Sample conversation

To end this lesson, we will give you a conversation as an example.

A: すみませんが…
sumimasen ga...
Excuse me…

B: はい、何でしょうか。
hai, nan deshō ka?
Yes, can I help you?

A: 今は何時ですか?
ima wa nan ji desu ka?
What's the time, please?

B: ええ…今はX時Y分です。
ee... ima wa X ji Y fun desu
Mmm... It's now X Y.

A: ありがとうございます。
arigatō gozaimasu
Thank you very much.

B: どういたしまして。
dō itashimashite
You're welcome.

Hours 時 (ji)		Minutes 分 (fun)	
一時	*ichi ji*	一分	***ippun***
二時	*ni ji*	二分	*ni fun*
三時	*san ji*	三分	*san pun*
四時	***yo ji***	四分	*yon pun*
五時	*go ji*	五分	*go fun*
六時	*roku ji*	六分	***roppun***
七時	***shichi ji***	七分	*nana fun*
八時	*hachi ji*	八分	***happun***
九時	***ku ji***	九分	*kyū fun*
十時	*jū ji*	十分	***jippun / juppun***
十一時	*jū ichi ji*	十一分	***jūippun***
十二時	*jū ni ji*	十二分	*jū ni fun*
何時？	*nan ji?*	何分？	*nan pun?*
Special readings in bold type			

This conversation could easily be taking place right now in Kamakura, for instance, or in any other place in Japan. All you need to do is change the X and Y for the corresponding hour and minutes. Give it a try!

今は八時です。
ima wa hachi ji desu
It's now eight o'clock.

今は五時十五分すぎです。
ima wa go ji jū go fun sugi desu
It's now a quarter past five.

今は三時半です。
ima wa san ji han desu
It's now half past three.

今は十一時十五分まえです。
ima wa jū ichi ji jū go fun mae desu
It's now a quarter to eleven.

漫画例：*Manga-examples*

As well as illustrating the contents of the theory pages with manga panels, we will use the manga-examples in this lesson to learn a little about Japanese culture. We are talking about the translation of part of an information leaflet from Hiroshima's Peace Memorial Museum.

a) 3:30

Sekiguchi: 3時24分…タイムリミットは3時半…。
san ji ni jū yon pun... taimu rimitto wa san ji han...
3 hour 24 minute... time limit 3 hour half...
It's 3:24... The time limit is half past 3...
それまでにやらなきゃ…。
sore made ni yaranakya...
then before do (expressing obligation)...
It must be done by that time...

In this example we have two times, 3時24分 (*san ji ni jū yon pun*, 3:24) and 3時半 (*san ji han*, half past 3). In the last case, we could also say 3時30分 (*san ji san juppun*, 3:30). We find here as well the katakana タイムリミット (*taimu rimitto*), which comes from the English "time limit."

b) What's the time?

Kintarō: そうだ今何時だ!?
sō da ima nan ji da!?
that be now what time be!?
That's right! What's the time?

Miyuki: 12時10分よ。
jū ni ji juppun yo
12 hours 10 minutes (excl.)
It's 10 past 12.

We will use this example to illustrate two of the points we saw in the previous pages. The first point is how to ask the time. We saw the formal way, 今は何時ですか？ (*ima wa nan ji desu ka?*). Here, Kintarō uses the informal way (slightly rough, but OK among friends), 今何時だ (*ima nan ji da*). This last way does without the *wa* particle and uses the simple form of the verb です (*desu*, to be), (see Lesson 9). The second point is the answer, where Miyuki says 12時10分 (*jū ni ji juppun*), 10 past 12.

c) 6:10

Kei: 6時10分を指していたよ。
roku ji juppun o sashiteita yo
six hours indicate (past) EP
The time was 10 past 6.

Kei is talking about a clock, that's why she uses the verb 指す (*sasu*), "to point (at the hours)." This time, the example is 6時10分 (*roku ji juppun*), 10 past 6.

d) The Hiroshima bomb

はじめに

　1945（昭和20）年8月6日午前8時15分、広島は世界で初めて原子爆弾による被害を受けました。まちはほとんどが破壊され、多くの人びとの生命がうばわれました。かろうじて生き残った人も、心と体に大きな痛手を受け、多くの被爆者がいまなお苦しんでいます。

　平和記念資料館は、被爆者の遺品や被爆の惨状を示す写真や資料を収集・展示するとともに、広島の被爆前後の歩みや核時代の状況などについて紹介しています。

　資料の一つ一つには、人びとの悲しみや怒りが込められています。原爆の惨禍からよみがえったヒロシマの願いは、核兵器のない平和な社会を実現することです。

はじめに：1945（昭和20）年8月6日午前8時15分、広島は世界で初めて原子爆弾による被害を受けました。

hajime ni: 1945 (shōwa 20) nen 8 gatsu muika gozen hachi ji jūgo fun, hiroshima wa sekai de hajimete genshi bakudan ni yoru higai o ukemashita

start: 1945 (year showa 20) 8 month 6 day morning eight hours fifteen minutes, Hiroshima world in first of all atomic bomb by damage suffer

Introduction: At 8:15 a.m., August 6, 1945, the world's first atomic bomb exploded over Hiroshima.

8時15分で止まった時計

８時15分で止まった時計
hachi ji jūgo fun de tomatta tokei
eight hours fifteen minutes stopped watch
This watch stopped at 8:15.

This is part of the information leaflet from Hiroshima's Peace Memorial Museum, in its Japanese version. We can see a date and a time in it. If you like, take a look at Lesson 6 to review dates. In this case, the time is ８時15分 (*hachi ji jūgo fun*), which means "a quarter past eight."

1 Translate the following words into English, and give their Japanese pronunciation: 七分, 三時, 四分 and 九時.

2 Translate the following words into Japanese and give their pronunciation: ten minutes, eight o'clock, two minutes, and five o'clock.

3 Translate the following sentence into Japanese: "it's seven o'clock."

4 Translate the following sentence into English, and give its Japanese pronunciation: 今は六時です。

5 Translate the following sentence into Japanese: "it's a quarter past three."

6 Translate the following sentence into English, and give its Japanese pronunciation: 今は八時十五分まえです。

7 In what two different ways can you say in Japanese "it's half past nine?"

8 Translate the following sentence into Japanese: "It's 4:33." Note: You may have to review Lesson 9.

9 Ask what time it is.

10 Answer question 5, giving the exact time right now.

第13課：形容詞

Lesson 13: "i" adjectives

In this lesson we will learn one of two kinds of Japanese adjectives: the "i" adjectives. An adjective is a noun-qualifying word, that is, it indicates a quality of the noun. For example, in "expensive car," the word "expensive" is an adjective showing a quality in the car, in this case that it costs a lot of money.

Why "i" adjective?

In Japanese there are two kinds of adjectives, unlike in English, where there is no distinction. The so-called "i" adjective is one of these. The other kind is the so-called "na" adjective. Why "i?" The reason these adjectives belong to the "i" kind is that they all end in the letter "i," with no exceptions. Obviously, "na" adjectives end in "na," but that is another subject, and we will explain it in Lesson 14.

In Japanese, like in English, adjectives always go before the noun they modify. For example, "tall tree" is 高い木 (*takai ki / takai* = tall, *ki* = tree), and "blue sky" is 青い空 (*aoi sora / aoi* = blue, *sora* = sky).

漢字 kanji	ローマ字 rōmaji	翻訳 translation
小さい	*Chiisai*	Small
大きい	*Ookii*	Big
易しい	*Yasashii*	Easy
難しい	*Muzukashii*	Difficult
白い	*Shiroi*	White
赤い	*Akai*	Red
青い	*Aoi*	Blue
黒い	*Kuroi*	Black
黄色い	*Kiiroi*	Yellow
高い	*Takai*	Tall / Expensive
安い	*Yasui*	Cheap
低い	*Hikui*	Low
新しい	*Atarashii*	New
古い	*Furui*	Old
暗い	*Kurai*	Dark
明るい	*Akarui*	Bright

"i" adjectives are inflected

We have reached the most difficult point about Japanese adjectives. Not only are there two kinds ("i" and "na"), which work in different ways, but we also find "i" adjectives are inflected. Read carefully, because as it is a concept that doesn't exist in English, doubts and misunderstandings may arise.

Fortunately, there are only four kinds of inflection, present-affirmative, past-affirmative, present-negative, and past-negative. The formation of these four inflections is illustrated in the table on the next page. Let's look at them, one by one, with examples.

The four inflections

Present-affirmative: This is the easiest form, it is the adjective as it is, with no changes. For example: bright day 明るい日 (*akarui hi / akarui* = bright, *hi* = day), white book 白い本 (*shiroi hon / shiroi* = white, *hon* = book).

Past-affirmative: The final "i" in the adjective is' replaced with "*katta*", past ending. For example: day that was bright 明るかった日 (*akarukatta hi*), book that was white 白かった本 (*shirokkata hon*).

Present-negative: The final "i" in the adjective is replaced with "*kunai*", negative ending. For example: day that isn't bright 明るくない日 (*akarukunai hi*), book that isn't white 白くない本 (*shirokunai hon*).

Past-negative: This is a combination of the two last ones. The final "i" in the adjective is replaced with "*kuna*," negative ending, + "*katta*," past ending. For example: day that was't bright 明るくなかった日 (*akarukunakatta hi*), book that wasn't white 白くなかった本 (*shirokunakkata hon*).

Inflection of "i" adjectives		Affirmative	Negative
Present	Rule	いです	~~い~~くないです
	Example	やすいです	やすくないです
	Rōmaji	*yasui desu*	*yasukunai desu*
	Translation	**It's cheap**	**It isn't cheap**
Past	Rule	~~い~~かったです	~~い~~くなかったです
	Example	やすかったです	やすくなかったです
	Rōmaji	*yasukatta desu*	*yasukunakatta desu*
	Translation	**It was cheap**	**It wasn't cheap**

Now let's try with the adjective *atatakai* (warm), but read carefully as it gets very complicated.

Inflection of "i" adjectives		Affirmative	Negative
Present	Rule	い	~~い~~くない
	Example	あたたかいです	あたたかくないです
	Rōmaji	*atatakai desu*	*atatakakunai desu*
	Translation	**It's warm**	**It isn't warm**
Past	Rule	~~い~~かった	~~い~~くなかった
	Example	あたたかかったです	あたたかくなかったです
	Rōmaji	*atatakakatta desu*	*atatakakunakatta desu*
	Translation	**It was warm**	**It wasn't warm**

Sentences with the verb desu (to be)

Remembering Lesson 9 (basic grammar) is essential to understand this lesson perfectly, since we will assume there are many things you already know.

How do you construct sentences such as "This bag is heavy." or "That dog is dangerous?" The answer is using the verb *desu* (to be), and mastering the words *kono* (this), *sono* (that one here), and *ano* (that one over there). We will give you some sample sentences.

このかばんは重いです。
kono kaban wa omoi desu
This bag is heavy.
(*kaban* = bag, *omoi* = heavy)

あのマンガはおもしろくないです。
ano manga wa omoshirokunai desu
That manga is not interesting.
(*omoshiroi* = interesting)

その犬は危なかったです。
sono inu wa abunakatta desu
That dog was dangerous.
(*inu* = dog, *abunai* = dangerous)

あの肉はおいしくなかったです。
ano niku wa oishikunakatta desu
That meat wasn't good.
(*niku* = meat, *oishii* = good, delicious)

As you can see, adjectives are inflected, and the verb to be is not conjugated—it always remains the same, that is, in its infinitive form.

A warning!

A sentence like this is completely wrong:

　　* その犬は危ないでした。　　*sono inu wa abunai deshita (That dog was dangerous).

This is a completely wrong sentence, because, instead of inflecting the adjective, the verb has been conjugated. You have to take care with this special characteristic of "i" adjectives, constructing wrong sentences is extremely easy, because the concept of inflecting adjectives and leaving the verb in the infinitive doesn't exist in English.

However, in spoken language and manga, which reflect the spoken language, the verb *desu* is usually left out, and, therefore, the sentence would be: その犬は危なかった (*sono inu wa abunakatta*, that dog was dangerous).

漫画例: *Manga-examples*

As usual, we have selected some manga panels to illustrate what was explained in the theory pages.

a) Present-affirmative (1)

Raishinshi: 速い！！！
hayai!!!
That's fast!

As we mentioned above, in spoken language the verb *desu* is usually left out when using "i" adjectives. This is a very clear case, where the adjective is used on its own. When translating into English, leaving the adjective on its own wouldn't sound natural ("Fast!," in this case), and so, something must be added, as in our suggestion: "That's fast!!"

b) Present-affirmative (2)

Sakura: かっこいい…。
kakkoii...
He's handsome...

This use of the "i" adjective is exactly the same as the previous one, that is, without the verb *desu* (to be). This time our option in the translation is adding the personal pronoun "he", plus the omitted verb, "is."

Kakkoii is a word used by women when referring to a handsome man (among other usages). The other way around, when a man wants to say a woman is beautiful, he can say 美しい (*utsukushii*) or 美人です (*bijin desu*). *Utsukushii* is also an "i" adjective.

c) Past-affirmative

Kishi: 相手が悪かったな。
aite ga warukatta na
rival SP bad EP
You chose a bad rival...

The main word in this example is 悪かった (*warukatta*), the past affirmative form of the adjective 悪い (*warui, bad*). In the translation, we have used the verb "to choose," which doesn't appear in the original, because the literal translation doesn't sound correct. By the way, the opposite of *warui* (bad) is いい (*ii*, good).

d) Present-affirmative (3)

Wolf:	あ！その肉あまってんのか…？
	a! sono niku amatten no ka...?
	oh! that meat leaft EP Q?
	Oh! Was there still that meat left...?

おかしいと思った…！！
okashii to omotta...!!
odd CP thought…!!
That's odd!

The "i" adjective we want to show you in this example is おかしい (*okashii*), "odd, strange." It comes in its present-affirmative form, so it isn't inflected. Another point worth making about this example is the expression と思った (*to omotta*), "I thought that..." We haven't translated it, leaving "that's odd" on its own. The reason for this is that, in Japanese, the expression "think that..." is extremely common, whereas it may sometimes sound unnatural in English.

e) Present-negative

And to end this Lesson, we will see an "i" adjective in its present-negative form. It's こわくない (*kowakunai*), and its dictionary form is *kowai*, "scary." Also, we see here a point mentioned in Lesson 7 (personal pronouns). The girl, Mio, doesn't use the second person personal pronoun (you) to talk to the boy, instead, she uses his name. Were we to translate it literally, the sentence would be: "Tadaomi is not afraid of me?" It might seem they are talking in the third person, that is why we have added "you" in the translation.

Mio:	忠臣くんあたしがこわくないの？
	Tadaomi-kun atashi ga kowakunai no ?
	Tadaomi me SP not afraid Q?
	Tadaomi, aren't you afraid of me?

1 What are "i" adjectives? Why are they called that?

2 With regard to the noun, in what position do Japanese adjectives always go?

3 Translate the following words into English and give their Japanese pronunciation: 赤い, 古い, 大きい, and 高い.

4 Translate the following words into Japanese and give their pronunciation: small, blue, dark, cheap.

5 How are the "i" adjectives inflected in the past?

6 And how about the negative inflection?

7 Inflect the past-negative of the adjective 白い (shiroi, white.)

8 Inflect the present and past affirmative, and the present and past negative of the adjective 黒い (kuroi, black.)

9 Translate the following sentence into Japanese: "This mountain is low." (mountain: 山 (yama)).

10 Is the following sentence correct: このねこはおとなしいではありません。 (kono neko wa otonashii de wa arimasen)? (Neko: cat / otonashii: meek ("i" adj.) Why?

In the previous lesson we talked about one of two kinds of adjectives in the Japanese language: the "i" adjectives. Now we are going to talk about the "na" adjectives, which have a different construction to the "i" adjectives. We recommend reviewing the previous lessons; this time, take a good look at Lessons 9 (basic grammar) and 13 ("i" adjectives).

Why "na" adjectives?

As we explained in Lesson 13, there are two kinds of adjectives in Japanese, "i" and "na" adjectives. You may remember "i" adjectives are called that because they all end in "i." Well, "na" adjectives are named this way for the same reason: they all end in "na," with no exceptions. You can have a look at the vocabulary table to confirm this rule.

Just like "i" adjectives, "na" adjectives always go before the noun they modify. Here are some examples:

下手な大工 (heta-na daiku)
Clumsy carpenter (heta-na = clumsy / daiku = carpenter)
好きな女 (suki-na onna)
The woman I like (suki-na = that one likes / onna = woman)

漢字 kanji	ローマ字 rōmaji	翻訳 translation
大変な	Taihen-na	Serious, difficult
静かな	Shizuka-na	Calm
きれいな	Kirei-na	Pretty
ひまな	Hima-na	Spare time
丈夫な	Jōbu-na	Healthy, strong
元気な	Genki-na	Cheerful, strong
親切な	Shinsetsu-na ~~Taisetsu-na~~	Kind
危険な	Kiken-na	Dangerous
安全な	Anzen-na	Safe
上手な	Jōzu-na	Skillful
下手な	Heta-na	Clumsy
大切な	Taisetsu-na	Important
有名な	Yūmei-na	Famous
大丈夫な	Daijōbu-na	Sure, safe
好きな	Suki-na	To like
嫌いな	Kirai-na	To dislike

Then, if they are similar in everything up to this point, what are the differences between them?

Adjectives "na" are NOT inflected

Here we come to the most important difference between the two kinds of Japanese adjectives. In Lesson 13 we explained how "i" adjectives had four forms: present-affirmative, past-affirmative, present-negative, and past-negative. The verb *desu* (to be) was always left in the infinitive.

"na" adjectives are NOT inflected: the verb "to be" is conjugated instead, as you can see in the table of the forms of the "na" adjectives.

Then, how do "na" adjectives work?

Handling "na" adjectives is much simpler than "i" adjectives because they are not inflected. All you need to do to construct sentences with the verb "to be" is to conjugate this verb, and remove the "na" ending of the adjective. In this page you have a table with all the possible conjugations. We have added its "formal" and "simple" forms. The first is used in formal situations, and the second one when talking with friends. The simple form is used more often, by far, in manga, as we will see in Lessons 19 and 20.

Forms of "na" adjectives		Affirmative		Negative	
		desu form	Simple form	*desu* form	Simple form
Present	**Rule**	春です	春だ	春ではありません	春ではない
	Example	有名です	有名だ	有名ではありません	有名ではない
	Rōmaji	*yūmei desu*	*yūmei da*	*yūmei de wa arimasen*	*yūmei de wa nai*
	Translation	**Is famous**		**Isn't famous**	
Past	**Rule**	春でした	春だった	春ではありませんでした	春ではなかった
	Example	有名でした	有名だった	有名ではありませんでした	有名ではなかった
	Rōmaji	*yūmei deshita*	*yūmei datta*	*yūmei de wa arimasendeshita*	*yūmei de wa nakatta*
	Translation	**Was famous**		**Wasn't famous**	

Sentences with the verb desu (to be)

In this section you have a table explaining how to construct sentences with the verb *desu* (to be) and "na" adjectives. However, for a better understanding, we will construct some illustrative sentences.

この本は大切です。(formal pres. aff.)
kono hon wa taisetsu desu
This book is important.
(*hon* = book / *taisetsu* = important)

あの道は危険ではない。(simple pres. neg.)
Ano michi wa kiken de wa nai
That road isn't dangerous.
(*michi* = road / *kiken* = dangerous)

私は魚が大嫌いでした。(formal past aff.)
Watashi wa sakana ga daikirai deshita
I didn't like fish at all.
(*watashi* = I / *sakana* = fish / *daikirai* = not like at all)

その花はきれいではなかった。(sple. past neg.)
Sono hana wa kirei de wa nakatta
That flower wasn't pretty.
(*hana* = flower / *kirei* = pretty)

You have probably noticed that "na" adjectives work just like nouns, so once you master Lesson 11 you should have no problem.

When do we leave "na," and when do we remove it?

As you have observed, the "na" particle sometimes disappears, and sometimes stays. When does this happen? You only keep the "na" particle when the adjective comes before a noun, as in the examples we saw earlier:

下手な大工 *(heta-na daiku)*
Clumsy carpenter

The "na" particle disappears when the adjective comes before the verb "to be", as in:

この大工は下手です。
kono daiku wa heta desu
This carpenter is clumsy.

As you can see, the "na" adjective we have used is the same in both examples, 下手な (*heta-na*, clumsy). We keep the "na" particle in the first example, and we remove it in the second one, following grammatical rules.

A warning!

You may remember towards the end of Lesson 13 we mentioned "i" adjectives could go without the verb "to be" in informal situations, as for example:

試験は難しかった（です）。

shiken wa muzukashikatta (desu) → it is omitted

The exam was difficult.

(*shiken* = exam / *muzukashikatta* = was difficult)

With "na" adjectives, the verb "to be" must always be there, whether in the simple form or in the formal one, as for example in:

試験は大変だった。

shiken wa taihen datta

(*taihen* = difficult)

The exam was difficult.

Muzukashii and *taihen-na* are synonymous here. The second is a "na" adjective, and therefore always needs the verb *desu*. Whereas the "i" adjective can go without this verb.

漫画例：*Manga-examples*

We will now see the practical use and the differences of use of "na" adjectives. We will review once more what we saw in the theory pages.

a) Present-affirmative

Takara: 大丈夫だよ。
daijōbu da yo
well/correct be EP
It's okay. / Don't worry.

In this first example, we see a "na" adjective in a sentence with the verb *desu* (to be.) As we saw in the table, we have here a simple form in the present-affirmative. The simple form is much used in manga, being as it is the chosen form in an informal conversation with friends, family, etc. The "na" adjective in this example 大丈夫な (*daijōbu-na*) is very commonly used in Japanese. Its approximate translation into English would be "I'm okay," "Don't worry."

b) Past-affirmative

> Zorg: 残念だったな…。
> *zannen datta na...*
> pity be (past) EP
> **What a pity...!**

Here we have another inflection example, this time the simple form of the past-affirmative. The words in the literal translations marked as EP are particles which emphasize the sentence; in this example we have *na*, in the first example we have *yo*, and in the last example we have *wa*. They have different nuances, which we will see in a later lesson (Lesson 17). *Zannen-na* means "what a pity," "what a shame."

c) Present-negative

> Tatsuhiko: なんだ、元気じゃねーか。
> *nan da, genki ja nee ka*
> what be, healthy be (neg.) Q?
> **What's wrong?**
> **Aren't you feeling well?**

We see here the simple form of the present-negative of the adjective 元気な (*genki-na*.) The *de wa* part in *genki de wa nai* is often contracted, becoming *ja*, as in this example, where we have *genki ja nai*.

In addition, Tatsuhiko is talking in the Kanto dialect (Tokyo and its surroundings), and so we have yet another contraction, dialectal this time: *nai* becomes *nee*. Thus, what in standard Japanese would be *genki de wa nai*, here becomes *genki ja nee*. *Genki-na* means "strong," "healthy," "lively."

d) Past-negative

Nanako: あたしちっともイヤじゃなかった。
atashi chittomo iya ja nakatta
I nothing unpleasant not be (past)
I didn't find it unpleasant at all.

And to complete the set, we have the past-negative form of the adjective *iya-na*. It is written in katakana in this example, but the kanji version 嫌な (*iya-na*) is very common as well. According to the dictionary, *iya-na* means "unpleasant," "offensive," "lousy," "nasty," "disgusting," and "repulsive." This word appears very often in manga. In this example, we also have the contraction we saw in the Tatsuhiko example, *de wa* in *de wa nakatta* becomes *ja (ja nakatta)*.

e) When do we keep the "na" particle?

Tamiko: イヤな予感がするわ…。
iya-na yokan ga suru wa...
unpleasant foreboding SP do EP
I have a horrible foreboding...

To end this lesson's examples section, we will give you an example of when we do NOT remove the *na* particle in "na" adjectives. As we previously said, we only keep the *na* particle when there's a noun after the adjective, as in this case, where we have the noun *yokan* (foreboding). Therefore, as Tamiko says, the sentence is not *iya yokan ga suru wa*, but *iya-na yokan ga suru wa*. The sentence would be wrong without the *na*. Otherwise, the adjective here is *iya-na* once more, and like in the previous example, it is written in katakana instead of kanji.

1 What are "na" adjectives? Why are they called that?

2 What is the difference between "i" and "na" adjectives?

3 What happens to the "na" adjective when it comes before the verb *to be*?

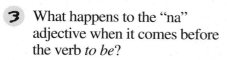

4 Translate the following words into English and give their Japanese pronunciation: 丈夫な, 親切な, 好きな, and ひまな.

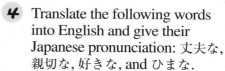

5 Translate the following words into Japanese and give their pronunciation: dangerous, pretty, famous, and skillful.

6 How do we conjugate the past of "na" adjectives in both forms, *desu* and simple? Give an example with any "na" adjective you like.

7 Conjugate the past negative (*desu* form) of the adjective 大変な (*taihen-na*, difficult, serious).

8 Conjugate the present and past affirmative, and the present and past negative (*desu* and simple forms) of the adjective 元気な (*genki-na*, strong, lively).

9 Translate the following sentence into Japanese: "That road was safe," using the *desu* form (*road*: 道 (*michi*)). We suggest reviewing Lesson 9.

10 Translate the following construction into Japanese: "quiet park" (park: 公園 (*kōen*)).

We will see another feature of the Japanese language in this lesson: suffixes for proper names, very much related to Japanese ways and their hierarchical society. We already mentioned this hierarchical aspect in Lesson 7 (personal pronouns).

Social hierarchy

Theoretically, Japan is an egalitarian society, but practice proves distances are quite marked, mainly among people of different ages. The relationship *senpai-kōhai* (senior–junior) or *sensei-gakusei* (teacher–student), and many others, turn out to be very important, to the extent that the way of talking about oneself changes completely, both grammatically and lexically. For example, a 25-year-old man talks in an informal–vulgar way with his friends, but with his *sensei* his way of talking changes radically. We already saw an aspect about these hierarchies in Lesson 7, in the first person personal pronouns.

Suffixes for proper names

Japanese obviously has several characteristics which are totally different from Western languages. One of them is the use of suffixes after people's names. That is, in Japanese, when we refer to someone by their given name or surname, we must always add a suffix after that name. The most common suffix is *–san*. For example, if we refer to *Tanaka*, we will not just say *Tanaka*, but always *Tanaka-san*. The sentence "Tanaka is handsome" would be:

田中さんはカッコイイです。
Tanaka-san wa kakkoii desu
Tanaka SP handsome be

Adding the suffix *–san* to proper names is very important, for, if we don't do it, we will be considered very rude. So we should be careful to remember.

Formal? Informal?

The suffix *–san* implies a certain formality. It would be equivalent to adding Mr., Mrs., or Ms. to somebody's name in English. We have other options, of course, and we will now explain them one by one, from more formal to less so:

–dono: this is an extremely formal suffix, as well as old-fashioned, and is only used in samurai films or the likes. Try not using it, unless you are playing samurais.

–sama: very formal suffix, used mainly in written language or in the client–shop assistant relationship. The shop assistant will always address the client using *–sama*, as, for example, in the expression *o-kyaku-sama* (Mr./Mrs./Ms. client). Letters are always addressed to Tanaka-sama, and not Tanaka-san. Using *–san* in letters means a lack of respect, so take care. *–sama* is also used when a subject is talking to a king. In the past, children would address their parents using *–sama*.

–san: we have already explained the use of this suffix. It is the most commonly used.

–kun: this expression is quite often used "when senior speaks to junior," when the first is referring to the second. However, it is also used among young people when they are not too familiar with each other yet. It may be the equivalent of "Mr.," "Mrs.," or "Ms.," but is not as strong as *–san*. It is usually used with male names, and if the speaker is a woman, it shows some familiarity towards the male interlocutor.

–chan: affectionate suffix used with children names. It can be used with more grown-up girls as well, when speakers know each other very well. Take care not to use it with a man, because it would sound as if you were talking to a child or a girl.

The name alone:

finally, among fairly close friends, young people, parents to children, etc., people are nowadays being called by their name alone. Take care when calling someone without suffix, it has to be a close and young friend. If that is not the case, using any of the previous suffixes is a better option, except *–dono*, *–sama*, and *–chan* (the latter, when talking to boys, and not girls).

The easiest option for a foreigner who knows little Japanese is to always use *–san*, in order to avoid misunderstandings.

A warning!

NONE of these suffixes are ever used to refer to oneself: *Watashi wa Tanaka desu* (I am Tanaka) is the right form of introducing oneself, saying *Tanaka-san* here is a terrible mistake.

Shop names

As you can see, this lesson's vocabulary table deals with different shop names. What relationship does this have with proper name suffixes? Well, you have probably noticed shop names usually end with the word 屋 (*ya*), which means "shop." However, when talking about a specific store, the suffix *–san* is very often added. This is a very curious honorific use. We don't usually say 本屋 (*honya*) but 本屋さん (*honya-san*) when referring to the bookstore and, at the same time, to the bookseller.

漢字 kanji	ローマ字 rōmaji	翻訳 translation	漢字 kanji	ローマ字 rōmaji	翻訳 translation
本屋	*Hon-ya*	Bookstore	ラーメン屋	*Rāmen-ya*	*Ramen* shop
八百屋	*Yaoya*	Grocery	肉屋	*Niku-ya*	Butcher's shop
靴屋	*Kutsu-ya*	Shoe shop	果物屋	*Kudamono-ya*	Fruit store
魚屋	*Sakana-ya*	Fishmonger	文房具屋	*Bunbōgu-ya*	Stationery store
酒屋	*Saka-ya*	Wine shop	うどん屋	*Udon-ya*	*Udon* shop
居酒屋	*Izaka-ya*	Pub	お茶屋	*O-cha-ya*	Tea store
お菓子屋	*O-kashi-ya*	Bread shop	寿司屋	*Sushi-ya*	*Sushi* shop
電気屋	*Denki-ya*	Electric appliance store	お弁当屋	*O-bentō-ya*	*Bentō* store

漫画例：*Manga-examples*

Here is the example section, where we will try to illustrate with manga the contents of the previous pages. Given name suffixes are not translated into English, but we will see some of them.

a) –kun

> Kotono: 気を付けてね　愛天くんっ！！
> *ki o tsukete ne aiten-kun !!*
> spirit DOP put EP Aiten (noun suf.)!!
> **Take care, Aiten!**

In the first example we see the suffix –*kun*, which Kotono, the girl, adds to her interlocutor's name, Aiten. This is an affectionate use of –*kun*, used with male names. Furthermore, we have the expression *ki o tsukete* (take care), mentioned in Lesson 4.

b) –san

> Nina: ロッソさん！
> *rosso – san!*
> Rosso (noun suf.)!
> **Mr. Rosso!**

When Mary meets her old boss, she calls him by his name and adds the suffix –*san*. Since Rosso is older than her, and her boss as well, the use of –*san* showing respect is compulsory here.

c) –senpai

A very frequent way of showing respect is adding the person's title instead. Here we see the suffix –*senpai*, a very Japanese concept meaning "person who studies or works with me, but who started earlier, and is more experienced." Other such suffixes are *sensei* (teacher), *buchō* (head of a department), *shachō* (company director), *gakuchō* (university rector), etc. It is always much more correct and it sounds better if you use the interlocutor's title rather than –*san*, -*kun*, etc.

Tetsuharu: 麻美先輩！！
asami – senpai
Asami (noun suf.)!!
Asami!

d) –chan

Matsu: ま…まってくれ！梓ちゃん！
ma... matte kure! azusa – chan!
w... wait (receive)! Azusa (noun suf.)!
W... wait, Azusa!

In this panel we have the suffix –*chan*. As we mentioned before, it is used with children names or, as is the case here, with girls. When it is used with girl names, it implies some familiarity. It is an affectionate way of calling a girl.

e) –sama

> Musashimaru: お…およびでございますか　隆起さま！
> *o... o-yobi de- gozaimasu ka　Ryūki sama!*
> (formal) call be Q? Ryūki (noun suf.)!
> **Ha... have you called me, Mr. Ryūki?**

The suffix *–sama* is seldom used in present-day Japanese. As we mentioned earlier, it isn't uncommon in the client–shop assistant relationship, but it isn't quite used in other situations. The manga in this example takes place two or three hundred years ago, and *–sama* was still used then when talking to one's master.

f) –dono

> Yūji: 清花殿　　傷の手当てありがとうでござる。
> *Sayaka –dono　kizu no teate arigatō de-gozaru*
> Sayaka (noun suf.) wound PoP take care thank you be
> **Thank you for taking care of my wounds, Mrs. Sayaka.**

We have here a sample of the way ancient Japanese samurais used to speak. In this way of speaking, extremely formal in all cases, the suffix *–dono* is always used (translated here as "Mrs."), as well as the verb *–de gozaru*, equivalent to present-day *desu* (to be).

1 What are proper name suffixes, and in which situations are they used?

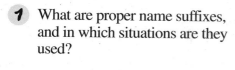

2 You are a 20-year-old man. What suffix would you use after your best childhood female friend's name?

3 You are a 15-year-old girl. What suffix would you use after a male classmate's name?

4 You are a shop assistant. What suffix would you use after your best client's name?

5 You are a samurai, 300 years ago. What suffix would you use when referring to someone else?

6 When don't you need to use proper name suffixes?

7 When in doubt, or to make sure, which is the all-purpose personal name suffix?

8 Write the following words in Japanese and give their pronunciation: bookstore, wine shop, *ramen* shop, butcher's shop.

9 Our company director's name is 樋口 (*Higuchi*). If we want to call him by his name, which would be the best proper name suffix? (not forgetting he is our director).

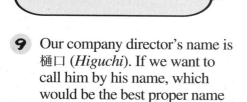

10 Is the following sentence correct: 私はマークさんです。 (*Watashi wa Maaku-san desu*)? *Maaku*: Mark (given name).

第 1 課

練習

Exercises

第16課：助詞

We will now begin with what probably is one of the most difficult aspects in Japanese grammar: the particles. Therefore, you'll have to concentrate as much as you can. We will be dealing as well with basic grammatical concepts, such as direct object, subject, and so on, so please try to keep these concepts in mind as you read.

What is a particle?

A particle is a small word with no meaning, usually consisting of only one, or two at the most, hiragana characters.

The role of particles is purely grammatical; a particle is like a marker which follows a word and indicates this word's function in a sentence. Particles are a sentence's framework and you can't construct a Japanese sentence without them.

The usual explanatory table has an essential role in this lesson, and we will base our exposition on it. We have the most important and basic particles in the table, with their function and an example sentence.

Particle	Function	Example sentence	Vocabulary
は ha (wa)	Topic	私は学生です。 *watashi wa gakusei desu* **I am a student.**	私 (*watashi*) I 学生 (*gakusei*) student です (*desu*) to be
が ga	Subject	きょうは雨が降る。 *kyō wa ame ga furu* **It's raining today.**	きょう (*kyō*) today 雨 (*ame*) rain 降る (*furu*) to fall (rain)
の no	Possessive	これは私の本です。 *kore wa watashi no hon desu* **This is my book.**	これ (*kore*) this 本 (*hon*) book
に ni	a) Direct Contact	a) 黒板に字を書く。 *kokuban ni ji o kaku* **I write letters on the blackboard.**	黒板 (*kokuban*) blackboard 字 (*ji*) letter 書く (*kaku*) to write
	b) Place (existence)	b) ここに犬がいる。 *koko ni inu ga iru* **There is a dog here.**	ここ (*koko*) here 犬 (*inu*) dog いる (*iru*) to be
	c) Indirect object	c) 太郎にビデオをあげる。 *Tarō ni bideo o ageru* **I give Taro a video tape.**	ビデオ (*bideo*) video tape あげる (*ageru*) to give
で de	a) Place (no existence)	a) 図書館で勉強する。 *toshokan de benkyō suru* **I study in the library.**	図書館 (*toshokan*) library 勉強する (*benkyō suru*) to study
	b) Means	b) 電車で行く。 *densha de iku* **I go by train.**	電車 (*densha*) train 行く (*iku*) to go
へ he (e)	Direction	日本へ行く。 *nihon e iku* **I go to Japan.**	日本 (*nihon*) Japan
を wo (o)	Direct object	りんごを食べる。 *ringo o taberu* **I eat an apple.**	りんご (*ringo*) apple 食べる (*taberu*) to eat
と to	a) with, and	a) 花子と太郎は結婚する。 *Hanako to Tarō wa kekkon suru* **Hanako and Tarō get married.**	結婚する (*kekkon suru*) to marry
	b) quote	b)「愛している」と言う。 *"ai shite iru" to iu* **He says "I love you."**	愛 (*ai*) love 言う (*iu*) to say

Some particles are pronounced differently from the way they are written. The correct pronunciation for those particles is between brackets underneath its "standard" reading. Thus, は is pronounced *wa* instead of *ha*, を is *o* instead of *wo*, and へ is *e* instead of *he*.

Basic explanation

We will now see the particles, one by one, using the table as a basis.

は (*wa*) The word before it is the topic, "the thing we are talking about," "the topic we want to emphasize." In the example, *watashi wa gakusei desu*, we are talking about *watashi*, that is, about "I." This is the topic, what is important in the sentence. If we change it slightly, and leave it as *gakusei wa watashi desu* (The student am I), with the particle *wa* we are emphasizing that what is important in the sentence—the topic—, is "student."

が (*ga*) It indicates the word before it is the subject in the sentence, "the performer of the verb's action." *Ame* (rain) performs the action (to rain), therefore, the particle *ga* indicates *ame* is the subject. The particles *wa* and *ga* are very often confused, and they are one of the most difficult points for students of Japanese.

の (*no*) Possessive particle, that is, "whose." The word before it owns the word after it. In the example, *watashi no hon*—I (*watashi*) own the book (*hon*)—, means, in other words, "my book."

に (*ni*) Particle with several functions:
   a) Direct contact ("where," "in which place"). *kokuban ni kaku*: to write on the blackboard.
   b) Place ("where," "situation"). When the verb in the sentence means existence, such as *iru*, *aru* (there is/ there are), *sumu* (to live), etc., the *ni* particle is used. When the verb is different, the particle to be chosen is *de*.
   c) The word that it follows is an indirect object, that is, "to whom," "to what" does the subject's action affect. In the example, Tarō is who receives the video tape.

で (*de*) It has two basic functions:
   a) Place ("where"). When the verb doesn't indicate existence (most verbs). It is easy to confuse with *ni*, another difficult point for the student.
   b) Means of transport. The previous word is the "means" to go somewhere. *Densha de iku*, "to go by train," *jitensha de iku*, "to go by bycicle," *basu de iku*, "to go by bus."

へ (*e*) It indicates direction, that is, "where to," and it is used with the verbs *iku* (to go), *kuru* (to come), *kaeru* (to return), and other verbs with a similar meaning.

を (*o*) The previous word is the direct object ("what receives the verb's action"). *Ringo o taberu* "to eat an apple", *ocha o nomu* "to drink tea".

と (*to*) To conclude, another multipurpose particle. We will explain two of its uses:
   a) "And, with." For comprehensive lists, or to indicate "company." *Pen to fude to gomu* (ballpoint pen, and pencil, and eraser), *Watashi to Keiko* (Me and Keiko.)
   b) To quote somebody else's words.

In this lesson we have given you a very global vision in a small space, so you can get a general idea. It is normal if you don't fully understand it yet: the important thing here is to get the gist of it and, then, with practice and further study, you'll get to use particles properly.

漫画例：*Manga-examples*

We will now see a few practical examples of the use of particles. Look at the glossary of terms at the beginning of the book to understand the abbreviations used here.

a) Topic particle wa

Kindaichi: まさか　犯人はクリス…？
masaka　hannin wa Kurisu…?
oh, no! criminal ToP Chris…?
Impossible! The murderer, Chris?

We have here an example of the use of the particle *wa*. As we mentioned earlier, this particle indicates the previous word is the topic, "what we are talking about." The topic in this sentence is the word *hannin* ("criminal," although in this case we translate it as "murderer," for context reasons). Supposing we wanted to give importance to the name Chris and not *hannin*, we could correctly say *Kurisu wa hannin desu* (Chris is the murderer.)

Another feature to point out in this sentence is the word *masaka*, which in a direct translation would mean something like "oh, no!," "don't tell me…" In this case, we thought it better not to translate the word directly, and use the more appropriate exclamation "impossible!"

b) Direct object particle o

Tomo: これをかしてあげよう。
kore o kashite ageyō
this DOP lend give
I'll lend you this.

Here we have a very clear example of the use of the particle *o*. This particle indicates the previous word is a direct object, that is "the thing that receives the verb's action." In this case, the verb is *kasu* (to lend) and what is lent is *kore* (this). Therefore, the particle we must place after *kore* is *o* because this is what receives the verb's action.

The form *–shite ageru* is used in the sense of "doing something for somebody," and when the verb ends in *–yō* it means "to be going to do something," "let's do something."

c) Possessive particle no

We have here a very simple example in a really difficult lesson. It is the use of the particle *no*. This particle indicates "possession," "to belong to," and, also, "description." In this case, the previous word "owns" (describes) what comes after. In this example the word *tane* (seed, stone) is from a *momo* (peach). And so it has been translated as "peach stone."

Yūzen: 桃の種……?
momo no tane......?
peach PoP seed...?
A peach stone...?

d) Direction particle e

Pipy: さようなら もう水の中へ帰らないかもしれない。
sayōnara mō mizu no naka e kaeranai kamo shirenai
goodbye any more water PoP inside DP not return perhaps
Goodbye. I might never be able to return to the sea again.

In this example we have the use of two different particles, the first one (*no*) indicates "possession," and the second one (*e*), "direction, where to." The particle *e* is usually used with the verbs *iku* (to go), *kuru* (to come), and *kaeru* (to return). In this panel it is used with the verb "to return." The form *kamo shirenai* at the end of a sentence suggests doubt, something that is not sure, and it is usually translated as "might (do)," "perhaps."

さようなら もう水の中へ 帰らないかも しれない

e) Existence particle ni

Akiko: なあ なあっ!! ここに あたしの手裏剣あるかっ!?
naa naa!! *koko ni atashi no shuriken aru ka!?*
hey, hey!! here PP I PoP shuriken there is Q!?
Heeey, heeey!! **Are my *shuriken* here?**

In this last example we see Akiko looking desperately for her ninja stars (called *shuriken* in Japanese). The particles used are: *ni*, particle of "place, existence," and once more the possessive particle *no*. The particle *ni* indicates that the previous word is the place where something is, and it is usually used with the verbs *iru* (to be, animals, and people), and *aru* (to be, things). In this case, *koko* (here) are (*aru*) Akiko's ninja stars (*shuriken*), and therefore the particle *ni* goes after the word showing the place, that is *koko*. Another important particle is the one right at the end of the sentence, *ka*, which is always used in that position to indicate question, it is like the equivalent of our question mark (?). But we will deal with this kind of particles in the next lesson. By the way, the small hiragana character *tsu* っ at the end of the sentence means the sound ends suddenly.

なあ なあっ!!
ここに あたしの手裏剣あるかっ!?

1 What are particles, and what do we use them for?

2 What is the actual pronunciation of the hiragana characters は, へ, and を when they are used as particles?

3 When do we use the particle は?

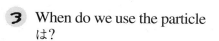

4 When do we use the particle に?

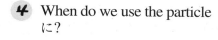

5 When do we use the particle の?

6 When do we use the particle へ?

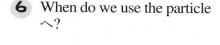

7 Translate the sentence これはあなたの車です。(*kore wa anata no kuruma desu*) into English. (*Kore*: this / *anata*: you / *kuruma*: car).

8 Translate the sentence "to give a flower to Hanako" into Japanese. (To give: あげる (*ageru*) / flower: 花 (*hana*) / Hanako: 花子) Take a look at Lesson 15!

9 Translate the sentence 中国へ行く。(*Chūgoku e iku*) into English. (*Chūgoku*: China / *iku*: to go).

10 Translate the sentence "to make a plastic model" into Japanese. (Plastic model: プラモデル (*puramoderu*) / to make: 作る (*tsukuru*))

Continuing with the last lesson's subject (particles), we will now explain the use of the so-called end-of-sentence particles, very common in spoken Japanese and, of course, plentiful in manga.

What do we use them for?

As we explained in the previous lesson, a particle is a word usually formed by only one hiragana character, which equals two letters in English. Examples of end-of-sentence particles are *ne*, *yo*, *zo*, *na*, etc., as you can see in the explanatory table on the next page.

Be careful, you mustn't confuse "normal" particles, which have a grammatical function in the sentence and which we explained in the previous lesson, with end-of-sentence particles, which we will now explain.

These kinds of particles are always placed at the end of a sentence, and usually have different connotations. The particle *zo*, for example, indicates the speaker is a self-confident man, besides placing a special emphasis on the sentence. We should state that these particles are almost exclusively used in spoken Japanese and, moreover, in informal situations. The only acceptable particles in formal spoken Japanese are *ka*, *ne*, and *yo*.

The Japanese language distinguishes between male and female ways of speaking and, consequently, this tendency can be seen in the end-of-sentence particles too: there are particles used only by men, and vice-versa.

How to use end-of-sentence particles: an outline

We will try to define the use of the different end-of-sentence particles, always basing these definitions on the explanatory table.

か (*ka*) This particle would be, more or less, the equivalent of our question mark (?), which, strictly speaking, is not necessary in Japanese, although it is very often used, due to its great expressive power. The particle *ka* turns a sentence into a question. Thus:

ね (*ne*) This particle is also used very often in Japanese. It has two functions:

a) It gives the sentence a confirmation tone. It would be equal to "isn't it?," "you know..."

b) When suggesting something, you usually soften your suggestion with the particle *ne* at the end, so as not to sound too sharp. It would be something like "Okay...?"

あなたはお寿司が好きです。
anata wa o-sushi ga suki desu
You like sushi. (statement)

あなたはお寿司が好きですか？
anata wa o-sushi ga suki desu ka?
Do you like sushi? (question)

We can see the two sentences are exactly the same but for the final *ka*, which turns the sentence into a question.

よ (*yo*) Just like *ne*, it is a very common particle. It has two main functions:
  a) To state, to give the sentence a degree of certainty, and to sound convincing.
  b) At the end of a sentence which expresses an order or a wish, the particle *yo* has the function of "insistence," "pressure."

ぞ (*zo*) A particle used only by men in informal language. Its function is very similar to the a) function of よ (*yo*), that is, it states and gives the sentence some certainty.

ぜ (*ze*) The two functions of this particle are almost identical to those of よ (*yo*), but with the peculiarity that it is only used by men in very informal situations.

な (*na*) This particle has two very different functions that should not be confused:
  a) Used mainly by men, it implies the wish to do something which is theoretically very difficult to do.
  b) Particle of the negative imperative, that is, straight orders which indicate prohibition. Used mainly by men.

わ (*wa*) Female version of ぞ (*zo*) and (*ze*). *Wa* is used exclusively by women, otherwise, it has more or less the same functions as these particles.

の (*no*) It has two main functions:
  a) Informal version of the particle *ka*, that is, it turns a sentence into a question.
  b) A particle basically used by women and children to give an informative nuance to the sentence. It could be translated as "you know."

Particle	Function	Example sentence	Vocabulary
か ka	Question	お寿司がすきですか。 *o-sushi ga suki desu ka* **Do you like sushi?**	お寿司 (*o-sushi*) sushi 好き (*suki*) like です (*desu*) to be
ね ne	a) Affirmation statement	a) あの映画はおもしろいね。 *ano eiga wa omoshiroi ne* **That film is interesting, isn't?**	あの (*ano*) that 映画 (*eiga*) film おもしろい (*omoshiroi*) interesting
	b) Softens a suggestion	b) あしたは来てね。 *ashita wa kite ne* **Come tomorrow, okay?**	あした (*ahista*) tomorrow 来て (*kite*) come (you)
よ yo	a) Emphasis Statement	a) 日本語はやさしいよ。 *nihongo wa yasashii yo!* **Japanese is easy!**	日本語 (*nihongo*) Japanese やさしい (*yasashii*) easy
	b) Suggestion	b) 歌を歌ってよ。 *uta o utatte yo!* **Sing a song, come on!**	歌 (*uta*) song 歌って (*utatte*) sing (you)
ぞ zo	Emphasis Statement (M, informal)	めっちゃ疲れたぞ。 *metcha tsukareta zo!* **I'm all in!**	めっちゃ (*metcha*) very much (informal) 疲れた (*tsukareta*) tired
ぜ ze	a) Emphasis Statement	a) あれは千円だぜ。 *are wa sen en da ze!* **Hey, that's one thousand yen!**	あれ (*are*) that 千円 (*sen en*) one thousand yen だ (*da*) to be (informal)
	b) Suggestion (M, informal)	b) いっぱい遊ぼうぜ。 *ippai asobō ze!* **Let's have some good fun!**	いっぱい (*ippai*) a lot 遊ぼう (*asobō*) let's have fun
な na	a) Emphasis Statement, Wish (M)	a) 中国へ行きたいな。 *Chūgoku e ikitai na* **I'd love to go to China!**	中国 (*Chūgoku*) China 行きたい (*ikitai*) to want to go
	b) Negative imperative (M)	b) これを壊すな。 *kore o kowasu na!* **Don't break this!**	これ (*kore*) this 壊す (*kowasu*) to break
わ wa	Emphatic statement (F)	聖家族教会は感激するわ。 *Seikazoku kyōkai wa kangeki suru wa!* **The Sagrada Familia is impressive!**	聖家族教会 (*Seikazoku kyōkai*) Sagrada Familia (Barcelona) 感激する (*kangeki suru*) to be deeply impressed
の no	a) Question (informal)	a) あしたは来るの？ *ashita wa kuru no?* **Will you come tomorrow?**	あした (*ashita*) tomorrow 来る (*kuru*) to come
	b) Statement (F)	b) タイへ行くの。 *Tai e iku no* **I'm going to Thailand, you know?**	タイ (*Tai*) Thailand 行く (*iku*) to go

漫画例：*Manga-examples*

The end-of-sentence particles take up all the manga-examples in this lesson. We will see how the most important ones function in a real context.

a) Question (1)

死ぬ か…？

Heartnet: 死ぬ か…？
shinu ka...?
die Q?
Will you die…?

In this first manga-example we see how the particle *ka* works: it is the equivalent to our question mark (?). Question marks don't exist in traditional Japanese, although, as we can see in this panel, it is often used in manga, due to its expressive power. The question mark is actually not needed here, because the particle *ka* has the same function.

The verb *shinu* means to die. Just by adding *ka* after the verb *shinu* the minisentence becomes a question. Making questions is as simple as adding *ka* to a sentence.

b) Question (2)

Keiko: じゃお大事に。
ja o-daiji ni
well (set phrase)
Well, take care.

Keitarō: もう帰るの？
mō kaeru no?
already go home Q?
Are you going already?

The important particle in this panel is *no*. It is an informal version of *ka*, which we saw in the previous example; therefore, it is used to form questions in an informal or colloquial context. You might remember we talked about "normal" particles in the previous lesson, and the particle *no*, indicating possession, was among them. Their use being different, you should take care not to confuse these two particles. Reviewing Lesson 16 (particles) is recommended.

There is a set phrase in this panel which cannot be translated word by word. It is *o-daiji ni*, a farewell aimed at sick people. Our suggested translation is: "take care."

c) Insistence, pressure

John: 僕を撃てよ……。
boku o ute yo...
me DOP shoot EP...
Shoot me...

In this shocking panel, John, a boy, asks his sister to shoot him. The particle used by John in his sentence is "*yo.*" This particle indicates "insistence," "pressure" at the end of a sentence where an order or a wish is expressed. That is, at the end of the imperative sentence *boku o ute* (shoot me), John further reinforces his order adding this commonly used particle. The suggested translation is much briefer, but no less sharp.

d) Emphasis

Shingo: 今度はお前ん家行こーぜ！
kondo wa omae n chi iko — ze!
next time ToP you PoP home go EP!
Next time we'll go to your place!

The particle to be mentioned in this panel is *ze*, used only by men in very informal situations, basically among friends. *Ze* gives the sentence a nuance of insistence and assertion. The dash in the word 行こー has the function of making the sound longer than usual.

e) Double use of end-of-sentence particles

This panel will illustrate the fact that sometimes two end-of-sentence particles are used together in the same sentence. Here, the statement particle *yo* is used together with the male confirmation particle *na*. Other common combinations are, for example, *yo+ne*, *wa+ne*, *wa+yo*, etc., mainly used in female language. Sometimes, it seems one sole particle is not enough, and two are used to give the sentence a stronger emphatic tone, as in this example.

Sr. Schüle: 約束10時にあったよな。
Yakusoku jū ji ni atta yo na
promise 10 o'clock IP be EP EP
You had an appointment at 10, didn't you?

1 What is an end-of-sentence particle? When do we use them?

2 Are end-of-sentence particles usually used in written Japanese?

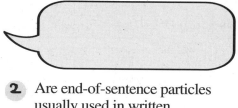

3 What does the end-of-sentence particle よ *yo* indicate?

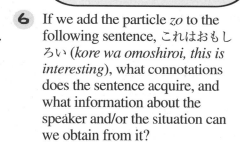

4 What does the end-of-sentence particle わ *wa* indicate?

5 What does the end-of-sentence particle ぞ *zo* indicate?

6 If we add the particle *zo* to the following sentence, これはおもしろい (*kore wa omoshiroi, this is interesting*), what connotations does the sentence acquire, and what information about the speaker and/or the situation can we obtain from it?

7 Turn the following sentence into a question: きょうはメキシコに行く (*kyō wa Mekishiko ni iku*, you are going to Mexico today). There are two options.

8 Translate the following sentence into English: アイスを食べるな。(*aisu o taberu na*). (*aisu*: ice-cream / *taberu*: to eat). Is the speaker a man or a woman?

9 Translate the following sentence into Japanese: "Nice weather, isn't it?" (Nice weather: いい天気 (*ii tenki*) / to be: です (*desu*).

10 Can we use end-of-sentence particles in formal conversations?

第 ⑱ 課：ある・いる

Lesson 18: The verbs aru / iru (there is, there are)

We will start verbs in this lesson. As a prelude to the next lesson (verbs I), we will see two of the most basic verbs in Japanese: *aru* and *iru*. Both mean "there is / are, to have, to be (somewhere)," but are used in different situations.

Two verbs that have exactly the same meaning?

We mentioned earlier that *iru* and *aru* both mean "there is, there are, to have." But what is the difference? The difference is that the verb *iru* is used when the subject is a person or an animal (that is, an animate being), and the verb *aru* is used with things (inanimate objects and beings.) Be careful with this difference, as it is a very important one.

As we said in Lesson 9 (basic grammar), Japanese verbs always go at the end of the sentence, with no exceptions. Japanese is said to have an SOV structure (Subject + Object (Direct object) + Verb), while English is SVO. Example:

> English: **I have a flower.**
>   S V   O
>
> Japanese: Watashi wa hana ga aru.
>   S   O   V
> (*watashi* = I / *hana* = flower / *aru* = to have)

This particular order must be kept in mind when forming sentences. (*wa* and *ga* are grammatical particles (see Lesson 16: particles).

Conjugations

The verbs *aru* and *iru* are conjugated in the following forms: present, past, negative, and past negative. You can look up the conjugations in the table below.

As usual with Japanese, verbs have several conjugations depending on the formality level. A standard student of Japanese will first learn the so-called *masu* form, named like this because all the present forms end in –*masu*: in this case, *iru* = *imasu*, *aru* = *arimasu*. This variety is used in formal situations.

But, since this course can be used to be able to read manga, we must also explain the so-called simple form, or dictionary form, used in informal and vulgar situations. It is called dictionary form because this is the form in which verbs appear in dictionaries. It is by far the most used in manga, and that is why we must explain it so early (a student usually learns the dictionary form after at least a year of studies).

	Verb *iru* (people, animals)		Verb *aru* (things, plants)	
	Formal	Dictionary form	Formal	Dictionary form
Present (There is)	います *imasu*	いる *iru*	あります *arimasu*	ある *aru*
Past (There was)	いました *imashita*	いた *ita*	ありました *arimashita*	あった *atta*
Negative (There isn't)	いません *imasen*	いない *inai*	ありません *arimasen*	ない *nai*
Past negative (There wasn't)	いませんでした *imasendeshita*	いなかった *inakatta*	ありませんでした *arimasendeshita*	なかった *nakatta*

120 The verbs *aru* / *iru* (there is, there are)

Basic sentences

We will give basic structures to form simple sentences using the verbs *aru* and *iru*. You will need to know the words *koko, soko, asoko, doko* (here, there, over there, where), which we commented on in Lesson 9 (basic grammar).

Depending on the sentence, the verbs *aru* and *iru* have two meanings. They can mean both "there is/are" and "to have." The first structure explains the meaning "there is / are."

With the meaning of "There is / are"

A) ここに _____ が（ある・いる）。
koko ni _____ ga (aru / iru)
here (PP) _____ (SP) there is / are
There is/ are ____ here.
1-ここに亀がいる。
koko ni kame ga iru
There is a turtle here.
2-そこに財布がありました。
soko ni saifu ga arimashita
There was a wallet there.

日本語 Japanese	ローマ字 Romaji	翻訳 Translation
はえ	Hae	Fly
とら	Tora	Tiger
亀	Kame	Turtle
くも	Kumo	Spider
熊	Kuma	Bear
さめ	Same	Shark
花	Hana	Flower
さくら	Sakura	Cherry tree
バラ	Bara	Rose
桃	Momo	Peach
すいか	Suika	Watermelon
財布	Saifu	Wallet
花びん	Kabin	Flower pot
めがね	Megane	Glasses
はし	Hashi	Chopsticks
コップ	Koppu	Glass

We have used the dictionary form of the verb *iru* in the present tense in the first sentence. Notice how the subject is "turtle," an animate being, and therefore, the appropriate verb is *iru*. Whereas in the second example, we have used the formal form in the past tense of the verb *aru*. The subject is "wallet," an inanimate object, and thus the appropriate verb is *aru*.

With the meaning of "to have"

B) 私は _____ が（ある・いる）。
watashi wa _____ga (aru / iru)
I (SP) _____ (SP) have
I have____.
1-私はとらがいません。
watashi wa tora ga imasen
I don't have a tiger.
2-私はももがあった。
watashi wa momo ga atta
I had a peach.

In the first example, "tiger" is an animate being, and therefore, we need the verb *iru*. Whereas in the second example, "peach" is a fruit. It's a living thing, but inanimate: we use *aru*. Regarding conjugations, in the first sentence we have used the negative formal form of *iru*, and in the second one, we have chosen the dictionary form of *aru* in the past tense. Try making different sentences with the help of the conjugation and vocabulary tables.

IMPORTANT NOTE: In actual Japanese, the verbs *aru* and *iru* are not always used in the sense of "to have," which we have just explained. Generally, other verbs, such as 持つ (*motsu*, to have, to own), or 飼う (*kau*, to keep, to raise) in the specific case of animals are used.

漫画例：*Manga-examples*

In the theory pages we have mentioned *iru* and *aru* have different meanings depending on the sentence. We have commented on sentences where these verbs can be translated as "there is / are", and "to have," but there is one more meaning: "to be somewhere."

a) Aru = there is / are

Suzuki: ここにスズが2つある…。
koko ni suzu ga futatsu aru...
here PP bell two there are
There are two bells here.

This first manga-example illustrates the meaning of "there is" of the verb *aru*. The structure of this kind of sentences usually is: "place + particle *ni* + thing + particle ga/wa + verb *aru / iru*." We find an identical structure in this example. Besides, since the word *suzu* names a thing, the chosen verb must be *aru*. In this case, the situation being an informal one, the speaker chooses the dictionary form.

ここにスズが
2つある…

b) Iru = to be somewhere

An example of the meaning "to be somewhere." Note the particle following the word for place is always *ni*. There is never an exception to this rule, whatever the verb is, *aru* or *iru*. Note too the use of the end-of-sentence particle *yo*, already mentioned in Lesson 17.

Rabbit: ぼくはここにいるよ。
boku wa koko ni iru yo
I SP here PP to be EP
I'm here!

c) Iru = to be somewhere—negative form

Teacher: みんなの机の中にはいないな？
minna no tsukue no naka ni wa inai na
everybody PoP desk PoP inside PP/SP not be EP
Isn't it inside any of your desks?

Pupil: いませーん。
imaseeen
not be
Nooo!

We see here the two options of the present negative form of the verb *iru*. The teacher uses the dictionary or colloquial form (*inai*, "not to be"), whereas the pupil, showing respect, uses the polite form (*imasen*). We must point out that they are looking for the class hamster, and, consequently, they use the verb *iru*, for living beings.

d) Aru = there is / are—negative form

もぉ
逃
げ
場
は
あ
り
ま
せ
ん
よ

Mori:	もぉ逃げ場はありませんよ。

mō nigeba wa arimasen yo
any more means of escape SP there isn't EP
You can't escape now.

We see in this example the use of the –*masu* form, that is, the formal use of the verb *aru*. Mr. Mori conjugates the negative form of the verb (*arimasen*), so the translation into English is "there isn't." Since the word *nigeba* (means of escape) is not a living being, but a concept, the verb *aru* is used, and not *iru*. Usually, the –*masu* form is used when you don't know the interlocutor too well, that is, in formal situations. It would be roughly similar to the use in English of "Mr.," "Mrs.," or "Ms." with the surname.

e) Iru = there is / to exist—past

We see in this last example the past form of the verb *iru* in its colloquial form (*ita*, there was). Since Kido is talking about a man, he uses the verb *iru* and not *aru*.

Pointing out that in Japanese there are different ways of speaking depending on the formality level is essential, and they should all be mastered somehow. We can't go to Japan

オ
レ
に
似
て
い
る
男
が
、
本
当
に
い
た
ん
だ

and talk to our Japanese teacher like we would talk to our closest friend. Neither can we go out and talk like most characters do in manga, where the tendency is to use an extremely colloquial and vulgar language. This is why we are stressing both vulgar and formal expressions in this course.

Kido:	オレに似ている男が、本当にいたんだ。

ore ni niteiru otoko ga, hontō ni ita n da
I resemble man SP really there was to be
There really was a man who looked like me.

1 When do we use the verb *iru*? And how about the verb *aru*?

2 Conjugate the past tense of the dictionary form of the verb *aru*.

3 Conjugate the negative of the formal form (or –*masu* form) of the verb *aru*.

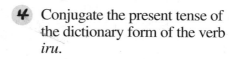

4 Conjugate the present tense of the dictionary form of the verb *iru*.

5 Translate the following sentence into Japanese: "There is a peach there." (2 answers: formal and dictionary).

6 Translate the following sentence into English: ここにさめがいませんでした。(*koko ni same ga imasendeshita*).

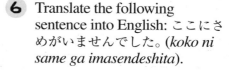

7 Translate the following sentence into Japanese: "I didn't have a spider." (two answers: formal and dictionary).

8 Translate the following sentence into English: わたしはすいかがない。(*watashi wa suika ga nai*).

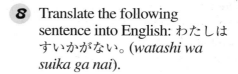

9 When do we use the formal form (or –*masu* form)? What would it be equal to in English?

10 Which of the two forms (formal / dictionary) would we use with our closest friend?

第 19 課：動詞（Ⅰ）：ます形

Lesson 19: Verbs (I): –masu form

Just as we mentioned in the previous lesson, we will deal fully with verbs in this chapter. Japanese verbal conjugations are very simple compared to other languages. The most obvious difficulty lies in the degree formality: there are two different conjugations depending on this fact. In this lesson we will first explain the polite form of verbs, that is, the *–masu* form, which we already gave a brief introduction on in Lesson 18.

Sentence structure

We have already mentioned Japanese verbs always go at the end of the sentence. To form a sentence we first have the subject, then the object or adverbial, and finally the verb.

After the subject and the object or adverbial, we need to add a grammatical particle which will function as a "joint" between the different sentence parts (we recommend reviewing Lesson 16.) Here are some examples:

> 私はパンを食べます。
> *watashi wa pan o tabemasu.*
> **I eat bread.**
> (*watashi* = **I** (subject) / *pan* = **bread** (direct object) / *tabemasu* = **to eat** (verb))

The words *wa* and *o* are particles (see Lesson 16), which indicate that the previous words are, respectively, topic and direct object.

> 私はジョセフに本を貸しました。
> *watashi wa josefu ni hon o kashimashita*
> **I lent Joseph a book.**
> (*watashi* = **I** (subject) / *josefu* = **Joseph** (indirect object) / *hon* = **book** (direct object) / *kashimashita* = **to lend**, past tense (verb))

The words *wa* and *o* have the same function as in the previous example, the word *ni* is the marker for the indirect object.

Conjugations

The *–masu* form of verbs, that is the formal way for conjugating them, is fairly simple. First, there are no different conjugation forms depending on person; that is, whatever the subject, "I," "you," "he," "we," or "they," the verbal form never changes.

For example:

> *watashi wa yomimasu* (I read.)
> *kare wa yomimasu* (he reads.)

While in English the verb changes (read / reads), in Japanese it is always *yomimasu*. You can review Lesson 7 for a reminder on pronouns.

Note on pronunciation: in all forms ending in *–masu*, the final *u* is hardly pronounced, and its pronunciation resembles "–mas."

Conjugation table

Let's have a look now at this lesson's conjugation table.

We have divided the table into three groups, Group 1 (invariable), Group 2 (variable), and Group 3 (irregular). The division won't be very relevant in this lesson, but it is worth knowing that there are three groups.

We will first look at the table from top to bottom.

First group: we eliminate the infinitive's –*ru* and add –*masu* to obtain the –*masu* form.

Second group: this one is more complicated. The –*masu* ending changes according to the verb ending. Verbs ending in *su* change *su* for *shimasu*, verbs ending in *tsu* change it for *chimasu*, and the same happens with: *u → imasu, ru → rimasu, ku → kimasu, gu → gimasu, bu → bimasu, mu → mimasu*, and *nu → nimasu*. Generally speaking, we change *u* for *i* and add –*masu*.

The **third group** is formed by the irregular verbs.

If we look at the table from left to right, we will find the dictionary form in bold type, which we could call the "infinitive." We will have a closer look at this form in the next lesson.

Then we have the –*masu* form. We see all the verbs in this column end in –*masu*, and that is where the name comes from.

The past is formed by replacing the *su* part of the –*masu* form with *shita*. Example: *machimasu*. We take off *su* = *machima*. We add *shita* = *machimashita*.

The negative is formed by replacing the *su* part of the –*masu* form with *sen*.

The past negative is formed by replacing the *su* part of the –*masu* form with *sendeshita*. We will further clarify these concepts in the examples.

		Dictionary f.	–masu f.	Translation	Past	Negative	Past negative
Group 1: Invariable		教える **oshieru**	教えます oshiemasu	teach	教えました oshiemashita	教えません oshiemasen	教えませんでした oshiemasendeshita
		起きる **okiru**	起きます okimasu	wake up	起きました okimashita	起きません okimasen	起きませんでした okimasendeshita
Group 2: Variable	A	貸す **kasu**	貸します kashimasu	lend	貸しました kashimashita	貸しません kashimasen	貸しませんでした kashimasendeshita
		待つ **matsu**	待ちます machimasu	wait	待ちました machimashita	待ちません machimasen	待ちませんでした machimasendeshita
	B	買う **kau**	買います kaimasu	buy	買いました kaimashita	買いません kaimasen	買いませんでした kaimasendeshita
		帰る **kaeru**	帰ります kaerimasu	return	帰りました kaerimashita	帰りません kaerimasen	帰りませんでした kaerimasendeshita
	C	書く **kaku**	書きます kakimasu	write	書きました kakimashita	書きません kakimasen	書きませんでした kakimasendeshita
	D	急ぐ **isogu**	急ぎます isogimasu	hurry	急ぎました isogimashita	急ぎません isogimasen	急ぎませんでした isogimasendeshita
	E	遊ぶ **asobu**	遊びます asobimasu	play	遊びました asobimashita	遊びません asobimasen	遊びませんでした asobimasendeshita
		飲む **nomu**	飲みます nomimasu	drink	飲みました nomimashita	飲みません nomimasen	飲みませんでした nomimasendeshita
		死ぬ **shinu**	死にます shinimasu	die	死にました shinimashita	死にません shinimasen	死にませんでした shinimasendeshita
Group 3: Irregular		する **suru**	します shimasu	do	しました shimashita	しません shimasen	しませんでした shimasendeshita
		来る **kuru**	来ます kimasu	come	来ました kimashita	来ません kimasen	来ませんでした kimasendeshita

漫画例：*Manga-examples*

As usual, the manga-examples will help us put into practice what was explained in the previous pages: the different conjugations of verbs in their –*masu* form.

a) The present tense (1)

> Fishbone: 私はミスターササキに命を挙げます。
> *watashi wa misutaa sasaki ni inochi o agemasu*
> I SP mister Sasaki IP life DOP give
> **I'll give my life for Mr. Sasaki.**

We see here the present tense of the verb *ageru* (to give), that is, *agemasu*. Japanese verbs don't have either number or gender, and therefore, as in this panel, when the subject is *watashi* (I), the verb in the present tense is *agemasu*. When the subject is *anatatachi* (you, plural), the present tense is also *agemasu*, and the same happens with *kare* (he), *watashitachi* (we), *anata* (you), etc.: the verb never changes because it has neither number nor gender. We have chosen the future (I will give) for the translation, as we thought it more appropriate. In Japanese there is no future form, and the idea of future is usually expressed with the infinitive, as in this case. A last note: the text in bubbles is usually written from top to bottom, and from right to left. In this case, we find the text written horizontally and from left to right. This is used when a non-Japanese speaker appears in a manga, and we are offered a "translation" of what he or she is saying.

b) The present tense (2)

Another example of the use of the present tense. In this case the verb is *iu* (to say), its *–masu* form being *iimasu*. The subject in the sentence is *o-shishō-sama* (Mr. teacher), and, as you can see, the verb is not conjugated in a different way. Something else to point out is the use of the respect suffix *–sama*, which we saw in Lesson 15.

Bukichi: 何を言いますかお師匠様！！
nani o iimasu ka o-shishō-sama!!
what? DOP say Q? teacher (respect suf.)
Pardon me, sir?

c) The negative (1)

We see in this panel the negative form of the verb *makeru* (to lose) in its *–masu* form. The *–masu* form in the present tense of *makeru* is *makemasu*. The negative is formed replacing *su* with *sen*. For example, *makemasu* / we remove *su*: *makema* / we add *sen*: *makemasen* (not to lose). The literal translation of this sentence would be "I don't lose," but we have used the construction with "going to," for a more natural translation. Take a look as well at the end-of-sentence emphatic particle *yo*, already explained in Lesson 17.

Sawada: 負けませんよ。
makemasen yo
lose (neg.) EP
I'm not going to lose.

d) The past tense

> Urfina: わかりました…。
> *wakarimashita...*
> understand (past)
> **I see...**

In this case we have an example of the past tense. The verb is *wakaru* (to understand, to know), its –*masu* form being *wakarimasu*. To form the past we replace the *su* with *shita*: *wakarimashita* (I understood). *Wakarimashita* is often used in expressions such as: "I see," "Fine," "OK," "Sure, I get you…"

e) The negative (2)

> Nina: 何も知りません。
> *nani-mo shirimasen*
> nothing know (neg.)
> **I know nothing.**

Another example of the negative form. This time the verb is *shiru* (to know), the –*masu* form in the present tense being *shirimasu*. The negative we see in this example is *shirimasen* (not to know). We should emphasize that the –*masu* form is part of the formal, polite language, and if we looked for an equivalent, the closest we would get in English would be addressing somebody using either "sir," or "Mr.," "Mrs.," or "Ms." with their surname. We will seldom see this form in manga, since the dictionary form is far more common.

1 Why are formal verbs called verbs in –*masu* form?

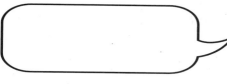

2 Which form is usually used in manga, the –*masu* form or the dictionary form?

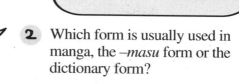

3 Conjugate the negative of the verb 書きます *kakimasu* (to write).

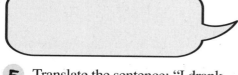

4 Conjugate the present tense of the verb 食べます *tabemasu* (to eat).

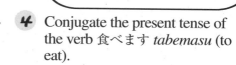

5 Translate the sentence: "I drank beer" into Japanese. (To drink = 飲みます (*nomimasu*) / beer = ビール (*biiru*) / Direct object particle = を (*o*))

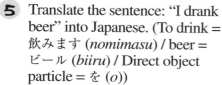

6 Translate the sentence 彼は遊びませんでした。(*kare wa asobimasendeshita*) into English. (*kare* = he / *wa* = Subject particle)

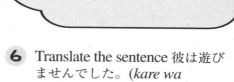

7 Translate the sentence: "She doesn't run" into Japanese. (She = 彼女 (*kanojo*) / to run = 走ります (*hashirimasu*) / Subject particle = は (*wa*))

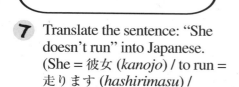

8 Translate the sentence 私は花を買います。(*watashi wa hana o kaimasu*) into English. (*hana* = flower / *o* = Direct object particle)

9 The past tense of the verb *wakaru* (to understand) is *wakarimashita*. What two senses can this verb in the past tense have in English?

10 When we see a bubble in a manga with the words written horizontally, what does it mean?

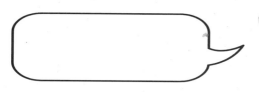

第 19 課

練習

Exercises

第(20)課：動詞（Ⅱ）：辞書形

Lesson 20: Verbs (II): Dictionary form

In Lesson 20 we will supplement the theory on verbs explained in the previous lesson. While in Lesson 19 we saw the polite verb conjugation, in this lesson we will see the informal one: the so-called "simple form," or "dictionary form."

Dictionary form

The simple or dictionary form is used in informal situations, when we talk with friends or family. That is why it is the most common form in manga. It is called "dictionary form" because when looking up a verb in dictionaries, the verb will always appear in this form; it would be the equivalent to the infinitive in English.

This form's special characteristic is that it always ends in *u* (see the table below), and contrary to the –*masu* form (see Lesson 19), its conjugation is much more complex. In the table, you have the conjugation of the different groups of verbs, and the rules for the past tense and negative form conjugations. Let's have a closer look at the table.

		Dictionary f.	Translation	Past	Rule	Negative	Rule	Past negative
Group1: Invariable		教える *oshieru*	teach	教えた *oshieta*	吞 た 吶 ta	教えない *oshienai*	吞 ない 吶 nai	教えなかった *oshienakatta*
		起きる *okiru*	wake up	起きた *okita*		起きない *okinai*		起きなかった *okinakatta*
Group 2: Variable	**A**	貸す *kasu*	lend	貸した *kashita*	恚 した 吶 shita	貸さない *kasanai*	恚 さない 吶 sanai	貸さなかった *kasanakatta*
	B	待つ *matsu*	wait	待った *matta*	㞢 った 㞢 tta	待たない *matanai*	㞢 たない 㞢 tanai	待たなかった *matanakatta*
		買う *kau*	buy	買った *katta*	㞢 った 㞢 tta	買わない *kawanai*	㞢 わない 㞢 wanai	買わなかった *kawanakatta*
		帰る *kaeru*	return	帰った *kaetta*	吶 った 吶 tta	帰らない *kaeranai*	吶 らない 吶 ranai	帰らなかった *kaeranakatta*
	C	書く *kaku*	write	書いた *kaita*	㞢 いた 㞢 ita	書きません *kakanai*	㞢 かない 㞢 kanai	書かなかった *kakanakatta*
	D	急ぐ *isogu*	hurry	急いだ *isoida*	㞢 いだ 㞢 ida	急かない *isoganai*	㞢 がない 㞢 ganai	急がなかった *isoganakatta*
	E	遊ぶ *asobu*	play	遊んだ *asonda*	㞢 んだ 㞢 nda	遊ばない *asobanai*	㞢 ばない 㞢 banai	遊ばなかった *asobanakatta*
		飲む *nomu*	drink	飲んだ *nonda*	㞢 んだ 㞢 nda	飲まない *nomanai*	㞢 まない 㞢 manai	飲まなかった *nomanakatta*
		死ぬ *shinu*	die	死んだ *shinda*	㞢 んだ 㞢 nda	死なない *shinanai*	㞢 なない 㞢 nanai	死ななかった *shinanakatta*
Group 3: Irregular		する *suru*	do	した *shita*	There is no rule.	しない *shinai*	There is no rule.	しなかった *shinakatta*
		来る *kuru*	come	来た *kita*		来ない *konai*		来なかった *konakatta*

From top to bottom, we see three divisions: Groups 1, 2, and 3.

Group 1: "Invariable" verbs, we will later see the reason for their name.

Group 2: "Variable" verbs. There are 5 divisions: A, B, C, D, and E.

Group 3: Irregular verbs; there are only 2, the verbs *suru* and *kuru*, and we should learn them by heart, because, since they are irregular, conjugation rules are obviously not applied to them.

From left to right we have:

• Simple form, equivalent to the English infinitive. Notice how all verbs end in *u*.

• Translation.

• Past tense.

• Rules for the past tense.

Verbs in Group 1 always end in *ru*, and the past tense is formed by removing this *ru* and replacing it with *ta* (hence their name: invariable.) Example: *oshieru*. We remove *ru* = *oshie* / we add *ta* = *oshieta* (I taught).

Verbs in Group 2 are more complicated:

Verbs ending in *su* (A) always replace *su* with *shita*.

Verbs ending in *tsu*, *u* or *ru* (B) always replace the last syllable with *tta*. Be careful! There are verbs which end in *ru* both in Groups 1 and 2, and this can cause confusion. You can only tell a verb ended in *ru* corresponds to Group 1 or 2 by learning it by heart.

Verbs ending in *ku* (C) always replace *ku* with *ita*.

Verbs ending in *gu* (D) always replace *gu* with *ida*.

And, finally, verbs ending in *bu*, *mu* and *nu* (E) always replace the last syllable with *nda*.

• The negative form of verbs.

• Rules for the negative form.

As usual, the verbs in Group 1 are easy: we replace the *ru* in the simple form with *nai*. Example: *okiru*. We remove *ru* = *oki* / we add *nai* = *okinai* (I don't wake up.)

In Group 2, as a general rule, we replace the last *u* in the simple form with an *a* and we add *nai*. Example: *nomu*. We remove *u* = *nom* / we add *a* = *noma* / we add *nai* = *nomanai* (I don't drink.)

Pay attention to verbs ending in *tsu*, the last syllable doesn't become *tsa* but *ta* (*matsu* = *matanai*), and verbs ending in *u*, where *u* is replaced with *wa* (*kau* = *kawanai*).

• Past negative form.

In this case, we have not added a column for rules because the rule is very easy. Starting from the negative form of any verb, we simply replace the last *i* with *katta*. Example: *kaku*. Negative form of the verb *kaku* = *kakanai* / we remove the last *i* = *kakana* / we add *katta* = *kakanakatta* (I didn't write.)

Now you could try forming your own sentences with these verbs, plus the information in Lessons 7, 9, 16, 18, and 19.

漫画例：*Manga-examples*

We will see now some examples taken from Japanese manga in its original version. We will be looking at how Japanese verbs are conjugated in their dictionary form.

a) Infinitive

Maruko:	まる子の今日は今からはじまるよ。	さあさあ。
	maruko no kyō wa ima kara hajimaru yo	*saa saa*
	Maruko PoP today SP now from start EP	come now
	Maruko's day starts now.	**Here we go.**

We start the manga-examples with the use of the present tense in its dictionary form: the verb *hajimaru* (to start). We must emphasize the fact that Japanese verbs are not conjugated like English verbs (see Lesson 19). Japanese verbs have neither gender nor number. For instance: *watashi wa hajimaru* (I start); *anatatachi wa hajimaru* (you start (second person plural)); *kanojo wa hajimaru* (she starts). While the verb changes in English ("start, starts"), in Japanese it is always the same (*hajimaru*).

The expression *saa saa* used by Maruko in the second bubble conveys an idea of haste, impatience. Its translation as "Here we go!" sounded appropriate.

b) Past tense (1)

<table>
<tr><td>Tom: どうしたの？ジェニー。
dōshita no? jenii
what is the matter? Jenny
What's wrong, Jenny?</td><td>Jenny: 酔った。
yotta.
feel dizzy (past)
I feel dizzy.</td></tr>
</table>

We see here a verb in the past tense of the dictionary form. It is the verb *you* (to feel dizzy.) Since the verb ends in *u* (group 2, B in the table), the past is formed removing the *u* of the infinitive and adding *tta*. Thus: *you* / we remove *u* = *yo* / we add *tta* = *yotta*. Since a literal translation was not suitable in the context, we have chosen to translate it as "I'm dizzy."

c) Past tense (2)

Rooster: トウモロコシ村に朝がきたぞーい。
tōmorokoshi mura ni asa ga kita zo—i
Corn village PP morning SP come EP
Morning has come to Corn Village!

トウモロコシ村に
朝がきたぞーい

We see in this example the past form of one of the two irregular verbs in Japanese, *kuru*. As we saw in the theory section's table and in this example, the past tense of *kuru* is *kita*. Irregular verbs don't follow conjugation rules and, therefore, we must learn them by heart. Still, there are only two irregular verbs in Japanese, whereas in English there are many more.

There is also a half-irregular verb. That is the verb *iku* (to go), its past tense being *itta* and not *iita*. It is worth remembering.

d) Negative

Maria: 竜次くんいっしょに入らない？
ryūji kun isshoni hairanai?
Ryūji-kun together enter (neg.)?
Shall we bathe together, Ryūji?

This panel offers us the negative conjugation of the verb *hairu* (to enter / get into), which is *hairanai* (not to enter / not to get into). In this context, they are talking about getting into the bath, the word "bath" having been omitted. In English, a better translation would be "bathe." The literal translation of Maria's sentence would be something like: "We don't enter together?" We use this negative form to make questions, and we think the translation we have offered you is closer to the original.

e) Past negative

Raishin: 十郎には、できなかったもので。
jūrō ni wa, dekinakatta mono de...
Jūrō IP SP, be able to (past neg.) thing
As Jūrō couldn't do it...

To conclude, an example of the past negative form of the verb *dekiru* (to be able to / to know), which is *dekinakatta*. To conjugate this form you have to follow the following steps:
Infinitive: *dekiru* / what group does it belong to? Group 1 / how do we form the negative in this group? we replace *ru* with *nai* (*dekinai*) / how do we form the past negative? we replace the *i* in the negative form with *katta* (*dekinakatta*.) That's it.

1 What is another name for verbs in dictionary form? Why is this verb form called "dictionary form?"

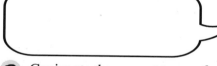

2 Which are the rules for the negative form? Give one example using a verb from group 1, and two examples using verbs from group 2.

3 Conjugate the present tense of the verb 遊ぶ (*asobu*, to play), simple and –*masu* forms (review Lesson 19 for the –*masu* form).

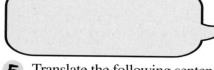

4 Conjugate the negative form of the verb 飲む (*nomu*, to drink), simple and –*masu* forms (review Lesson 19 for the –*masu* form).

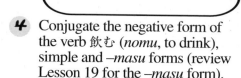

5 Translate the following sentence into Japanese: "I bought a book." (to buy = 買う (*kau*) / book = 本 (*hon*) / Direct object particle = を (*o*))

6 Translate the following sentence into English: "彼女は英語を教えなかった。" (*kanojo wa eigo o oshienakatta*) (*kanojo* = she / *eigo* = English / *wa* = Subject particle / *o* = Direct object particle)

7 Translate the following sentence into Japanese: "Tanaka doesn't wake up." (*Tanaka* (proper name) = 田中 / Subject particle = は (*wa*) Look out!: Lesson 15).

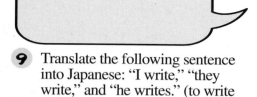

8 Translate the following sentence into English: "私はマリアさんを待つ。" (*watashi wa Maria-san o matsu*) (*watashi* = I / *Maria* = Maria / *wa* = Subject particle / *o* = Direct object particle)

9 Translate the following sentence into Japanese: "I write," "they write," and "he writes." (to write = 書く (*kaku*) / I = 私 (*watashi*) / they = 彼ら (*karera*) / he = 彼 (*kare*) / Subject particle = は (*wa*))

10 Name the two Japanese irregular verbs, and conjugate all their forms. There is another half-irregular verb, which one is it, and how do we conjugate it?

第21課：家族

> **Lesson 21: The family**

In this lesson we will slow down on the grammar and theory, and we will basically learn vocabulary: the family is our theme here. Japanese language is quite special as far as the family is concerned, so you should read carefully.

My family

As usual, we will base our explanations on the table supplementing the text.

Let's have a look at the first table: "My family." Japanese use different names when talking about relatives, depending on whether it is one's own family or someone else's.

Generally speaking, words used to talk about one's own relatives are shorter than those used to refer to somebody else's relatives. We will see why later.

You can study the vocabulary using the table. The only peculiarity about Japanese is that you have a different word for each brother and sister: elder brother (兄, *ani*), elder sister (姉, *ane*), younger brother (弟, *otōto*), and younger sister (妹, *imōto*).

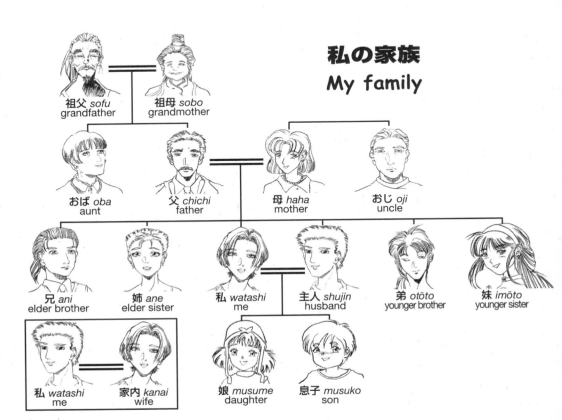

私の家族
My family

祖父 *sofu* grandfather

祖母 *sobo* grandmother

おば *oba* aunt

父 *chichi* father

母 *haha* mother

おじ *oji* uncle

兄 *ani* elder brother

姉 *ane* elder sister

私 *watashi* me

主人 *shujin* husband

弟 *otōto* younger brother

妹 *imōto* younger sister

私 *watashi* me

家内 *kanai* wife

娘 *musume* daughter

息子 *musuko* son

Somebody else's family

In the second table, "Tanaka's family," we have the words we use when talking about somebody else's family. All these words are imbued with great respect. This is due to the extreme respect Japanese have for other people, and, consequently, for their families. Using the words meant for one's own family when talking about someone else's relatives is a serious mistake and in seen as a lack of respect. Generally speaking, these words are longer and most of them have the suffix for respect –*san*, which we saw in Lesson 15. Learning these words by heart and using them accordingly is essential.

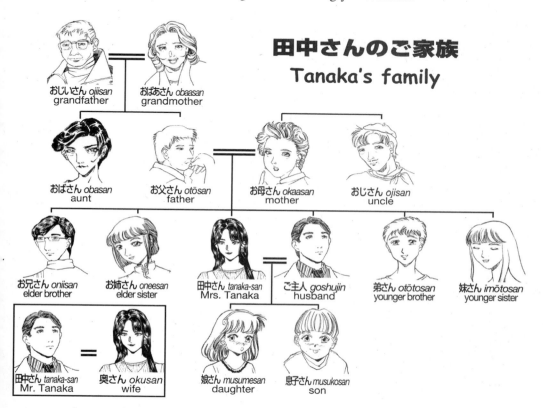

田中さんのご家族
Tanaka's family

And what about the mother-in-law?

We can't see any words for "in-laws" in this table. These words are seldom used, and, even if they do exist, they are hardly ever used in normal conversations. Usually, the son-in-law calls his mother-in-law *okāsan* (mother) and his father-in-law *otōsan* (father) and, more often so, he calls them by their name plus –*san*. When talking about other people, we would usually say "your daughter's husband" or "your wife's mother."

Some examples

Here are some sample sentences:

私の姉は先生です。

watashi no ane wa sensei desu

My elder sister is a teacher.

あなたのお姉さんは先生です。

anata no onēsan wa sensei desu

Your elder sister is a teacher.

As you can see, we have used the word *ane* in the first example and the word *onēsan* in the second one. They both mean "elder sister," the difference lying in that the first example refers to **my** sister, whereas the second one refers to **your** sister.

漫画例: *Manga-examples*

The family is a complex matter and not as easy as it seems, at least in Japanese. Let's see some examples in manga panels which will confirm what was said in the lesson and will offer other possibilities.

a) Somebody else's family

Komeyoshi: お子さん...いや、お孫さんですか？
okosan... iya, omagosan desu ka?
son/daughter/child... no, grandchild be Q?
Is this your daughter? No… your granddaughter?

Bernhart: いや。
iya
No.

We can see in this first example how to refer to somebody else's relatives. We must always use the formal words in the second table from the theory pages. Make sure you don't use the words meant for one's own family members, as this is a terrible mistake.

We see here two words not found in the previous table, *okosan* and *omagosan*. The first can be translated as "son," "daughter," or "child," and the second one means "grandson," "granddaughter," or "grandchild." When talking about one's own grandchild we use the word 孫 *mago*.

b) One's own family

あいつは俺の息子…

Risei: あいつは俺の息子…。
aitsu wa ore no musuko...
that guy SP I PoP son
That's my son...

A very clear example of how to use the words for family members, and how they change depending on whose family we are talking about, our own or someone else's. Here, Risei is talking about his son, therefore, he uses the word *musuko* (son). If Risei talked about somebody else's son he would use the word *musuko-san* (son).

c) Alternative words

Minako: おふくろと叔母さんのことか？
ofukuro to obasan no koto ka?
mother and aunt PoP (nominalizer) Q?
Are you talking about my mother and my aunt?

おふくろと叔母さんのことか？

Very often words we have not seen before in the vocabulary tables are used to talk about the closest family members. There are several words to talk about parents. We see here the word *ofukuro*, used by men to talk about their mothers. Another word men use, to talk about their fathers, is 親父 *oyaji*. Also very common are 父親 *chichioya* (father) and 母親 *hahaoya* (mother), which have formal and distant respect connotations. The words パパ *papa* and ママ *mama* are also used in Japanese, meaning "mummy" and "daddy."

In this example we also have the word *obasan* (aunt). Curiously enough, depending on the kanji used to write it, this word can mean "father / mother's younger sister" (叔母さん), or "father / mother's elder sister" (伯母さん). It is the younger sister in this example.

d) When talking about non-relatives

Tomoko: あ・・・お姉さん 大丈夫？
a... onēsan daijōbu?
oh... elder sister be well?
A... are you okay?

Words like "elder sister" are often used to refer to young women whose name we don't know, as in this manga-example. The little girl, Tomoko, is referring to the woman as *onēsan*, even though she isn't actually her sister. We have chosen to omit it in the translation. Other words used with the same intention, that is, to refer to people whose name we don't know, are *oniisan* (for a young man, literally meaning "elder brother"), *ojisan* (for a 40- or -so-year-old man, meaning "uncle"), *obasan* (for a 40- or -so-year-old woman, meaning "aunt"), *ojiisan* (for an old man, meaning "grandfather"), or *obāsan* (for an old woman, meaning "grandmother").

e) Affectionate way of calling relatives

Nina: お兄ちゃんに狙いをつけたの。
oniichan ni nerai o tsuketa no
elder brother IP aim DOP take EP
I took aim at my brother...

Another very common tendency in Japanese is to call one's siblings in an affectionate way, using the corresponding word plus the suffix *–chan*. Thus, we have *oniichan* (elder brother) or *onēchan* (elder sister.) Calling one's own parents *otōsan* (father) and *okāsan* (mother) is also very usual. It is an affectionate use which has nothing to do with the formal usage previously seen in the second table in the theory pages.

Likewise, calling one's own uncle and aunt *ojisan* (uncle), *obasan* (aunt), and one's grandparents *ojiisan* (grandfather) and *obāsan* (grandmother) is also very common.

1 Why are different words used in Japanese to refer to one's own family or to somebody else's?

2 What's the name for one's own wife? And for somebody else's wife? How about the name for the husband (in both cases)?

3 English only distinguishes between "brother" and "sister." How about Japanese? Which are the eight words we can use? (including the words used to refer to "my family" and to "somebody else's family")

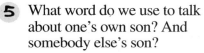
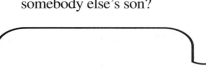

4 What word do we use to talk about one's own uncle? And somebody else's uncle?

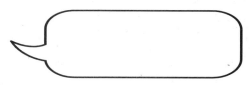

5 What word do we use to talk about one's own son? And somebody else's son?

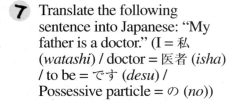

6 How do we translate the word 孫 (*mago*) into English? Is this one's own relative or somebody else's?

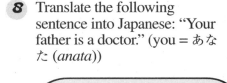

7 Translate the following sentence into Japanese: "My father is a doctor." (I = 私 (*watashi*) / doctor = 医者 (*isha*) / to be = です (*desu*) / Possessive particle = の (*no*))

8 Translate the following sentence into Japanese: "Your father is a doctor." (you = あなた (*anata*))

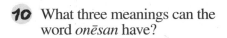

9 Name at least three words we can use to refer to one's own father.

10 What three meanings can the word *onēsan* have?

Having seen pronouns (Lesson 7), nouns (Lesson 11), adjectives (Lessons 13 and 14), grammatical particles (Lesson 16), and verbs (Lessons 18, 19 and 20), we are now going to study another part of speech: adverbs. As you know, adverbs are invariable words which modify the meaning of verbs, adjectives, or sentences. Words such as "today," "extremely," or "very" are adverbs.

How many adverbs are there?

Adverbs in Japanese, like in English, are one of the most difficult type of words to handle and to use correctly. We will mention, however, that there are many adverbs of many kinds, and that mastering at least the most basic ones is essential, because they are used a lot, both in conversation and in manga.

As you can see, there are grammar and vocabulary tables. In the vocabulary table, you will find a list of adverbs; they are probably the most commonly used in Japanese, and it is worthwhile learning them. We have divided them into four groups: time, place, manner, and quantity.

日本語 Japanese	ローマ字 rōmaji	翻訳 translation
今	ima	Now
今日	kyō	Today
昨日	kinō	Yesterday
明日	ashita	Tomorrow
まだ	mada	Still, yet
もう	mō	Already
いつ	itsu	When?
下に	shita ni	Under
上に	ue ni	On, over
側に	soba ni	Beside
前に	mae ni	In front of
後ろに	ushiro ni	Behind
きっと	kitto	Certainly
ゆっくり	yukkuri	Slowly
よく	yoku	Much, well
どんなに	donna ni	How?
いくら	ikura	How much?
何	nani	What?
大変	taihen	Very
たくさん	takusan	Much, many
十分	jūbun	Enough
だけ	dake	Only
少し	sukoshi	A little, some
ちょっと	chotto	A little; rather
もっと	motto	More

How to make adverbs

It is very easy to make adverbs from adjectives in English. In most cases all you have to do is add "ly" to the adjective, and we have an adverb. Example: easy = easily, high = highly, noisy = noisily, etc. In Japanese, there is a very similar way of forming adverbs from adjectives. As you know, there are two kinds of adjectives in Japanese: "i" adjectives (Lesson 13) and "na" adjectives (Lesson 14). The rules for the forming of adverbs change depending on the kind of adjective, as we can see in the grammar table.

1) "i" adjectives: we replace the final *i* with *ku*.

   Ex: *atarashii* (new). We remove the final *i* = *atarashi* / we add *ku* = *atarashiku* (newly).

2) Ex: *kantan-na* (easy) = we remove *na* and we add *ni* = *kantan-ni* (easily).

You can make your own adverbs from the adjective vocabulary tables in Lessons 13 and 14.

	Adjective	Translation	Rule	Adverb	Translation
Adj. "i"	新しい *atarashii*	new		新しく *atarashiku*	newly
	強い *tsuyoi*	strong	~~~い~~く ~~~i~~ *ku*	強く *tsuyoku*	strongly
	大きい *ookii*	big		大きく *ookiku*	in a large way
Adj. "na"	便利な *benri-na*	convenient		便利に *benri-ni*	conveniently
	静かな *shizuka-na*	quiet, calm	~~~な~~に ~~~na~~ *ni*	静かに *shizuka-ni*	quietly, calmly
	簡単な *kantan-na*	easy		簡単に *kantan-ni*	easily

Other kind of adverbs

There are other ways of making adverbs which we will briefly comment.

– Adding the suffix 的に (*-teki ni*).

Ex: 具体 (*gutai*, specific) =具体的に (*gutaiteki ni*, specifically).

– The gerunds and participles of many verbs can be used as adverbs:

喜んで (*yorokonde*, gladly) / はじめて (*hajimete*, for the first time).

– Some adverbs are formed by repeating a word:

時々 (*tokidoki*, sometimes), しばしば (*shibashiba*, often), いちいち (*ichiichi*, one by one).

Example sentences

Adverbs are usually placed before the verb or adjective they modify.

Ex: **to eat a lot** (a lot = adv.)

たくさん食べる。

takusan taberu (*takusan* (adv.) = a lot, *taberu* = to eat)

Let's now look at some sentences with adverbs.

a) Adverb of place 前に (*mae ni*, in front of):
   私はテレビをテーブルの前に置く。
   watashi wa terebi o teeburu no mae ni oku
   I SP television DOP table PoP in front of put
   I put the television in front of the table.

b) Adverb of manner ゆっくり (*yukkuri*, slowly):
   私は彼女をゆっくり抱く。
   watashi wa kanojo o yukkuri daku
   I SP her DOP slowly embrace
   I embrace her slowly.

c) Adverb of time まだ (*mada*, yet):
   料理はまだ出来ていない。
   ryōri wa mada dekite inai
   food SP yet be ready (neg. Gerund)
   The food is not ready yet.

d) Adverb of quantity ちょっと (*chotto*, a little):
   ちょっと待ってください。
   chotto matte kudasai
   a little wait please.
   Wait a moment, please.

e) Adverb of manner 静かに (*shizuka-ni*, quietly):
   彼は静かに勉強します。
   kare wa shizuka ni benkyō shimasu
   he SP quietly study do
   He studies quietly.

漫画例： *Manga-examples*

As usual, the second part of the lesson is devoted to the examples taken from Japanese manga which illustrate what was explained in the theory pages. Here are the adverbs.

a) Quickly

Sawada: なにしてんだ早くはいれ。
nani shiten da hayaku haire
what do be quickly get in (imperative)
What are you doing? Get in, quickly.

This panel is a very clear example of the use of an adverb derived from an "i" adjective. It is the adverb *hayaku* (quickly), derived from the adjective (quick). To form adverbs from "i" adjectives, all we need to do is to replace the *i* with *ku*. Therefore: *hayai* → *hayaku*.

With the word *hayai*, we should mention that, depending on the kanji used to write it, the word has two slightly different meanings. The first *hayai*, 早い, seen here, means "quick (in time), soon" and the second one 速い means "fast (in speed)."

b) Neatly

Spectator: きれいに抜いた!?
kirei ni nuita!?
neat (adv.) pass
Did it pass neatly?

In the previous example we saw how an adverb is formed from an "i" adjective. In this example we will see an adverb derived from a "na" adjective. As you have seen in the previous grammar table, "na" adjectives replace *na* with *ni* to form an adverb. Therefore: *kirei-na* → *kirei ni*.

In this example, the adjective *kirei-na* (beautiful, neat) becomes the adverb *kirei ni* (neatly, beautifully).

c) Now

One of the simpler adverbs of time, and very easy to use, is *ima* (now). It is used on countless occasions, as, for instance, in this panel.

We already saw a very clear example of the usage of the word *ima* in Lesson 12 (telling the time): To say "What's the time now?," the following sentence is very common:
今は何時ですか。
ima wa nanji desu ka
now SP what time be Q?
What's the time (now)?

Enemy: 今だ囲んでたたんじまえ!!
ima da kakonde tatanjimae!!
Now be surround hit (imp.)
Now! Surround him and down with him!

d) Hypothetically / completely

Kurama: 仮に 敵の力がまったく未知のものだったら…。
kari ni   teki no chikara ga mattaku michi no mono dattara...
supposing   enemy PoP strength SP completely unknown thing be
Supposing the enemy's strength is completely unknown...

There are many more adverbs in Japanese which have not derived from adjectives. Adverbs are probably some of the most difficult words to master in Japanese, because they usually give a very important nuance, essential to understand certain sentences. For instance, in this sentence we have two adverbs, *kari ni* (hypothetically, supposing that) and *mattaku* (completely, entirely), which give very important nuances to the sentence, that are essential to its comprehension.

e) For the first time

Kyōsuke: はじめてのんだお酒の味は…。
hajimete nonda o-sake no aji wa...
for the first time drink (past) sake PoP taste SP
The taste of liquor the first time I drank…

There are other ways to form adverbs. A very common way is adding the suffix 的に *(teki ni)* to certain nouns, as for example, in the word 積極的に *(sekkyokuteki ni*, positively), derived from the noun 積極 *(sekkyoku*, positive). Another way is using the gerund of certain verbs, like in this example, where Kyōsuke uses the adverb はじめて *(hajimete*, for the first time), gerund of the verb はじめる *(hajimeru*, to start). A last remark: the word *sake* has two meanings in Japanese. The first one obviously is the famous Japanese liquor made from rice and called *sake*. However, the second one, used much more often in everyday life, covers any kind of alcoholic drink (beer, whisky, etc.).

1 What does the adverb 側に (*soba ni*) mean? What kind of adverb is it (time, manner…)? How about the adverb まだ (*mada*)?

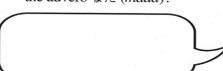

2 What is the rule of formation for adverbs derived from "i" adjectives?

3 Form an adverb from the adjectives すごい (*sugoi*, amazing), 低い (*hikui*, short), and 熱い (*atsui*, hot). How do you translate these newly formed adverbs into English?

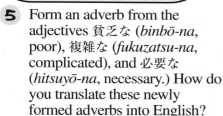

4 What is the rule for the formation of adverbs from "na" adjectives?

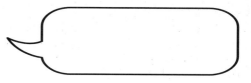

5 Form an adverb from the adjectives 貧乏な (*binbō-na*, poor), 複雑な (*fukuzatsu-na*, complicated), and 必要な (*hitsuyō-na*, necessary.) How do you translate these newly formed adverbs into English?

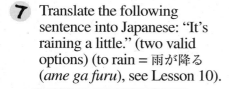

6 Translate the following sentence into English: "この試験は大変難しいです" (*kono shiken wa taihen muzukashii desu.*) (*shiken* = exam / *muzukashii* = difficult).

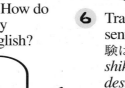

7 Translate the following sentence into Japanese: "It's raining a little." (two valid options) (to rain = 雨が降る (*ame ga furu*), see Lesson 10).

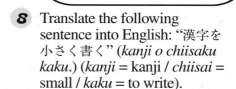

8 Translate the following sentence into English: "漢字を小さく書く" (*kanji o chiisaku kaku.*) (*kanji* = kanji / *chiisai* = small / *kaku* = to write).

9 Which two words can be pronounced *hayai*? How do we write them and what do they mean?

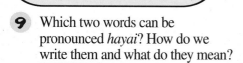

10 What are the two meanings for 酒 (*sake*)? Which is most commonly used?

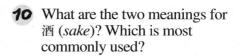

第23課：汚い言葉

Lesson 23: Swearwords and insults

We will be dealing with insults and swearwords in this lesson, a subject all good manga fans should be familiar with to be able to understand fully the manga in original version they want to read, as they appear quite often.

A warning

Insults are actually seldom used in Japanese society, so we can hardly expect to go to Japan and learn insults and swearwords on the streets. The Japanese DON'T usually use this kind of words.

However, they are used quite often in manga. As many of you will actually use this course to be able to understand manga—and we really encourage this—we think it would be good for manga fans to know which are the main Japanese swearwords.

We have a vocabulary table as usual, with twenty insulting terms. Many of them are not often used and we hardly ever come across them. The most common insults and dirty words are: *baka* (and derivatives), *aho,* and *kuso.*

The other swearwords in the list have a rather limited use and we seldom see them.

What would you say if your bike was stolen?

An experiment carried out by the author in Japan was related to insults. The experiment consisted of asking several people what would they say if they got to the place they had left their bike and found out it had been stolen. This is the typical case when someone would let fly with a string of insults and swearwords, which would not exactly flatter the alleged thief.

Well, the almost unanimous answer to the question "What would you say if you found out your bike had been stolen?" was *shinjirarenai*! (I can't believe it!). At most, there were some who said *kuso*! (shit!).

This suggests the Japanese don't use swearwords the same arbitrary way as we do. They don't usually insult other people either. That is something people frown upon in a society where the natural thing is to keep a poker face, remaining impassive, very often with a false smile, even though they may be cursing their interlocutor's ancestors. Losing one's control in Japan is bad manners and very much frowned upon.

Main swearwords

Let's review the contents of the vocabulary table. Almost all translations into English have been taken from the Japanese–English dictionary published by *Kenkyūsha*.

Note: The table always gives the kanji writing of the corresponding swearword. However, swearwords are usually written in the katakana syllabary in manga, due to its visual impact.

The top swearword in Japan is *baka*. This word has numerous possible translations and many derivatives, such as *bakamono* or *bakayarō*. It is the most commonly used.

Next, we have the word *ahō*, and most times we will find it in katakana: アホ (*aho*). The dictionary considers the words *baka* and *aho* synonymous. However, in Osaka and its surroundings, *aho* is a rather non-offensive word, whereas *baka* is an explosive word. In Tokyo and its surroundings, we find exactly the opposite, so you must be careful with the usage of these words.

The words *baka* and *kuso* can work as pejorative suffixes before certain nouns. It would be equivalent to our "damn," or "fucking." Example: *kuso-keisatsu* (damn policeman), *baka-sensei* (fucking teacher), etc.

kanji-kana	Meaning	kanji-kana	Meaning
馬鹿 *baka*	fool, simpleton, ass, dunce, idiot, silly, stupid, fathead, nut	くそったれ *kusottare*	swine, son of a bitch
馬鹿者 *bakamono*	→*baka*	糞食らえ *kusokurae*	go to hell!, damn you!
馬鹿野郎 *bakayarō*	fool, stupid, son of a bitch	下手糞 *hetakuso*	good-for-nothing, awful
馬鹿にする *baka ni suru*	to make fun of, make a fool of, to hold someone cheap	屑 *kuzu*	rubbish, scum, dregs, junk
馬鹿を言う *baka o iu*	to talk nonsense, (rubbish, rot)	畜生 *chikushō*	beast, brute, dumb animal, damn it!, gosh!, the devil take you!
馬鹿馬鹿しい *bakabakashii*	absurd, ridiculous, ludicrous	気持ち悪い *kimochiwarui*	Unpleasant, disgusting, sick
阿呆 *ahō*	→*baka*	気色悪い *kishokuwarui*	→*kimochiwarui*
ドジ *doji*	(to make a) mess of it, blunder	化け物 *bakemono*	spook, monster, goblin
ブス *busu*	ugly woman, plain looking	タコ *tako*	pervert, disgusting, octopus
糞 *kuso*	Shit, excrement, dung, damn it!, heck!	間抜け *manuke*	half-wit, ninny, blockhead, fool, moron

漫画例：*Manga-examples*

Let's have a look at the swearwords in the examples taken from manga. But remember: avoid using all these words unless it is absolutely necessary. You will be considered extremely rude if you use them as often as you use swearwords in English.

a) Baka

Ryūtsu: ば　ばか苦しいっどけ！
ba　baka kurushii doke!
i... idiot painful move off (imperative)
You... idiot! You're hurting me! Move off!

This is a clear example of the use of the top swearword in Japanese: *baka*. The second sentence in the panel, which hasn't been translated, says: "I'll make *sukiyaki* out of you," *sukiyaki* being a delicious Japanese veal dish.

b) Baka ni suru

> Kazuhiro: バカにするなっ !!!
> *baka ni suru na !!!*
> fool P make (neg. imperative)
> **Don't make a fool of me! / Do you think I'm stupid?**

There are two translation options for this sentence: the first one is more faithful to the original, whereas the second one is freer. The expression *Baka ni suru* means "to make a fool of someone." We find the word *baka* written in katakana here, while in the previous example it was written in hiragana. Writing this word in hiragana, katakana or kanji is arbitrary: the writer decides.

c) Busu / urusai

> Kazuki: うるせぇ　ブス !!
> *urusee busu!!*
> noisy ugly
> **Shut up, you frights!**

Here we have two rude expressions in one example. The word *urusai* is pronounced here in a dialect belonging to the area of Tokyo and its surroundings, where *ai* becomes *ee* (*urusai* → *urusee*.) This word literally means "noisy," but most times it is used to make somebody shut up. It would be the equivalent of "shut up," "shut your mouth," or "you're a pain…"

The second expression is *busu*. Although literally translated as "ugly," we should mention *busu* is the most offensive word you can say to a woman, and it should be avoided. Don't mistake *busu* for *basu* (bus)!

d) Kuso

We have here an example of what was mentioned at the end of the theory pages. Very often words such as *kuso* (shit) or *baka* (fool) are used pejoratively before certain nouns. This usage is very similar to our "fucking," or "damn."

Sōma:	このクソネコー	またおまえか。
	kono kuso-neko	*mata omae ka*
	this shit cat	again you Q?
	You again,	**damn cat!**

e) Chikushō

Chikushō is quite a strange word. Originally, *chikushō* refers to what we know as "wild animal" or "beast." Oddly enough, the sense in which it is most often used nowadays derived from this original meaning: "damn it," "gosh." That is, this expression is used when something doesn't go right, when there is a setback, or a bad reversal of fortune.

To conclude, we must emphasize the fact that insults are seldom used in Japan. The most obvious proof of this is the limited number of insults in Japanese compared to the richness of swearwords in English. But they are worth knowing just in case.

Yamazaki:	ちくしょうー。
	chikushō
	Damn it!

1 Which language is richer in insults, English or Japanese?

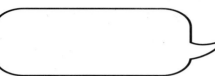

2 Why do you think the Japanese hardly ever use insults?

3 Write at least three derivatives of the insult *baka*.

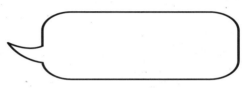

4 What does the word くず (*kuzu*) mean?

5 What important regional difference lies between the words *aho* and *baka* in Osaka and Tokyo?

6 How would we say "damn it" in Japanese?

7 How do we usually find swearwords written in manga, in hiragana, katakana, or kanji? Why?

8 Write a rude way of making somebody shut up.

9 What is the most insulting expression against a woman in Japanese?

10 Translate into Japanese the following words: "damn teacher" (teacher = 先生 *sensei*), and "fucking computer" (computer = コンピューター *konpyūtā*).

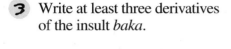

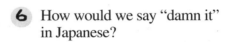

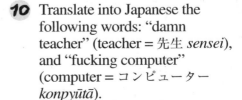

第 24 課：動詞（Ⅲ）：－て形

Lesson 24: Verbs (III): –te form

The –*te* form is a verb conjugation in Japanese, essential in the formation of many basic grammatical expressions.

In this lesson we will see only two of the most basic grammatical expressions formed with the –*te* form: the gerund and a form of request. However, there are many more, and mastering the –*te* conjugation is indispensable if we really want to learn Japanese.

Conjugation

The way we conjugate verbs in their –*te* form is identical to the formation of the past tense of verbs in their simple form, which we saw in Lesson 20. Having studied that lesson well, you shouldn't have any problem in learning the –*te* form. The only difference between the –*te* form and the past tense is that all –*ta* and –*da* past tense endings will be replaced with –*te* and –*de*. For more information, you have a conjugation table for the –*te* form and its conjugation rules.

		Dictionary f.	Translation	Imperative	Rule
Group 1: *Invariable*		教える *oshieru*	teach	教えて *oshiete*	る て ru *te*
		起きる *okiru*	wake up	起きて *okite*	
Group 2: *Variable*	A	貸す *kasu*	lend	貸して *kashite*	す して su *shite*
	B	待つ *matsu*	wait	待って *matte*	つ って tsu *tte*
		買う *kau*	buy	買って *katte*	う って u *tte*
		帰る *kaeru*	return	帰って *kaette*	る って ru *tte*
	C	書く *kaku*	write	書いて *kaite*	く いて ku *ite*
	D	急ぐ *isogu*	hurry	急いで *isoide*	ぐ いで gu *ide*
	E	遊ぶ *asobu*	play	遊んで *asonde*	ぶ んで bu *nde*
		飲む *nomu*	drink	飲んで *nonde*	む んで mu *nde*
		死ぬ *shinu*	die	死んで *shinde*	ぬ んで nu *nde*
Group 3: *Irregular*		する *suru*	do	して *shite*	Irregular verbs: There is no rule.
		来る *kuru*	come	来て *kite*	

Gerund

If we use the gerund when forming our sentences, our Japanese level will have considerably gained in quality. We will go from a very basic level to a much higher level.
The formation of the gerund is very easy if we have mastered the –*te* form. As we can see in the grammar table, all we need to do is add *iru* to any verb in the –*te* form. Thus, we will be able to form sentences such as: "I'm doing X."
Since Japanese verbs have neither gender nor number, there is one only conjugation for all genders and persons. For example, the sentences *oshiete iru* can mean either "I am teaching," or "they are teaching," or "she is teaching." One conjugation is good for all.

Request

Another way of using the –*te* form conjugation is the forming of request sentences.
All you need to do is add –*kudasai* after a verb in the –*te* form. You have some examples of the usage of this expression in the table. The form –*te kudasai* is extremely common in Japanese, and mastering it is undoubtedly advisable, plus being very useful. In spoken Japanese, and in manga by extension, –*kudasai* tends to be omitted when making requests.

A very common expression in Japan, *ganbatte*, is actually *ganbatte kudasai*, but when we express it in an informal and friendly way, we do without the –*kudasai* part. *Ganbatte* comes from *ganbaru*, a verb in Group 2 (B) which means "persevere, bear up, hold out." The expression *ganbatte kudasai* (or just *ganbatte*), extremely popular among the Japanese, would be translated as "stick to it, show your nerve, come on."

～て＋いる -te + iru	Gerund (to be doing)	待っている *matte iru*	To be waiting
		遊んでいる *asonde iru*	To be playing
		教えている *oshiete iru*	To be teaching
～て＋ください -te + kudasai	Request (please, do. . .)	待ってください *matte kudasai*	Please, wait
		遊んでください *asonde kudasai*	Please, play
		教えてください *oshiete sudasai*	Please, teach

-suru verbs

They have nothing to do with the –*te* form, but now that we have the chance they are worthwhile mentioning. These kinds of verbs are originally nouns, but once we add the verb *suru* (one of the two irregular verbs in Japanese) they become verbs. With these verbs conjugation is simple: we just conjugate *suru*. Here is an example: 勉強 (*benkyō*, "study")

Present tense: 勉強する (*benkyō suru*, "to study")
Past tense: 勉強した (*benkyō shita*)
Negative form: 勉強しない (*benkyō shinai*)
-*te* form: 勉強して (*benkyō shite*)

Other *suru* verbs: 運転する (*unten suru*, "to drive"), 結婚する (*kekkon suru*, "to marry"), 質問する (*shitsumon suru*, "to ask"), and many more.

Theory 157

漫画例：*Manga-examples*

We will see in the manga-examples in this lesson, the three grammatical points explained in the previous pages: the formation of the gerund, a form of request, and *suru* verbs.

a) Gerund

We have a clear example of the use of the Japanese gerund in this first panel. The formation of the gerund (we call it gerund so as to make concepts clearer, but it very often works differently to the English gerund), could be schematized in the following way: "*–te* form + conjugated verb *iru*." The verb here is *nokoru* (remain, be left). To conjugate the *–te* form of this verb *nokoru*, we have to check which group it belongs to. *Nokoru* belongs to Group 2 (B), and following the table's conjugation rules we will see the *–te* form of *nokoru* is *nokotte*. Adding the verb *iru* we obtain the gerund, *nokotte iru* (remaining). The final translation here is different due to context reasons. We can also conjugate the past tense, negative form, and past negative form just by conjugating the verb *iru*, as we saw in Lesson 18. Past tense: *nokotte ita*, negative: *nokotte inai*, past negative: *nokotte inakatta*.

Kindaichi: この「証拠」がこの会場に残っているんだ！！
kono "shōko" ga kono kaijō ni nokotte iru n da!!
this "proof" SP this assembly hall PP remain (ger.) be
The proof is still in this assembly hall!

b) Informal gerund

Takashi: サトミっ　まだ動いてるっ。
Satomi   mada ugoiteru
Satomi   still move (ger.)
Satomi! It's still moving!

This second example will help us illustrate a feature seen in spoken Japanese and, by extension, in most manga. In the formation of the gerund, –*te* form + conjugated verb *iru*, the *i* in the verb *iru* is very often removed. Spoken Japanese is actually quite different from written Japanese, just like English. Clearly, manga is a written medium, but it tries to copy the spoken language. Therefore, in manga we find colloquial language, contractions, and, sometimes, dialect forms. The gerund of the verb *ugoku* would be *ugoite iru*, but if we remove the *i* of the verb *iru*, turning it into spoken Japanese, we will have *ugoiteru*, as in this example.

c) Request form

Another possible use of the –*te* form is in a very common request form in Japanese. The formation is very simple: "–*te* form + *kudasai*", and it could be translated as "(verb), please". The verb in this example is *daku* (to hug), its –*te* form being *daite*. Adding *kudasai*, we obtain daite *kudasai* (hug me, please).

Kotomi: 抱いて下さい。
daite kudasai
hug please
Hug me, please.

Manga-examples 159

d) –suru verb

Here is a very simple example of a *–suru* verb. The verb in question is *kekkon suru* (to marry). The word *kekkon* means "wedding, marriage," but adding the verb *suru* (to do), the words *kekkon suru* become a verb which works just like all other verbs. The conjugation of these verbs is made just by conjugating the verb *suru* and leaving the other part untouched (the noun *kekkon* here). We saw the conjugation of the verb *suru* in Lessons 19–20, but we will repeat it here with the example of *kekkon*: Present tense: *kekkon suru* (to marry) / past tense: *kekkon shita* (married) / negative: *kekkon shinai* (doesn't marry) / past negative: *kekkon shinakatta* (didn't marry). There are many *–suru* verbs and it's worth knowing their conjugation.

Ralph: 盗賊と結婚する。
tōzoku to kekkon suru
thief CP marry do
I'm marrying a thief.

e) Ganbatte!

The request form "*–te* form + *kudasai*" can be simplified in spoken Japanese removing the word *kudasai*, as in this example. What Yamomoto actually wants to say is *ganbatte kudasai*, but removing *kudasai* and leaving *ganbatte* alone is much more informal and friendly.

ロドニーさん
がんばってー

Yamamoto: ロドニーさん　がんばってー。
Rodonii-san ganbatte –
Rodney (noun. suf.) hold out (ger.)
Come on, Rodney!

1 What do we use the *–te* form for, and why is it important that we know it?

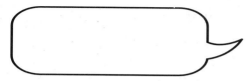

2 Conjugate the *–te* form of the verbs 飛ぶ (*tobu*, to fly), 見る (*miru*, to look → Group 1), and 座る (*suwaru*, to sit → Group 2).

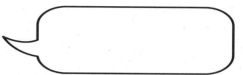

3 Form the gerund in the present tense of the verbs 寝る (*neru*, to sleep → Group 1), 転ぶ (*korobu*, to fall), and 笑う (*warau*, to laugh).

4 Form the past gerund and the negative gerund of the verbs in question 3.

5 Translate the following sentence: "They are playing." (they = かれら (*karera*) / to play = 遊ぶ (*asobu*))

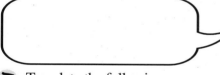

6 How do we form one of the most common and useful request forms?

7 Translate the following sentence: "Eat an apple, please." (to eat = 食べる (*taberu*, Group 1) / apple = りんご (*ringo*) / Direct object particle = を (*o*))

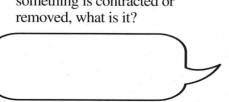

9 What happens to the gerund in colloquial spoken Japanese? If something is contracted or removed, what is it?

8 Conjugate the *–suru* verb 発生する (*hassei suru*, to occur) in the present and past tenses, and in the present and past negative forms.

10 What happens to the *–te* + *kudasai* form in colloquial spoken Japanese? If something is contracted or removed, what is it?

第24課

練習

Exercises

We will see in this lesson one of the most strange and disconcerting aspects of Japanese: the so-called counters.

What do we use counters with?

As we mentioned in several previous lessons, Japanese doesn't tell the difference between male, female, singular, or plural in nouns. We commented the male–female problem at length in Lesson 11 (nouns), and we also mentioned counters in passing.

Our intention in this lesson is to broaden our knowledge on the usage of these curious words called counters. Counters are words combined with nouns that indicate number, we use them to say "how many" things are there.

In English we say, for example, "I want six apples." To indicate "how many" apples we want, all we do is add the corresponding number, "six" in this case. In Japanese, we must add a suffix to that number six. This suffix is called "counter," and depending on the noun we want to count we will choose from a great number of counters. The choice will depend on the noun we want to count: if they are long things, we will choose *hon*, if they are people, we will choose *nin*, if they are machines *dai*, etc. In the table on the next page, you will find the main counters.

Reviewing Lessons 5 (numerals) and 6 (days of the week and months), is highly recommended in order to thoroughly review the numbers in Japanese.

I want six apples

The sentence we saw above, "I want six apples," easy as it may be in English, cannot be translated straight into Japanese as りんごを六ください。 (*ringo o roku kudasai*, *ringo* = apple, *o* = DOP, *roku* = 6, *kudasai* = please). A counter must be added to number *roku* (6) for the sentence to be correct. Let's analyze an apple: it is a small rounded object. The most convenient counter for it is *ko*, because we use it to count small rounded things. Then, the correct sentence would be: りんごを六個ください。 (*ringo o rokko kudasai*), because, just as we see in the table, number *roku* (6) + counter *ko* become *rokko* and not *rokuko* due to phonetic reasons. Irregular readings are indicated in bold type in the table.

Nevertheless, there is a counter that can be used with everything, and we can use it with any word without fear of getting it wrong. It is *tsu*. However, all the readings in the *tsu* line are irregular and they must be learned by heart. Still, it is much better knowing how to use counters and using the right counter on each occasion, rather than resorting to *tsu*.

Types of counters

つ (*tsu*):　universal counter. It can always be useful when in trouble.

人 (*nin*):　to count people. Watch out for special readings *hitori* (one person) and *futari* (two people), very much used.

枚 (*mai*):   for papers and flat things (CDs, blankets…)
台 (*dai*):   for machines (cars, tape recorders, computers, televisions…)
本 (*hon*):   for long and slender things (pencils, ball-point pens, trees…) Also video or audio tapes, telephone calls…
匹 (*hiki*):   small animals (mice, cats…) Large animals are counted with 頭 (*tō*), and birds with 羽 (*wa*)
冊 (*satsu*): books, magazines, printed and bound material
階 (*kai*):   building floors
個 (*ko*):   small things (and very often, rounded things) (apples, croquettes, stones…)

Example sentences

ここにえんぴつが三本あります。
koko ni enpitsu ga sanbon arimasu
There are three pencils here.
Enpitsu = pencil. Counter = *hon*

本を五冊ください。
hon o gosatsu kudasai
Give me five books, please.
hon = book. Counter = *satsu*

Don't confuse *hon* (book) with the counter *hon*, both written and pronounced the same way 本.

家の前に子供が二人います。
ie no mae ni kodomo ga futari imasu
There are two children in front of the house.
kodomo = child. Counter = *nin* (*futari*, irregular reading)

桃を三つください。
momo o mittsu kudasai
Give me three peaches, please.
momo = peach. Counter = it should actually be *ko* (small and round things), but we have used *tsu*, the universal counter, which can be used with anything.

	つ general counter	人 people	枚 papers, flat things	台 machines	本 slender, long things	匹 small animals	冊 books	階 building floors	個 small things
1	一つ *hitotsu*	一人 *hitori*	一枚 *ichimai*	一台 *ichidai*	一本 *ippon*	一匹 *ippiki*	一冊 *issatsu*	一階 *ikkai*	一個 *ikko*
2	二つ *futatsu*	二人 *futari*	二枚 *nimai*	二台 *nidai*	二本 *nihon*	二匹 *nihiki*	二冊 *nisatsu*	二階 *nikai*	二個 *niko*
3	三つ *mittsu*	三人 *sannin*	三枚 *sanmai*	三台 *sandai*	三本 *sanbon*	三匹 *sanbiki*	三冊 *sansatsu*	三階 *sangai*	三個 *sanko*
4	四つ *yottsu*	四人 *yonin*	四枚 *yonmai*	四台 *yondai*	四本 *yonhon*	四匹 *yonhiki*	四冊 *yonsatsu*	四階 *yonkai*	四個 *yonko*
5	五つ *itsutsu*	五人 *gonin*	五枚 *gomai*	五台 *godai*	五本 *gohon*	五匹 *gohiki*	五冊 *gosatsu*	五階 *gokai*	五個 *goko*
6	六つ *muttsu*	六人 *rokunin*	六枚 *rokumai*	六台 *rokudai*	六本 *roppon*	六匹 *roppiki*	六冊 *rokusatsu*	六階 *rokkai*	六個 *rokko*
7	七つ *nanatsu*	七人 *nananin*	七枚 *nanamai*	七台 *nanadai*	七本 *nanahon*	七匹 *nanahiki*	七冊 *nanasatsu*	七階 *nanakai*	七個 *nanako*
8	八つ *yattsu*	八人 *hachinin*	八枚 *hachimai*	八台 *hachidai*	八本 *happon*	八匹 *happiki*	八冊 *hassatsu*	八階 *hakkai*	八個 *hakko*
9	九つ *kokonotsu*	九人 *kyūnin*	九枚 *kyūmai*	九台 *kyūdai*	九本 *kyūhon*	九匹 *kyūhiki*	九冊 *kyūsatsu*	九階 *kyūkai*	九個 *kyūko*
10	十 *too*	十人 *jūnin*	十枚 *jūmai*	十台 *jūdai*	十本 *juppon*	十匹 *juppiki*	十冊 *jussatsu*	十階 *jukkai*	十個 *jukko*
?	いくつ *ikutsu?*	何人 *nan nin?*	何枚 *nan mai?*	何台 *nan dai?*	何本 *nan bon?*	何匹 *nan biki?*	何冊 *nan satsu?*	何階 *nan gai?*	何個 *nan ko?*

漫画例：*Manga-examples*

We will now practice counting, which can be a rather demanding exercise, due to the existence of counters.

a) Counter for people and counter for long things

Shiraiwa: 四人が一度にロボトンの手と足を一本ずつねらえっ。
yonin ga ichido ni roboton no te to ashi o ippon zutsu nerae.
four people SP once TP Roboton PoP hand CP leg DOP one by one aim
Literal Translation: You four, take in unison one of Roboton's arms and legs each!
Final suggested translation: Take Roboton by his arms and legs between the four of you!

わかったな。
wakatta na
understand EP
Got it?

The essential words in this example are *yonin* (4 + counter for people) and *ippon* (1 + counter for long and slender things). The first use of a counter, *nin*, is obvious, since he is counting people. In the second one, the words "arm" and "leg" are being counted (to say "take an arm and a leg each"). Arms and legs are long, slender things, therefore, the counter is, undoubtedly, 本 (*hon*).

b) Counter for spoonfuls

Rosso: そして砂糖をいれたんだ。　　一杯、二杯…　　三杯、四杯…。
soshite satō o ireta n da　　*ippai, nihai...*　　*sanbai, yonhai*
then sugar DOP put in (aux) be.　one, two…　three, four…
Then he put the sugar in.　**One, two…**　**three, four spoonfuls…**

A very clear example of the counter 杯 (*hai*). This counter is used to count cups (tea, coffee...), glasses (milk, water, wine, whisky...), and spoonfuls, as in this example. Watch out for the special readings of *ippai* and *sanbai* (they are neither *ichihai* nor *sanhai*).

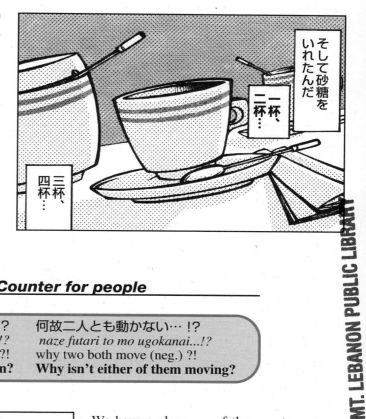

c) Counter for people

Tao Jun: なんなのそれは…!?　　何故二人とも動かない…!?
nan na no sore wa...!?　　*naze futari to mo ugokanai...!?*
what what this SP…?!　why two both move (neg.) ?!
But, what's going on?　**Why isn't either of them moving?**

We have a clear use of the counter for people 人 (*nin*) in this example. It is a much used counter in Japanese, but it has a very peculiar feature: two of its readings are completely irregular. 一人 is not read *ichinin*, the most obvious reading, but *hitori*, and 二人 is not read *ninin* but *futari*, as we can see in this example, and in the grammar table in the theory pages.

d) Counter for small animals

Asano:	くくくくっ。	一匹おわり！
	kukukuku	*ippiki owari!*
	(sound of laugh under one's breath)	one finish!
	He, he, he, he!	**One down!**

Here we have an example of the counter 匹 (*hiki*), used to count small animals (rats, cats...) But this counter is used here with a pejorative intention. Asano has actually defeated a person, but uses the counter *hiki* to humiliate and look down on the defeated opponent. These puns with the use of counters are frequent in manga.

e) Counter for tatami

Nanako:	大好きだったなあのアパート…。小さな6畳の中に。
	daisuki datta na ano apāto... chiisa-na rokujō no naka ni...
	be very fond of (past) EP that appartment… small 6 tatamis PoP inside PP
	I was very fond of that apartment… In that small 10 m² room…

We have given a list of the most common counters, but there are many more, which are used to count the most unlikely things. For instance, we have in this panel the counter 畳 (*jō*), used to count *tatami* (straw matting used to cover the floor in a house). Japanese houses are measured in tatamis (*jō*), just like we measure them in square meters (m²); a *tatami* is more or less 1.6 square meters (1.8m long x 0.9m wide).

1 What is a counter and what do we use it for?

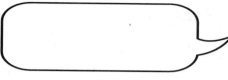

2 What does the use of one counter or another depend on?

3 Count from one to ten using the counter 枚 (*mai*). What do we use this counter with?

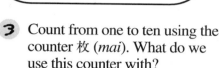

4 Count from one to ten using the counter 本 (*hon*). What do we use this counter with?

5 Were we to count books, what counter would we use? And with oranges?

6 Translate the following sentence into English: 道に車が六台あります。 (*michi ni kuruma ga rokudai arimasu*) (*michi* = road / *kuruma* = car / *arimasu* = there are / *ni* = Place particle / *ga* = Subject particle)

7 Translate the following sentence into Japanese: "Give me five cats, please." (cat = 猫 (*neko*) / please = ください (*kudasai*) / Direct object particle = を (*o*))

8 How do we say "one person?" And "two people?" And "three people?"

9 What do we use the counter 杯 (*hai*) with?

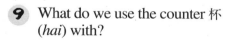

10 How many square meters is a 八畳 (*hachijō*) room?

第 26 課：体の呼び方

Lesson 26: The body

In this lesson we will basically look at vocabulary centered on the parts of the body. This time look at the three pictures full of words to be studied.

The body

The Japanese word for body is 体 (*karada*). In the illustration with the girl, we can see the main parts of the body. We have the kanji version, followed by a transcription in rōmaji, and, finally, each word's translation into English.

You should at least study the main ones, such as *kao*, *kubi*, *kaminoke*, *atama*, *mune*, *senaka*, *ude*, *te*, *onaka*, and *ashi* (see the references in the illustration). The remaining words are secondary, but they are also worth knowing.

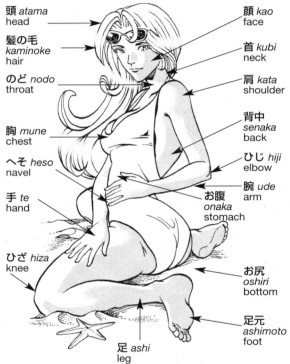

頭 *atama*
head

髪の毛 *kaminoke*
hair

のど *nodo*
throat

胸 *mune*
chest

へそ *heso*
navel

手 *te*
hand

ひざ *hiza*
knee

足 *ashi*
leg

顔 *kao*
face

首 *kubi*
neck

肩 *kata*
shoulder

背中 *senaka*
back

ひじ *hiji*
elbow

腕 *ude*
arm

お腹 *onaka*
stomach

お尻 *oshiri*
bottom

足元 *ashimoto*
foot

額 *hitai*
forehead

汗 *ase*
sweat

目 *me*
eye

鼻 *hana*
nose

口ひげ *kuchihige*
moustache

ひげ *hige*
beard

あご *ago*
chin

眉毛 *mayuge*
eyebrow

まつげ *matsuge*
eyelashes

耳 *mimi*
ear

ほお *hoo*
cheek

口 *kuchi*
mouth

歯 *ha*
tooth

舌 *shita*
tongue

Face and hand

In the illustration on the left we can clearly see the words referring to the parts of the face. The Japanese word for face is 顔 (*kao*). The basic vocabulary is: *me*, *kuchi*, *hana*, *mimi*, *shita*, *ha*, and *hige*.

And, finally, in the last illustration, we can see the hand of somebody who has passed away. The Japanese word for hand is 手 (*te*.) The basic vocabulary is: *yubi*, *tsume* and *tenohira*.

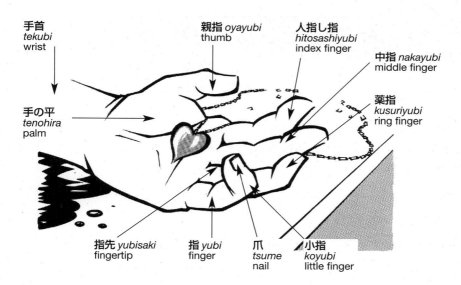

手首
tekubi
wrist

親指 *oyayubi*
thumb

人指し指
hitosashiyubi
index finger

中指 *nakayubi*
middle finger

薬指
kusuriyubi
ring finger

手の平
tenohira
palm

指先 *yubisaki*
fingertip

指 *yubi*
finger

爪
tsume
nail

小指
koyubi
little finger

Inside the body

In these illustrations we have seen a lot of vocabulary, but it only deals with the outside parts of the body. We will give a small list of organs:
頭脳 (*zunō*) brain / 心臓 (*shinzō*) heart / 血管 (*kekkan*) vein, artery / 肺臓 (*haizō*) lungs / 肝臓 (*kanzō*) liver / 腎臓 (*jinzō*) kidneys / 胃 (*i*) stomach / 腸 (*chō*) intestines / 生殖器官 (*seishoku kikan*) reproductive organs.

Feeling pain

Something very useful in any language is knowing how to say "X hurts me." Forming this sentence in Japanese is quite simple if we know the names for the different parts of the body, and if we use the following structure as a guide:

Xが痛いです。
X ga itai desu
X SP painful be.

Three practical examples to conclude:

頭が痛いです。(*atama ga itai desu*)
I have a headache.
おなかが痛いです。(*onaka ga itai desu*)
I have stomach pains.
心臓が痛いです。(*shinzō ga itai desu*)
My heart hurts me.

漫画例：*Manga-examples*

The vocabulary of the parts of the body may seem simple enough, and to a certain extent, it is. We will try to offer you a clearer view on the subject with these manga panels.

a) Tooth

Shigeko: 歯がかけちゃったー！！
ha ga kakechatta
tooth SP fall out (neg. result)
You have a missing tooth!

Sayaka: はっ !?
ha?
Uh?
Uuh?

We see in this first example one of the words we learnt in the previous pages: it is the word *ha* (tooth), written in kanji 歯. A grammatical note: when a sentence ends in *chatta* or *chau*, it usually implies the action indicated with the verb has a negative effect.

b) Body / soul

Title: PART 6 心も体も
pāto roku kokoro mo karada mo
part 6 heart too body too
Part six: In flesh and spirit

In this illustration, apart from the word *karada* (body), with which we are already familiar, we have the word *kokoro*. *Kokoro* means "heart," but it is a spiritual kind of heart, it is the mind, the soul, what is not the body, but what makes us human. The word *kokoro* can cause misunderstandings, due to the many meanings it covers. The word "heart," the physical organ which pumps the body's blood is called 心臓 (*shinzō*). We must not confuse both words (*kokoro* and *shinzō*) even though in English they are both called "heart."

The particle *mo* means "too." The literal translation of the sentence would be "the heart too and the body too," but we suggest "in flesh and spirit."

PART 6
心も体も

光線 (こうせん)

c) Medical vocabulary

銃弾が左中大脳動脈をかすめている

Just as in English, there are literally thousands of words which refer to the human body, most of them used only in medical fields. We have seen in this lesson the most common and general words related to the body, but seeing examples like this one is interesting in order to make us aware that the range is very wide. For example, brain 脳 (*nō*) is divided into three parts: 大脳 (*dainō*, brain), 小脳 (*shōnō*, cerebellum), and 間脳 (*kannō*, diencephalon.) We are told in this panel about a brain's artery, to be precise, and its literal translation would be "brain artery, center-left area." This very complex medical jargon is very common in medical manga.

Honma: 銃弾が左中大脳動脈をかすめている。
jūdan ga sachū dainō dōmyaku o kasumete iru
bullet SP center-left brain artery graze (gerund)
The bullet is grazing the center brain artery.

d) Something slightly more vulgar...

Just like in any other language, in Japanese the parts of the body, aside from their formal name, can have one or more vulgar names. We have an example here, where a female robot parodies Mazinger Z. The formal word for "breast" is *mune*, but she uses the word *oppai*, a word with the same sense and connotations as the English word "boobs." Another example is *ketsu*, the vulgar word for "bottom."

Robot: オッパイ　ミサイル
oppai misairu
boobs missile
Pectoral missile!

e) Feeling pain...

Toshio: 俺はいま頭が痛いんだ…。
ore wa ima atama ga itai n da...
I ToP now head SP painful be
I have a headache now...

At the end of the theory pages, we saw how to make sentences of the "X hurts me" sort. This is a real example of how to use this expression. The word *itai* (painful) is an "i" adjective and works as such (see Lesson 13). In English, instead, we have different expressions, where we use verbs such as "to hurt" or "to ache," or nouns such as "pain" or "ache." Mastering this structure is obviously very important.

1 What is the Japanese word for "body?" Write the most basic words for body parts in Japanese, and give their rōmaji reading.

2 What is the Japanese word for "face?" And for "hand?" Write the basic vocabulary for face and hand.

3 How do you say the following words in Japanese: brain, lungs, stomach?

4 Translate the following sentence into Japanese: "Your eyes are beautiful." (your = あなたの (*anata no*) / beautiful = きれいな (*kirei-na*) → watch out: this is a "na" adjective and you might need to review Lesson 14)

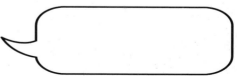

5 Translate the following sentence into English: 彼の腕は強いです。 (*kare no ude wa tsuyoi desu*) (*kare* = he / *no* = Possessive particle / *tsuyoi* = strong / *desu* = to be (Lesson 19))

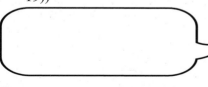

6 Translate into Japanese: "My back hurts."

7 Translate into English: 肩が痛いです。 (*kata ga itai desu*)

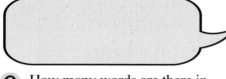

8 What two Japanese words can be translated as "heart," and what are their different senses?

9 How many words are there in Japanese which refer to the human body?

10 What is the vulgar equivalent of the word お尻 (*o-shiri*)? What about the word 胸 (*mune*)?

第 27 課：慣用表現

Lesson 27: Daily life expressions

In this lesson we will get a deeper insight into something we already studied in Lesson 4. We are talking about Japanese expressions used in daily life, many of which don't have a straight translation and require a more or less thorough explanation to be understood.

Good morning!

Following the usual pattern throughout this book, the center of this lesson will be the vocabulary table. We can find in it the main daily life expressions in the Japanese language. However, we have intentionally omitted the most common greetings, as we looked at them in depth in Lesson 4. Anyway, let's have a quick reminder:

Ohayō gozaimasu (good morning), *konnichi wa* (good afternoon—approximately from noon), *konban wa* (good evening), *oyasumi nasai* (good night—when somebody goes to bed). *O-genki desu ka?* (how are you?), the answer to which is *hai, genki desu* (I'm fine). *Sayōnara* (good bye), *mata ne* (see you later), and its different variations. *Arigatō* (thank you), and its answer *dō itashimashite* (you're welcome). This has been a very brief and condensed summary of Lesson 4.

However, Japanese daily expressions have a much broader range than these greetings. There are expressions for many situations, so we have made a graphic summary of some of them in the vocabulary table that comes along with this text.

Expression	Explanation	Translation
失礼します shitsurei shimasu	*Used when entering or exiting a place*	**Excuse me. / I'm leaving now. / Sorry to interrupt.**
ただいま tadaima	*Used when entering one's own home*	**I'm home.**
お帰りなさい o-kaeri nasai	*Answer to "tadaima"*	**Welcome home.**
行ってきます itte kimasu	*Used when leaving one's own home / work place*	**I'm leaving. / I'll be back soon.**
行ってらっしゃい itte rasshai	*Answer to "itte kimasu"*	**Bye–bye. / See you.**
お邪魔します o-jama shimasu	*Used when entering somebody else's home*	Lit. **I'm being rude.** Trans. **May I come in?**
いらっしゃい irasshai	*Answer to "o-jama shimasu"*	**Come in. / Welcome.**
ごめんください gomen kudasai	*When about to enter someone's home but there's nobody to greet*	**Is anyone home? / Excuse me?**
いらっしゃいませ irasshaimase	*Greeting from shop assistant / clerk to customer*	**Welcome! / May I help you?**

Expression	Explanation	Translation
ごめんなさい gomen nasai	*Apology, asking to be excused for something*	**Sorry.**
すみません sumimasen	*a) Apology* *b) To get someone's attention*	a) **Sorry.** b) **Excuse me.**
いただきます itadakimasu	*At the start of a meal*	Lit. **Let's accept.** Trans. **Bon appetit.**
ごちそう様 gochisō-sama	*At the end of a meal, expression of gratitude*	**It was very good.** **Thank you for the meal.**
お疲れ様 otsukare-sama	*When finishing a job or any other activity*	Lit. **Thanks for getting tired.** Trans. **Good job.**
ご苦労様 gokurō-sama	*Similar to "otsukare-sama"*	Lit. **Thanks for getting tired.** Trans. **Good job.**
おめでとうございます omedetō gozaimasu	*Expression of congratulation*	**Congratulations.**
宜しくお願いします yoroshiku o-negai shimasu	*After asking for a favor or when first meeting someone*	Lit. (see text below) Trans. **Please. / I beg you. /** **It's in your hands now. /** **Pleased to meet you.**

Expressions and culture

The Japanese culture is obviously very different from Western ones, and has many particular features. Languages reflect the character and the mentality of the people who use them. Clearly, Japanese is no exception. Why do we explain all this? Well, the point is that the characteristic features of the Japanese mentality are reflected much more in their daily expressions (which we are studying in this lesson) than those in Western languages.

One of the clearest cases is the extremely common expression *yoroshiku o-negai shimasu* (see table). This expression is used after having asked a favor of somebody, when we have just met somebody or when we leave some task in the hands of another person, as well as in many other circumstances.

The most literal translation of this expression would be something like "I humbly ask for your favorable consideration," which is a phrase that really says something about Japanese mentality: asking for a favor means placing responsibility on another person—not a very polite thing to do. Thus, we need to apologize when asking for something, and we have to be very humble about it.

I know it's something insignificant, but...

When a Japanese person gives a present to somebody, he or she will tend to reduce the importance of what he or she is giving, as an act of humility. The expression that is usually used when giving a present is: *tsumaranai mono desu keredo, dōzo...*, the literal translation of which would be "I know it's something insignificant, but please take it..." When a Western person hears this, he or she will think at once that if you are going to give a bad present, perhaps it would be better not to give it at all, or at least not to actually say it is bad. In fact, this "insignificant" present could very well be something very expensive that was bought in exchange for a considerable amount of yen.

Another curious expression is the one used by a Japanese person when he or she invites you to enter his or her house: *kitanai tokoro desu keredo, dōzo, agatte kudasai* means literally "this is a dirty place, but please, come in." The truth is that, in most cases, it is a very clean place.

Mastering Japanese does not only mean mastering the language, it also means understanding the culture behind it and being able to adapt oneself to it, which is maybe the most difficult part.

漫画例: Manga-examples

Even if we look for daily life expressions in our dictionary, the definition we find is not always good enough to understand them. As the saying goes "one picture is worth a thousand words," so . . . let's have a look at the manga-examples.

a) Entering and leaving a place

Marc: ただいまぁ。
tadaimaa
I'm home!

Ken: 行ってきます。
itte kimasu
I'm off!

One of the most difficult sets of fixed expressions in Japanese is who says what when entering or leaving a house. Here we see Marc arriving at his own <u>home</u> or office and Ken leaving his own <u>home</u> or office. The expression used by Marc to greet the people inside when he comes in is *tadaima*. If the people inside were to answer, they would say *o-kaeri nasai* (welcome). In Ken's case, the people inside would say goodbye to him with *itte rasshai* (bye, see you...), an expression which is the corresponding answer to *itte kimasu*.

However, when we enter or leave somebody else's place, the fixed set is as follows: Visitor when entering: *o-jama shimasu* / Answer of the host: *irasshai*. Visitor when leaving: *o-jama shimashita* / Answer of the host: *mata kondo kite kudasai*.

b) Sorry I kept you waiting

Waiter: お待たせしました。
o-matase shimashita
I made you wait
Sorry I kept you waiting.

Slime: おっ、メシだ メシだ。
o, meshi da meshi da!
oh, food be food be
Ah, here is my food!

We just saw some of the most common daily life expressions in Japanese in the theory section, but there are many more! For example, in this panel we have the expression *o-matase shimashita*, which literally means "I made you wait." The speaker is apologizing for the time the interlocutor has been made to wait. For instance, when we realize that, in an appointment, the other person has arrived earlier than us, we usually say *o-matase shimashita*. Another important expression we saw in example b) in Lesson 17 is お大事に (*o-daiji ni*), which means "Get well soon." We use it when saying goodbye to a sick person.

c) I'm hungry

Slime: 腹が減ったぜ…。
hara ga hetta ze...
stomach SP empty EP
I'm hungry...

Being able to say "I'm hungry." or "I'm thirsty." is very useful, and there are many ways of saying it depending on the speaker. **I am hungry**: *hara ga hetta* is quite a vulgar expression used by men. *Onaka ga suita* is the standard form, and *onaka ga peko peko* is often used by girls or children. **I am thirsty**: *nodo ga kawaita* is the standard form, and *nodo ga karakara* is the colloquial form.

d) Happy New Year

お明けましておめでとーございます

Maria: 明けましておめでとーございます。
akemashite omedetō gozaimasu
Happy New Year.

In this panel we have an expression that we have not yet seen: the New Year's greeting. *Akemashite omedetō gozaimasu* literally means "congratulations on the opening (of the new year)," although the adequate translation is "Happy New Year." This is usually followed by: *kotoshi mo yoroshiku o-negai shimasu*. *Kotoshi mo* means "this year too," and we already saw *yoroshiku o-negai shimasu* a few pages before.

Omedetō gozaimasu, on its own, means "congratulations" and is used on birthdays, successes, celebrations...

e) It's been a long time

Dr. Stark: お久しぶりです。ライヒワイン先生…。
o-hisashiburi desu raihiwain sensei...
It's been a long time, Dr. Reichwein.

The world of daily expressions is quite large. For example, as we have already seen, there are several greetings that can be used when meeting someone, (*konnichi wa, konban wa*, etc...). The expression *o-hisashiburi desu* could be added to this greetings category, and its approximate meaning is "it's been a long time (since we last met)."

In Lesson 4 we studied the many different ways of thanking someone (*arigatō, dōmo, arigatō gozaimasu*, etc.), and of saying goodbye (*sayōnara, mata ne, bai bai*, etc.). Likewise, apart from the well-known *gomen nasai*, there are many other ways of apologizing, from the colloquial *gomen ne* to the more formal 申し訳ない (*mōshiwake nai*), 申し訳ありません (*mōshiwake arimasen*), or 申し訳ございません (*mōshiwake gozaimasen*).

お久しぶりです
ライヒワイン先生…

1 It is 9 pm and you see someone you know in a bar. How do you greet him or her in Japanese?

2 It is 9 pm, you are really sleepy because you went out the night before, and you want to go to bed. How do you say goodbye?

3 You leave home. How do you say goodbye to your mother, who stays home? What is your mother's answer?

4 You are working in a Japanese McDonald's and a client comes in. What do you say?

5 Your friend has just passed a very important exam. How do you congratulate him or her?

6 You have to give a present to your Japanese boss (it is a formal situation). What do you say when handing it to him or her?

7 You are visiting a sick relative or friend, but you must leave now. How do you say goodbye?

8 How does a 22-year-old man say "I'm hungry" to his friends? And to his boss? And what if the speaker is a 5-year-old child?

9 Greet someone on New Year (the full expression).

10 What should I (the teacher) say to you (my students) when you have finished all these drills (two possibilities)?

第 28 課：名詞（Ⅳ）：なる

Lesson 28: Verbs (IV): the verb naru

Using the verb *naru* as an introduction, we will take the opportunity in this lesson to take a look at several grammatical structures. Reviewing Lessons 13, 14, 16, 19, 20, 22, and 24 is highly recommended.

The verb naru

One of the most frequent verbs in Japanese is the verb *naru*. It has no exact translation in English, although its use is very similar to that of "become."

In the table of the verb *naru*, we see the different inflections this verb asks of the word before it. For example, when this word is an "i" adjective (Lesson 13), we will replace the last *i* with *ku*. *Muzukashii* (difficult) = *muzukashiku naru* (to become difficult). With "na" adjectives (Lesson 14), *na* will be replaced with *ni*. *Ranbō-na*

The verb naru	Rule	Examples
Noun	＋になる +ni naru	先生になる *sensei ni naru* to become a teacher
"i" adjective	い＋くなる i + ku naru	強くなる *tsuyoku naru* to get strong
"na" adjective	な＋になる na+ni naru	静かになる *shizuka ni naru* to become quiet
Suru verb	Inf＋になる inf + ni naru	勉強になる *benkyō ni naru* to have learned something

(violent) = *ranbō ni naru* (to become violent). With nouns and *suru* verbs, *ni* must be added. *Shachō* (president of a company) = *Shachō ni naru* (to become president).

The verb *naru* is extremely common in any register and situation.

Conjugations: present tense = *naru* / past tense = *natta* / negative = *naranai* / past negative = *naranakatta* / –*masu* form = *narimasu* (see Lesson 19 for –*masu* form conjugations).

To go to...

The second grammatical structure in this lesson is very simple to learn as well as very useful. We will see how to say "I'm going to…" or "I'm coming to…" using a simple verb combination.

In Lesson 19, we explained the –*masu* form of verbs, and you might remember this form was characterized by the fact that all verbs always ended in –*masu*.

If we conjugate a verb in its –*masu* form, we remove the suffix –*masu* and we add the particle *ni* and the verb *iku* (to go), we will form sentences with the structure "to go to…"

ます＋に 行く ~~masu~~ V+ ni iku To go to...	買いに行く *kai ni iku* *kau / kaimasu*: to buy **To go to buy...**	見に行く *mi ni iku* *miru / mimasu*: to see **To go to see...**
ます＋に 来る ~~masu~~ V + ni kuru To come to...	遊びに来る *asobi ni kuru* *asobu / asobimasu*: to play **To come to play...**	書きに来る *kaki ni kuru* *kaku / kakimasu*: to write **To come to write...**

Let's look, for example, at the verb *kau* (to buy). If we conjugate its *–masu* form, we have *kaimasu*. Once we remove *–masu*, we have *kai*. Then, we just need to add *ni* + *iku* (*kai ni iku* = to go to buy...).

> 次郎さんは車を買いに行く。
> *jirō-san wa kuruma o kai ni iku*
> Jirō-(suf.) SP car DOP go buy
> **Jirō goes to buy a car.**

If we replace the verb *iku* (go) with *kuru* (come), we will form sentences with the structure "to come to…"

> 広美さんはテレビを見に来る。
> *hiromi-san wa terebi o mi ni kuru*
> Hiromi-(suf.) SP television DOP come watch
> **Hiromi comes to watch television.**

Ageru, morau, kureru

In this lesson's last table we see how to make sentences using the trio of verbs *ageru* (give), *morau* (receive), and *kureru* (receive). Completely understanding how these verbs work can be quite difficult, for the structure is not easy to grasp for an English speaker.

The verbs *ageru* and *morau* don't have any obvious problem, since they have an almost 100% correspondence in sense with the English verbs "to give" and "to receive."

However, the verb *kureru* is more difficult: *kureru* can also be translated as "to receive," just like *morau*. But *kureru* is used when the sentence's subject, the receiver, is either "I" or someone (emotionally) very close to "I."

You should now examine thoroughly the examples in the grammar table in order to understand who gives and who receives, who the subject in the sentence is, and who the indirect object is. Look closely as well at the use of the particles *ni* and *o*.

あげる *ageru* give	XさんはYさんにZをあげる。 *X-san wa Y-san ni Z o ageru* Mr. X gives Z to Mr. Y (X = gives / Y = receives)	太郎さんはマリアさんに本をあげる。 *tarō-san wa maria-san ni hon o ageru* Tarō-(suf.) SP Maria-(suf.) IP book DOP give **Tarō gives a book to Maria.**
もらう *morau* receive	XさんはYさんにZをもらう。 *X-san wa Y-san ni Z o morau* Mr. X receives Z from Mr. Y (X = receives / Y = gives)	山口さんは伊藤さんにたばこをもらう。 *yamaguchi-san wa itō-san ni tabako o morau* Yamaguchi-(suf.) SP Itō-(suf.) IP tobacco DOP receive **Mr. Yamaguchi receives tobacco from Mr. Itō**
くれる *kureru* receive	Xさんは私にZをくれる。 *X-san wa watashi ni Z o kureru* I receive Z from Mr. X (I = receive / X = gives)	鈴木さんは私にワインをくれる。 *Suzuki-san wa watashi ni wain o kureru* Suzuki-(suf.) SP I IP wine DOP receive **I receive wine from Mr. Suzuki.**

There is also a grammatical structure made with the *–te* form (Lesson 24) plus these three verbs. Let's see an example with the verb *ageru* which we can also apply to similar sentences with *morau* and *kureru*.

> 茂さんは花子さんに花を買ってあげた。
> *Shigeru-san wa Hanako-san ni hana o katte ageta* (*hana* = flower, *kau* = buy)
> **Shigeru bought a flower for Hanako.**

The meaning of this sentence with the *–te* form + *ageru* is like the sum of the verbs "buy" and "give" = buy (doing someone a favor.)

Conjugations:

Ageru / Past = *ageta* / Neg. = *agenai* / Past Neg. = *agenakatta*.

Morau / Past = *moratta* / Neg. = *morawanai* / Past Neg. = *morawanakatta*.

Kureru / Past = *kureta* / Neg. = *kurenai* / Past Neg. = *kurenakatta*.

漫画例：*Manga-examples*

Here is the lesson's illustrative section. This time the amount of
information is quite large, since we have explained three grammatical
structures in one lesson. We will try to make them clearer with these
graphic examples.

a) "i" adjective + naru / –te form + morau

Maya: 私のペチャパイも兄様にさわってもらったら大きくなるかも。
watashi no pechapai mo niisama ni sawatte morattara ookiku naru kamo
my flat breast also brother IP touch would receive big become maybe
Maybe, if you touched them, my small breasts might grow.

Here we have two examples in one panel. First, we see the usage of the verb *naru*
with the "i" adjective *ookii* (big). All we need to do is replace the last *i* with *ku*.
(*ookiku naru* = to get big; to grow).
Then, we have an example with the *–te* form + *morau* (receive): *sawatte morau* = to
receive the fact of being touched, to be granted the favor of being touched.

b) To come to...

マサオを殺しに来たんだろう？

Here is a good example of the –*masu* form verb + *ni* + *kuru* (come to…) structure.

Let's review how to make this structure using the same verb as Katsuya: *korosu* (kill). The –*masu* form of *korosu* is *koroshimasu*. After removing the suffix –*masu*, we have *koroshi*. We add the particle *ni* and the verb *kuru* (come) and then we have *koroshi ni kuru* (come to kill).

If we change the verb *kuru* (come) for the verb *iku* (go), then the sentence *koroshi ni iku* would mean "go to kill." The V *masu*+*ni*+*iku/kuru* construction is very useful and it's worthwhile learning it.

Katsuya: マサオを殺しに来たんだろう？
masao o koroshi ni kita n darō?
Masao DOP kill come to (aux.) I think
You've come to kill Masao, haven't you?

c) To give

Here is a practical example of the usage of the verb *ageru* (give). The usage of *ageru* is probably the easiest to understand in the trio formed by *ageru* / *morau* / *kureru* because it merely means "to give." The speaker is usually the one performing the action of giving and there is someone else receiving. It is different with *morau* and *kureru*, because there are many variations, and they can become very complex.

全部あげるわっ！！

Nami: 全部あげるわっ！！
zenbu ageru wa!!
everything give EP (fem.)
I'll give you everything!

d) –te ageru

わからないの!?だったら教えてあげるわ

This is a quite good example of the usage of a verb in the *–te* form with the verb *ageru*, similar to the example we saw at the end of the theory section. *Oshieru* means "to teach," but if we conjugate it in the *–te* form (*oshiete*) and add *ageru* (*oshiete ageru*), then we have a construction with the meaning "to teach doing a favor." However, this nuance is lost in the translation into English.

Likewise, if we used the other two verbs in the trio instead of *ageru*, we would have the following: *oshiete morau* "be granted the favor of being taught" / *oshiete kureru* "I or someone close to me is granted the favor of being taught." Remember the verb *kureru* is only used when the receiver is "I" or someone close to "I."

Karin:	わからないの!?だったら教えてあげるわ。
	wakaranai no!? dattara oshiete ageru wa
	understand (neg.) Q? then teach (-te form) give EP
	You don't understand? I'll show you then.

e) Order

ただな娘がお前を殺してくれといっとるんじゃ

Oyatsu:	ただな娘がお前を殺してくれといっとるんじゃ。
	tada na musume ga omae o koroshite kure to ittoru n ja
	only EP daughter SP you DOP kill (order) say that (aux.)
	I only know my daughter asked me to kill you.

A very frequent derivative of the *–te* form plus *ageru* / *morau* / *kureru* is the construction *–te* form plus *kure* (imperative of *kureru*). This construction is used to give orders in a way which is not very direct nor abrupt, but it isn't gentle either (it is a halfway solution). In this sentence, for instance, we have the construction *koroshite kure*. *Koroshite* is the *–te* form of the verb *korosu* (kill). Adding *kure* it becomes an order (*koroshite kure* = kill him). However, we will expand on the imperative in Lesson 30.

1 What does the verb *naru* mean? Conjugate the present and past tenses, and the negative and past negative of *naru* in its simple form.

2 Add the verb *naru* to the words やさしい (*yasashii*, easy), 便利な (*benri-na*, convenient), and 学生 (*gakusei*, student).

3 How do we conjugate "i" adjectives with the verb *naru*? How about "na" adjectives? And nouns?

4 Translate the following sentence into English: 彼は映画を見にく。 (*kare wa eiga o mi ni iku*) (*kare* = he / *eiga* = film / *miru* = see).

5 Translate the following sentence into Japanese: "He comes to write a novel." (*he* = 彼 (*kare*) / to write = 書きます (*kakimasu*) / novel = 小説 (*shōsetsu*).

6 What do the verbs あげる (*ageru*) and もらう (*morau*) mean? What is the difference between もらう (*morau*) and くれる (*kureru*)?

7 Translate the following sentence into English: フランクさんは道子さんに本をあげた。 (*Furanku-san wa Michiko-san ni hon o ageta*) (*Furanku* = Frank / *Michiko* = Michiko (girl's name) / *hon* = book).

8 Translate the following sentence into Japanese: "Mr. Smith receives a document from Mr. Brown." (Smith = スミス (*Sumisu*) / document = 書類 (*shorui*) / Brown = ブラウン (*Buraun*) (You should review Lesson 15.) What is the best verb in this case?

9 Translate the following sentence into English: 私は生徒さんに日本語を教えてあげる。(*watashi wa seito-san ni nihongo o oshiete ageru*) (*watashi* = I / *seito-san* = pupils / *nihongo* = Japanese / *oshieru* = to teach).

10 Ask someone to drink up their milk using the *-te* form + *kure*. (milk = 牛乳 (*gyūnyū*) / to drink = 飲む (*nomu*), see Lesson 24 for its *-te* form.

第 29 課：擬音・擬態語

Lesson 29: Gion and gitaigo

In this lesson we will study another of the idiomatic peculiarities of the Japanese language: sound symbolisms. There are two kinds, which we will now see.

Sound symbolisms

Sound symbolisms are almost always adverbs (Lesson 22). They are sound imitating words, or words that "describe" a state of mind, or a physical condition with no sound. This definition may be difficult to understand, but we will try to clarify it now with the help of some examples.

There are two basic kinds of sound symbolisms: *gion* and *gitaigo*.

Gion: the word *gion* means "to imitate a sound." Therefore, *gion* are "sound imitating words." The concept is very similar to our onomatopoeias. For example, the sound of a beating heart in Japanese is *dokidoki*. The *gion* called *dokidoki*, which imitates the sound of a beating heart, has the meaning of "being nervous, excited" (because heartbeats are faster at such times).

The same happens with words like *geragera*, which imitates the sound we make when we laugh boisterously, or *pekopeko*, which imitates the sound the stomach makes when we are hungry.

Gitaigo: the word *gitai* means "to imitate a state," and *go* is "word," therefore, *gitaigo* means "state imitating words." Unlike *gion*, which imitate perceptible sounds, *gitaigo* don't imitate any sound, they are completely conceptual words. There are two kinds of *gitaigo*: those which symbolize a physical condition and those which symbolize a state of mind.

In the *gitaigo* group which symbolizes a physical condition, we find *karakara*, which means something is dry, or by extension, that we are very thirsty (since our throat is dry); or the word *pikapika*, which means something is very bright, dazzling.

Symbolizing a state of mind, we find words such as *kutakuta* (to be tired, exhausted), or *iraira* (to be irritated).

Real usage

One might think such simple words are hardly ever used, or if so, that they are mainly used by very young children. That's far from correct: all Japanese, children and adults, use *gion* and *gitaigo* in real life, both in written and spoken Japanese. In manga, we find these words very frequently, and any student of Japanese should master the most basic ones at least.

These words are almost always used before a verb (since they are adverbs, and modifying a verb is the function of adverbs). The *gion* and *gitaigo* usually take a particular verb. For example, the word *guruguru* is almost always followed by the verb *mawaru* (to turn round). *Guruguru mawaru* = to go round and round. Or the word *pakupaku*, which is almost always followed by the verb *taberu* (to eat). *Pakupaku taberu* = to munch, eat with relish.

There are some *gion* and *gitaigo* that take the verb *suru* (to do), like, for instance, *iraira suru* (to be irritated) or *dokidoki suru* (to be nervous, excited).

Studying these words can be quite tough, because they all sound very alike and it is easy to get them mixed up.

Gion	Meaning
ぺらぺら perapera	(To talk) fluently
しくしく shikushiku	(To weep) silently
どきどき dokidoki	To be nervous (*doki* = sound of heartbeat)
げらげら geragera	(To laugh) boisterously
ぺこぺこ pekopeko	To be hungry (*peko* = noise of stomach)
ぱくぱく pakupaku	(To eat) with relish
がらがら garagara	(To open) a sliding door

Animal sounds

Having a look at the onomatopoeias used in different languages to name animal sounds is something very curious.

When we analyze how the Japanese interpret animal sounds, we are surprised by the incredible difference between English and Japanese.

A dog barks in English as "bow wow". In Japanese, it is *wan wan*. A cat (miaow in English) in Japanese mews like this: *nyan nyan*. A frog (croak croak) says *gero gero,* and a pig (oink oink) goes *buu buu* in Japanese.

Gitaigo	Meaning	Gitaigo	Meaning
いらいら iraira	To be fretful, irritated	ぐっと gutto	At once, suddenly
くたくた kutakuta	To be tired, exhausted	ぐるぐる guruguru	(To go) round and round
からから karakara	To be dry / to be very thirsty	びっしょり bisshori	To be soaked
しっかり shikkari	Decidedly, firmly, (to hold) tight	ぴかぴか pikapika	To shine, sparkle, glitter
じっと jitto	To stare	きらきら kirakira	To glitter, dazzle
めちゃくちゃ mechakucha	To be a mess	ほっと hotto	(To feel) relieved
すっきり sukkiri	(To feel) refreshed, fine	わくわく wakuwaku	To be nervous, excited

d) Nokonoko

We saw how in the previous examples *sukkiri* and *dokidoki* were written in the katakana syllabary. This happens once more here with *nokonoko* ("obtrusively, to be a nuisance"). *Gion* and *gitaigo* are some of the few words that can be written either in hiragana or katakana. Katakana is used more often than hiragana in manga due to its visual effect.

Eikichi: なんだぁ　今ごろノコノコと。
nanda　ima goro nokonoko to
what be　about this time brazenly
What a pain he is, coming right now!

e) Bark

Dog: ワンワンワンワン
wan wan wan wan
(sound of dog barking)
Bow wow bow wow!

Master: まてまて　しずかに！！
mate mate　shizuka ni!!
wait wait　calm (adv.)
Just a minute!　Hush…

Finally, we have an example of a Japanese dog barking. Unlike "English–speaking" dogs, who bark saying "bow wow," Japanese dogs' barking goes *wan wan*.

1 What are *gitaigo*?

2 What are *gion*?

3 What do the following words mean: しくしく (*shikushiku*), ほっと (*hotto*), ぐるぐる (*guruguru*), and ぱくぱく (*pakupaku*)?

4 How do we say in Japanese "to laugh boisterously," "to be exhausted," and "to glitter, dazzling" (there are two options for the last one)?

5 Translate the following sentence into English: 彼は日本語がぺらぺらです。 (*kare wa nihongo ga perapera desu*) (*kare* = he / *nihongo* = Japanese)

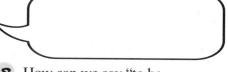

6 Translate the following sentence into English: ピカチュウのフラッシュはぴかぴかです。 (*Pikachū no furasshu wa pikapika desu*) (*Pikachū* = he / *furasshu* = flash)

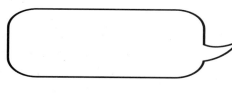

7 Are *gion* and *gitaigo* childish words?

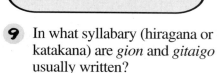

8 How can we say "to be surprised" in Japanese?

9 In what syllabary (hiragana or katakana) are *gion* and *gitaigo* usually written?

10 How does a Japanese dog bark? And how does a Japanese frog croak?

第(30)課：命令形

Here we are, at the end of our first foray into the world of Japanese! In this last lesson we will talk about orders, a somewhat knotty subject, but certainly interesting.

Orders

Those who already know some Japanese will probably be surprised we are talking about orders at such an early stage in the study of the Japanese language.

Indeed, in a "normal" Japanese course, the imperative form would not be dealt with until a much later stage. But this is not a "normal" course, because we have always tried to focus on these lessons from the point of view of spoken Japanese, widely used in manga.

In real life in Japan, orders are hardly ever used. Giving orders in a normal conversation is considered quite rude. Instead, the request form (-*te* form + *kudasai*, seen in Lesson 24), is used. The same happens in English, since it is much less straightforward to say "Could you bring me a pencil, please?" (using a request form) than "Bring me a pencil." (using an order).

However, orders are extremely frequent when it comes to manga, where colloquial and sometimes vulgar language is common. Therefore, we consider it necessary to explain orders at this early stage is quite.

Conjugation

In the grammar table we have, as usual, arranged the verbs according to the groups they belong to, and which we explained in Lessons 19, 20, and 24. The first two columns correspond to the dictionary form and the *–masu* form respectively (Lessons 19 and 20). The third column shows the translation of each verb.

In the fourth column we have the imperative, in its most straightforward and rude form. The conjugation of this form is quite simple:

Verbs in Group 1. We replace the *ru* in the dictionary form with *ro*.

Verbs in Group 2. As a general rule, we replace the last *u* in the dictionary form with *e* (*kaeru → kaere / kau → kae*).

Take care with the verbs ended in *–tsu*, these replace *tsu* with *te* and not *tse*.

The verbs in Group 3 are irregular, don't have conjugation rules, and we must learn them by heart.

Note: women virtually NEVER use this form of the imperative.

The "gentle" imperative

There is another imperative form which is neither as rude nor as straightforward as the "normal" imperative explained above. This is the *–nasai* form. This is mainly used by adults when giving orders to children (it is something like "would you please…?")

We have mentioned women hardly ever use the "normal" imperative. When a woman wants to order something with some authority she will usually use the *–nasai* form; as long as she is very familiar with the person who receives the order, her child, for example.

This form is also used between teacher and pupil or in situations where the speaker is or feels in a higher position than the interlocutor. However, this third use is rather uncommon. The conjugation is extremely simple and has no exceptions. We remove the *masu* in *–masu* form verbs and add *–nasai*.

Example: *kaku* → -*masu* form = *kakimasu* → we remove *–masu* = *kaki* → we add *–nasai* = *kakinasai*.

The –tamae form

There is a third imperative form, seldom used, but which may appear occasionally in manga. It is the *–tamae* form, and is used by a speaker who is or feels superior to the interlocutor (superior–subordinate / teacher–pupil…) It is formed exactly the same way as the *–nasai* form. That is, we remove the *masu* in *–masu* form verbs and add *–tamae*.

		Dictionary f.	–masu f.	Translation	Imperative	Rule	"Gentle" imperative	Rule
Group 1: In-variable		教える *oshieru*	教えます *oshiemasu*	teach	教えろ *oshiero*	～ろ *ro*	教えなさい *oshienasai*	*masu nasai* (ます なさい)
		起きる *okiru*	起きます *okimasu*	wake up	起きろ *okiro*		起きなさい *okinasai*	
Group 2: Variable	A	貸す *kasu*	貸します *kashimasu*	lend	貸せ *kase*	～せ *se*	貸しなさい *kashinasai*	
	B	待つ *matsu*	待ちます *machimasu*	wait	待て *mate*	～て *te*	待ちなさい *machinasai*	
		買う *kau*	買います *kaimasu*	buy	買え *kae*	～え *e*	買いなさい *kainasai*	
		帰る *kaeru*	帰ります *kaerimasu*	return	帰れ *kaere*	～れ *re*	帰りなさい *kaerinasai*	
	C	書く *kaku*	書きます *kakimasu*	write	書け *kake*	～け *ke*	書きなさい *kakinasai*	
	D	急ぐ *isogu*	急ぎます *isogimasu*	hurry	急げ *isoge*	～げ *ge*	急ぎなさい *isoginasai*	
	E	遊ぶ *asobu*	遊びます *asobimasu*	play	遊べ *asobe*	～べ *be*	遊びなさい *asobinasai*	
		飲む *nomu*	飲みます *nomimasu*	drink	飲め *nome*	～め *me*	飲みなさい *nominasai*	
		死ぬ *shinu*	死にます *shinimasu*	die	死ね *shine*	～ね *ne*	死になさい *shininasai*	
Group 3: Irre-gular		する *suru*	します *shimasu*	do	しろ *shiro*	*Irregular verbs:*	しなさい *shinasai*	
		来る *kuru*	来ます *kimasu*	come	来い *koi*	*There is no rule*	来なさい *kinasai*	

漫画例：Manga-examples

Orders are hardly ever used in "real" Japanese, that is, in everyday Japanese. However, they are extremely used in manga. Let's have a look at some examples.

a) Die!

Klangor: 死ねーっ！！！
shine ————-!!!
die (imp.)
Dieee!!!

In this panel we see violent Klangor in one of his attacks. Klangor is a man, and this is a fight scene. Therefore, in such a situation, Klangor is not given to good manners or tactfulness, and allows himself the use of the rudest imperative form.

The verb used here is *shinu* (to die), which belongs to Group 2 (see table). Let's review the rule for the imperative of verbs in Group 2: replace the last *u* with *e*. So: *shinu* (to die) → *shine* (die).

This imperative is very common, just like the –*te* + *kure* form which we saw in Lesson 28.

b) Shoot!

Soldier: 撃てェ。
ute
shoot (imp.)
Shoot!

A second example of the use of this imperative conjugation. The verb in dictionary form is *utsu* (to shoot). It belongs to Group 2 (they replace the last *u* of the dictionary form with the *e* of the imperative form), but it is slightly irregular: it replaces tsu with *te* and not *tse*.

c) "Gentle" imperative (1)

Girl:	さ…さあ…。	おりなさい！！	さあさあ。
	sa... sa...	*orinasai!!*	*saa saa*
	come on, come on	come down (imp.)	come on come on
	Come on, now...	**Come down.**	**Come on, now.**

An example of the "gentle" imperative form, that is, using the *–nasai* form. The speaker is a girl, and that is why she will never use the rude imperative conjugation.

d) "Gentle" imperative (2)

Kei: 待ちなさい！
machinasai!
wait (imp.)
Wait!

Another example of the use of the *–nasai* form. Even though the scene is a very tense and violent one, Kei lives up to the fact that she is a girl and doesn't use the rude imperative but the *–nasai* form of the verb *matsu* (to wait). To conjugate this form, we remove the ending *–masu* of the *–masu* form of the verb, and we add *–nasai*. Thus: dictionary form = *matsu* / *–masu* form = *machimasu* / we remove *–masu* = *machi* / we add *–nasai* = *machinasai*.

e) –tamae

In this example we have the imperative form *–tamae*. This form is seldom used, but we will come across it occasionally in manga. The conjugation of this form is identical to that of the *–nasai* form, and the speaker who uses it usually is or feels superior to his or her interlocutor. In this case, Sawada wants to impress the girl and, trying to look cool, he invites her into the car using the *–tamae* form with the verb *noru* (to get in, to ride). *Noru → norimasu → nori → noritamae*. We should also mention here the use of *o-matase*, a short and colloquial version of *o-matase shimashita* (Sorry I kept you waiting), which we saw in Lesson 27.

Sawada: おまたせ。　　　　乗りたまえ…。
o-matase　　　　*noritamae...*
kept waiting　　　get in (imp.)
Sorry I'm late.　Come on, get in…

1 Is the imperative commonly used in Japanese?

2 What are the three kinds of imperative? What is the difference between them?

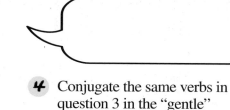

3 Conjugate the straightforward imperative of the verbs 見る (*miru*, "to see," Group 1), 聞く (*kiku*, "to hear," Group 2), 乗る (*noru*, "to ride," Group 2), and 洗う (*arau*, "to wash," Group 2).

4 Conjugate the same verbs in question 3 in the "gentle" imperative form (*–nasai*).

5 Conjugate the same verbs in question 3 in the *–tamae* imperative form.

6 Why would a woman never use the straightforward imperative? What imperative would she use instead?

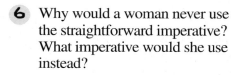

7 Translate the following sentence into English: 日本語講座を読め。 (*nihongo kōza o yome*). (*nihongo* = Japanese language / *kōza* = course / *o* = Direct object particle, see Lesson 16).

8 Translate the following sentence into Japanese using the straightforward imperative: "Buy the newspaper." (Newspaper = *shinbun* 新聞) Don't forget the corresponding particle!

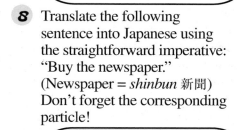

9 Translate the following sentence into Japanese using the "gentle" imperative (*–nasai*): "Sit on the chair." (To sit = *suwaru*, Group 2 / chair = *isu*). Remember the particle!

10 When is the *–tamae* form used? Is it a very commonly used form?

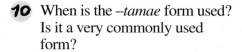

Answers

Lesson 1

1 Japanese doesn't use an alphabet the way we know it. Instead, there are two syllabaries (vowel plus consonant combinations) called hiragana and katakana. A hiragana character equals two Western characters when transcribed.

2 We use two syllabaries (hiragana and katakana) and a very complex system of ideograms called kanji.

3 They are usually written in the traditional style.

4 We use it to write strictly Japanese words when a word has no kanji, or when the author doesn't remember the corresponding kanji. Particles and verb endings are written in hiragana too.

5 *te*: て / *mu*: む / *i*: い / *sa*: さ

6 に: *ni* / る: *ru* / き: *ki* / え: *e*

7 *de*: で / *pi*: ぴ / *da*: だ / *za*: ざ

8 ぶ: *bu* / ず: *zu* / ぱ: *pa* / じ: *ji*

9 Combining the characters in the *i* line with those in the *y* line (these last written in a smaller size.) *cha*: ちゃ / *hyo*: ひょ / *jo*: じょ

10- It is pronounced like the "g" in "get."

Lesson 2

1 It is used to write foreign words which have been previously adapted to Japanese phonetics, non-Japanese people or place names, as well as for onomatopoeias. It is also used to give a striking effect in certain contexts.

2 Approximately 11% of Japanese words are foreign expressions. Almost all of them are written in katakana.

3 We would obviously use the katakana syllabary, because it is a non-Japanese name.

4 This answer depends on your name. If you are in doubt about certain combinations, check Lesson 8, where this subject is dealt with more thoroughly.

5 To replace the letter "l", which doesn't exist in Japanese, we use all characters in the *r* column of the katakana syllabary. *la* = ラ (*ra*) / *le* = レ (*re*), and so on.

6 They are vowels which are pronounced for a little longer than usual. In hiragana we represent them writing a hiragana *u* (う) after *u* and *o*. In katakana, we add a dash (-).

7 They are consonants that have a longer and more abrupt sound than normal ones. This effect is indicated by a small *tsu* (っ in hiragana, ッ in katakana) character before the consonant to be doubled.

8 *ho*:ホ / *ku*:ク / *wa*:ワ / *no*:ノ

9 ド: *do* / エ: *e* / ヨ: *yo* / ペ: *pe*

10 yes: はい (*hai*) / no: いいえ (*iie*)

Lesson 3

1   Kanji are characters which represent sound and meaning at the same time. They were imported from China into Japan in the fourth century A.D.

2   tree: 木 (*ki*) / river: 川 (*kawa*) / money: 金 (*kane*) / woman: 女 (*onna*)

3   水 (*mizu*): water / 男 (*otoko*): man / 山 (*yama*): mountain / 火 (*hi*): fire

4   *on'yomi* is the kanji's "Chinese reading," the reading kanji had before being imported into Japanese. This reading was further adapted to Japanese phonetics. *Kun'yomi* is the "Japanese reading," that is, the Japanese native pronunciation added to the kanji imported from China.

5   In 90% of cases it is read the *on'yomi* or Chinese way.

6   We usually use the *kun'yomi* or Japanese reading.

7   No, it is a terrible mistake. The character 山 in the word 富士山 must actually be read the *on'yomi* way, because it comes with other kanji. The *on'yomi* of the character 山 is *san* and the *kun'yomi* is *yama*.

8   There are over 45,000 kanji, but in everyday life we use around 3,000.

9   One only stroke. The kanji for "king" is 王 and the kanji for "ball" is 玉.

10 *Furigana* are hiragana characters written in a smaller size above the kanji which are most difficult to read. In manga aimed at children and young people, kanji usually have their reading written next to them in *furigana*.

Lesson 4

1- At 8 pm we already use the expression こんばんは。(*konban wa*, "good evening")

2   At 4 pm we always use こんにちは。(*konnichi wa*, "good afternoon")

3   私の名前はマルクです。(*watashi no namae wa maruku desu*) よろしくお願いします。(*yoroshiku o-negai shimasu*) Replace the word *maruku* (transcription of Marc) with your own name.

4   Mouth: 口 (*kuchi*) / yen: 円 (*en*) / university: 大学 (*daigaku*)

5   Any of the following is valid: ありがとう。(*arigatō*) / どうもありがとうございます。(*dōmo arigatō gozaimasu*) / ありがとうございます。(*arigatō gozaimasu*) / どうも (*dōmo*) / どうもありがとう。(*dōmo arigatō*).

6   どういたしまして。(*dō itashimashite*) or いいえ。(*iie*)

7   With the sentence: これはいくらですか。(*kore wa ikura desu ka?*)

8   Two options: すみません。(*sumimasen*) or ごめんなさい。(*gomen nasai*)

9   わかりません。(*wakarimasen*, "I don't understand").

10 Any of the following is valid: さようなら。(*sayōnara*) / それじゃまた明日会いましょう。(*sore ja mata ashita aimashō*) / じゃ、また明日。(*ja, mata ashita*) / じゃ、また。(*ja, mata*) / またね。(*mata ne*) / バイバイ。(*bai bai*) / 気をつけて。(*ki o tsukete*).

Lesson 5

1   Numbers are usually written in Arabic numbers in today's Japanese society. We will obviously find some exceptions, but generally speaking the use of Arabic numbers is much more widespread than that of native Japanese numbers.

2   十: *jū* (ten) / 八: *hachi* (eight) / 三: *san* (three) / 七: *nana* or *shichi* (seven)

3   50: *go jū* / 800: *happyaku* / 2,000: *ni sen*

4　The concept *man* stands for the number 10,000, which in Japanese is not interpreted as "ten thousand," but as "one *man*." 20,000: *ni man* / 400,000: *yon jū man*.

5　34,622: *san man yon sen roppyaku ni jū ni*

6　45,853: 四万五千八百五十三 (*yon man go sen happyaku go jū san*)

7　12,681, *ichi man ni sen roppyaku hachi jū ichi*

8　二百万 (*ni hyaku man*)

9　It corresponds to the number 40,000,000 (40 million).

10　They are formed by adding the prefix 第 (*dai*) before any numbers 4th: 第四 (*dai yon*) / 25th: 第二十五 (*dai ni jū go*).

Lesson 6

1　金曜日: Friday / 月曜日: Monday / 木曜日: Thursday

2　月曜日 (*getsuyōbi*) Monday / 火曜日 (*kayōbi*) Tuesday / 水曜日 (*suiyōbi*) Wednesday / 木曜日 (*mokuyōbi*) Thursday / 金曜日 (*kin'yōbi*) Friday / 土曜日 (*doyōbi*) Saturday / 日曜日 (*nichiyōbi*) Sunday

3　土: earth / 火: fire / 木: tree

4　Because the kanji 日 has two meanings: sun and day. Each of these meanings has a different reading. In the word 日曜日 the first 日 refers to the sun and the second to the day, therefore the meaning of this word is "day of the sun," or "sun day," like in English.

5　五月十五日 (*gogatsu jūgo nichi*)

6　3rd of March. These kanji are read *san gatsu mikka*.

7　January: 一月 (*ichigatsu*) / February: 二月 (*nigatsu*) / March: 三月 (*sangatsu*) / April: 四月 (*shigatsu*) / May: 五月 (*gogatsu*) / June: 六月 (*rokugatsu*) / July: 七月 (*shichigatsu*) / August: 八月 (*hachigatsu*) / September: 九月 (*kugatsu*) / October: 十月 (*jūgatsu*) / November: 十一月 (*jūichigatsu*) / December: 十二月 (*jūnigatsu*).

8　The 6th: 六日 (*muika*) / the 11th: 十一日 (*jūichinichi*)

9　The Heisei era began in the year 1989.

10　To 1945, the year the Second World War ended and the atomic bombs were dropped over the cities of Hiroshima and Nagasaki. (In the year 1926, the reign of Emperor Hirohito started, therefore 1926 was the year 1 of the Shōwa Era.)

Lesson 7

1　There are many. In English, and in most Indo-European languages, there is only one first person pronoun (I), one second person pronoun (you), and so on. Whereas, in Japanese, there are many pronouns, and they are used according to the speaker's sex, age, or social position, or according to the situation.

2　He probably would use the pronouns *watashi* or *watakushi*.

3　She probably would use *atashi*.

4　He probably would use *boku*.

5　He probably would use *ore*.

6　He probably would use *kimi*.

7　She probably would use *anta*.

8　If we are talking face to face with Mr. Takeda: "you are tall." If we are talking with someone who is not Mr. Takeda: "Mr. Takeda is tall."

9   He: 彼 (*kare*) / she: 彼女 (*kanojo*)
10 Because these pronouns are exclusively used by men. Japanese spoken by men and women is usually quite different (in fact, we talk about "female language" and "male language" in Japanese). Generally speaking, women usually speak in a more polite and formal way than men in any situation.

Lesson 8

1   It is used for several things. To transcribe foreign words into Japanese, both proper and place names, as well as isolated words which are seen as foreign expressions in Japanese; to write onomatopoeias; to highlight a word; or when looking for a striking effect.
2   The only independent consonant is ン (*n*).
3   We usually go to the column in question (in this case we want to transcribe the letter *s*) and we always choose the katakana "consonant + *u*," because the *u* is hardly pronounced in Japanese. Thus, in the case of the *s*, we will choose the katakana *s* + *u*, that is ス (*su*).
4   The syllables *tu* and *du* don't exist (we have *tsu* and *zu* instead). In this case, we will add an *o* to *t* and *d*, that is, when transcribing *t* we will use ト (*to*), and when transcribing d we will use ド (*do*).
5   They are consonants that are pronounced more abruptly than usual. They are represented writing a small *tsu* ッ character before the consonant to be doubled. Example: クラック (*kurakku*, crack).
6   We use *fu* + a small *i* beside it フィ.
7   We use *te* + a small *i* beside it ティ.
8   アメリカン (*amerikan*).
9   ファミリー (*famirii*, family) There are two problems: transcribing *fa* (see exercise 6, we have used *fu* + a small *a*), and *l*, which we have replaced with *r*.
10 This answer depends on your name.

Lesson 9

1   The verb always goes at the end of the sentence.
2   でした (*deshita*)
3   ではない (*de wa nai*) / じゃない (*ja nai*)
4   television: テレビ (*terebi*) / song: うた (*uta*) / cat: ねこ (*neko*) / bird: とり (*tori*)
5   Adding the hiragana か (*ka*) at the end of the sentence, and giving the sentence an interrogative intonation when pronouncing it.
6   This is not a photo.
7   That was not a bird.
8   Formal: それは漫画でした。(*sore wa manga deshita*) / Informal: それは漫画だった。(*sore wa manga datta*).
9   *Kore*: this / *sore*: that / *are*: that over there / *dore*: which?
10 We would obviously use the verbs in their simple conjugation, because it is a very informal situation.

Lesson 10

1   The Japanese archipelago is in the Northern Hemisphere.

2   Spring: 春 (*haru*) / summer: 夏 (*natsu*) / autumn: 秋 (*aki*) / winter: 冬 (*fuyu*)

3   The month of June coincides with the 梅雨 (*tsuyu*), or wet season. It rains almost every day during the whole month.

4   Wind: 風 (*kaze*) / cold: 寒い (*samui*) / moon: 月 (*tsuki*) / star: 星 (*hoshi*)

5   雪: *yuki* (snow) / 嵐: *arashi* (storm) / 熱い: *atsui* (hot) / 桜: *sakura* (cherry blossom)

6   More than 2,000 islands

7   本州 (*honshū*), 四国 (*shikoku*), 九州 (*kyūshū*), and 北海道 (*hokkaidō*)

8   Any of the following is valid: 東京 (*Tōkyō*) / 大阪 (*Ōsaka*) / 神戸 (*Kōbe*) / 名古屋 (*Nagoya*) / 横浜 (*Yokohama*) / 広島 (*Hiroshima*) / 札幌 (*Sapporo*).

9   Hokkaido has an almost Siberian climate: extremely cold with heavy snowfalls in winter, and cool summers. Okinawa has an almost tropical climate: generally good weather all through the year .

10 Starting with 寒いですね。(*samui desu ne*, "it's cold, isn't it?") if it is cold, or 暑いですね。(*atsui desu ne*, "it's hot, isn't it?") if it is hot. You will most probably receive a kind answer, and you can start up a conversation.

Lesson 11

1   Japanese nouns differ from English nouns in that they have neither gender nor number, that is, they never change. They can't tell plural from singular, nor female from male.

2   たばこ: *tabako* (tobacco) / たてもの: *tatemono* (building) / えいが: *eiga* (film) / スープ: *sūpu* (soup)

3   fish: さかな (*sakana*) / rice: ごはん (*gohan*) / noon: ひる (*hiru*) / restaurant: レストラン (*resutoran*)

4   車: *kuruma* (car) / 血: *chi* (blood) / ギター: *gitā* (guitar) / 酒: *sake* (liquor, Japanese sake)

5   Class: 教室 (*kyōshitsu*) / garden: にわ (*niwa*) / night: よる (*yoru*) / tear: 涙 (*namida*)

6   That is a magazine.

7   あれはてがみです。(*are wa tegami desu*)

8   This was a banana.

9   We will always have to deduce from the context what someone is talking about. For example, if we are shown one cat and we are told *are wa neko desu*, we will deduce we are being told "that is a cat" and not "those are several cats."

10 Counters are suffixes added to nouns to indicate "how many" things there are. There are many kinds of counters, and many uses as well, which we will see in Lesson 25.

Lesson 12

1   七分: *nana fun* (seven minutes) / 三時: *san ji* (three o'clock) / 四分: *yon pun* (four minutes) / 九時: *ku ji* (nine o'clock)

2   Ten minutes: 十分 (*juppun/jippun*) / eight o'clock: 八時 (*hachi ji*) / two minutes: 二分 (*ni fun*) / five o'clock: 五時 (*go ji*)

3   今は七時です。(*ima wa shichi ji desu*)

4   It's six o'clock. (*ima wa roku ji desu*)

5   今は三時十五分すぎです。(*ima wa san ji jū go fun sugi desu*)

6   It's a quarter to eight. (7:45h) (*ima wa hachi ji jū go fun mae desu*)

7   1)　今は九時半です。(*ima wa ku ji han desu*)

    2)　今は九時三十分です。(*ima wa ku ji san juppun desu*)

8   今は四時三十三分です。(*ima wa yo ji san jū san pun desu*)

9   今は何時ですか？(*ima wa nan ji desu ka*)

10 This depends, of course, on the time this question is answered.

Lesson 13

1   They are one of the two kinds of adjectives in the Japanese language. They are called that because they all end in "i," with no exception.

2   Japanese adjectives always go before the noun they modify.

3   赤い: *akai* (red) / 古い: *furui* (old) / 大きい: *ookii* (big) / 高い: *takai* (tall)

4   Small: 小さい (*chiisai*) / blue: 青い (*aoi*) / dark: 暗い (*kurai*) / cheap: 安い (*yasui*)

5   They are inflected replacing the last *i* with *katta*.

6   They are inflected replacing the last *i* with *nakatta*.

7   白くなかった (*shirokunakatta*) It wasn't white.

8   Present: 黒い (*kuroi*, black) / past: 黒かった (*kurokatta*, was black) / negative: 黒くない (*kurokunai*, is not black) / past negative: 黒くなかった (*kurokunakatta*, was not black)

9   この山は低いです。(*kono yama wa hikui desu*)

10 It isn't correct, because the negative form of the verb "to be" has been conjugated instead of inflecting the "i" adjective. The correct sentence would be: このねこはおとなしくないです。(*kono neko wa otonashikunai desu*)

Lesson 14

1   They are one of the two kinds of adjectives in the Japanese language. They are called that because they all end in "na," with no exception.

2   Apart from the fact that "i" adjectives end with the letter "i" and "na" adjectives end with the syllable "na," the main difference is that "na" adjectives are not inflected, whereas "i" adjectives are.

3   The last "na" syllable disappears.

4   丈夫な: *jōbu-na* (healthy, strong) / 親切な: *shinsetsu-na* (kind) / 好きな: *suki-na* (to like) / ひまな: *hima-na* (to have spare time)

5   Dangerous: 危険な (*kiken-na*) / pretty: きれいな (*kirei-na*) / famous: 有名な (*yūmei-na*) / skillful: 上手な (*jōzu-na*)

6   We remove the last "na" in the adjective and add the verb "to be" in the past tense. Example: clumsy (下手な, *heta-na*). The verb "to be" in the past tense is でした (*deshita*) in the *desu* form and だった (*datta*) in the simple form. We remove "na" from the word *heta-na* and we add the verb. *desu* form: 下手でした (*heta deshita*, was clumsy) / simple form: 下手だった (*heta datta*, was clumsy)

7   大変ではありませんでした。(*taihen de wa arimasen deshita*)

8   *desu* form. Present: 元気です。(*genki desu*) / past: 元気でした。(*genki deshita*) / negative: 元気ではありません。(*genki de wa arimasen*) / past negative: 元気ではありませんでした。(*genki de wa arimasen deshita.*) Simple forms. Present: 元気だ (*genki da*) / past: 元気だった。(*genki datta*) / negative: 元気ではない。(*genki de wa nai*) / past negative: 元気ではなかった。(*genki de wa nakatta*)

9　この道は安全でした。(*kono michi wa anzen deshita*)

10　静かな公園 (*shizuka-na kōen*)

Lesson 15

1　They are words we add to a proper name and they are used in practically all situations whenever we are talking about a second or third person.

2　ちゃん (*chan*), or none at all

3　君 (*kun*)

4　様 (*sama*)

5　殿 (*dono*)

6　Among family members (between brothers and sisters, and parents to children) you don't need a suffix with proper names. Likewise, with open-minded young friends with whom you are very familiar you can do without the suffix.

7　We will always use さん (*san*) whenever we are in doubt.

8　Bookstore: 本屋 (*hon-ya*) / wine shop: 酒屋 (*saka-ya*) / *ramen* shop: ラーメン屋 (*rāmen-ya*) / butcher's shop: 肉屋 (*niku-ya*)

9　Calling him by his title is essential, and since he is our company director, the best thing would be calling him 樋口社長 (*Higuchi-shachō*, Company director Higuchi)

10　No. When we talk about ourselves, we never use these suffixes for our proper name.

Lesson 16

1　They are small words without meaning, usually written with only one hiragana character. Their role is purely grammatical. Particles show the role played in a sentence by the word they follow.

2　は is usually pronounced *ha*, but when it works as a particle it is pronounced *wa*. へ is usually pronounced *he* but as a particle it is pronounced *e*. を is always pronounced *o* (since this character is only used as a particle)

3　To indicate the topic in the sentence. That is, "the thing" we are talking about.

4　It has three uses: a) to indicate direct contact ("where," "in which place.") / b) To indicate place, whenever the verb in the sentence means existence, such as "to be" or "to live" / c) To indicate indirect object, that is, "who", "what" is affected by the subject's action.

5　To indicate possession or description

6　To indicate direction, "where" we are going to.

7　This is your car. (The particle *wa* indicates topic, which is "this," and the particle *no* indicates possession: *anata no kuruma* = your car).

8　花子さんに花をあげる (*Hanako-san ni hana o ageru*). Hanako receives the flower, therefore she is the indirect object and needs the particle *ni*. Flower is the direct object, the given thing, and therefore needs the particle *o*. Don't forget the use of the suffix *–san* with proper names (Lesson 15).

9　To go to China. The particle *e* indicates direction, "where" we are going to.

10　プラモデルを作る (*puramoderu o tsukuru*). "What" are we making? The answer is "plastic model." Therefore "plastic model" is the direct object and needs the particle *o*.

Lesson 17

1   An end-of-sentence particle is a word (usually consisting of only one hiragana character) which, placed at the end of the sentence, indicates a certain emphasis or other connotations.

2   No. End-of-sentence particles are usually used exclusively in spoken Japanese. Only the particle か (*ka*), which indicates question, is usually used in written Japanese.

3   It has two main functions: a) to state, to give the sentence a degree of certainty, and to sound convincing. b) to express "insistence," "pressure" at the end of a sentence which expresses an order or a wish.

4   It is a particle used exclusively by women. It is used to state, to give the sentence a degree of certainty. It is also used to express admiration.

5   It is the masculine version of わ (*wa*). It is used to state and give the sentence some certainty, in very informal contexts.

6   The sentence becomes stronger and more certain. We can be sure that the speaker is a man and that he is talking with a friend or with someone very close to him, in an informal situation.

7   First possibility: add *ka*. きょうはメキシコに行くか？ (*kyō wa Mekishiko ni iku ka*, Are you going to Mexico today?) Second possibility: (in a rather informal situation) add *no*. きょうはメキシコに行くの？ (*kyō wa Mekishiko ni iku no*)

8   Don't eat ice-cream. The speaker is certainly a man.

9   いい天気ですね (*ii tenki desu ne*). The particle *ne* is used to give the sentence a confirmation tone, looking for an answer of the sort: "yes, you're right." It can often be translated into English as "isn't it?" (or its equivalent, according to the person and number used).

10 Yes, but with restrictions: the only acceptable particles in formal spoken Japanese are *ka*, *ne* and, to a lesser extent, *yo*.

Lesson 18

1   Verb *iru*: when we talk about animate beings (people, animals...) / Verb *aru*: when we talk about things and inanimate beings.

2   あった (*atta*)

3   ありません (*arimasen*)

4   いる (*iru*)

5   Dictionary form: あそこに桃がある。(*asoko ni momo ga aru*) / Formal form: あそこに桃があります。(*asoko ni momo ga arimasu*).

6   There wasn't a shark here.

7   Dictionary form: 私はくもがいなかった。(*watashi wa kumo ga inakatta*) / Formal form: 私はくもがいませんでした。(*watashi wa kumo ga imasendeshita*).

8   I don't have a watermelon.

9   In formal occasions or when we don't know our interlocutor. It would be equal to addressing our interlocutor with "Mr.," "Mrs.," or "Ms." before their surname.

10 We would naturally and logically use the dictionary form.

Lesson 19

1 Because the present tense of this verbal form always ends in –*masu*.

2 The dictionary form.

3 書きません (*kakimasen*)

4 食べます (*tabemasu*)

5 私はビールを飲みました。(*watashi wa biru o nomimashita*)

6 He didn't play.

7 彼女は走りません。(*kanojo wa hashirimasen*)

8 I buy a flower.

9 First sense (literal) = I understood / Second sense (phrasal) = fine / OK / Got it.

10 That the character is not speaking in Japanese, but we are offered a translation of what he or she says.

Lesson 20

1 Simple form. Because when we look up a verb in a dictionary we always find it in this form.

2 Group 1: we replace *ru* in the infinitive with *nai* (Ex: 教える *oshieru* = 教えない *oshienai*.) Group 2: we replace the last *u* in the infinitive with *a*, and we add *nai* (Ex: 書く *kaku* = 書かない *kakanai* / 貸す *kasu*= 貸さない *kasanai*)

3 Simple form = 遊ぶ (*asobu*) /–*masu* form = 遊びます (*asobimasu*)

4 Simple form = 飲まない (*nomanai*) /–*masu* form = 飲みません (*nomimasen*)

5 Simple form = 私は本を買った。(*watashi wa hon o katta*) /–*masu* form = 私は本を買いました。(*watashi wa hon o kaimashita*)

6 She didn't teach English.

7 Simple form = 田中さんは起きない。(*Tanaka-san wa okinai*) /–*masu* form = 田中さんは起きません。(*Tanaka-san wa okimasen*)

8 I wait for Maria.

9 I write: 私は書く。(*watashi wa kaku*) / they write: 彼らは書く。(*karera wa kaku*) / he writes: 彼は書く。(*kare wa kaku*)

10 The irregular verbs are する *suru* (to do) and 来る *kuru* (to come), and the half-irregular verb is 行く *iku* (to go).
present: する (*suru*) / past: した (*shita*) / negative: しない (*shinai*) / past negative: しなかった (*shinakatta*)
present: 来る (*kuru*) / past: 来た (*kita*) / negative: 来ない (*konai*) / past negative: 来なかった (*konakatta*)
present: 行く (*iku*) / past: 行った (*itta*) / negative: 行かない (*ikanai*) / past negative: 行かなかった (*ikanakatta*)

Lesson 21

1 Because the words used to refer to somebody else's family are used to express respect for the other person.

2 One's own wife: 家内 (*kanai*) / somebody else's wife: 奥さん (*okusan*) / one's own husband: 主人 (*shujin*) / somebody else's husband: ご主人 (*goshujin*).

3 Brothers and sisters are not only distinguished by sex, as in English, but also by their being older or younger. There are four words used to refer to one's own family: 兄 (*ani*, elder brother), 姉 (*ane*, elder sister), 弟 (*otōto*, younger brother), and 妹 (*imōto*, younger sister). And there are four more words used to refer to somebody else's family: お兄さん (*oniisan*, elder brother), お姉さん (*onēsan*, elder sister), 弟さん (*otōtosan*, younger brother), and 妹さん (*imōtosan*, younger sister).

4 One's own uncle: おじ (*oji*) / somebody else's uncle: おじさん (*ojisan*)

5 One's own son: 息子 (*musuko*) / somebody else's son: 息子さん (*musukosan*)

6 It means "grandchild" and it is one's own relative.

7 私の父は医者です。 (*watashi no chichi wa isha desu*)

8 あなたのお父さんは医者です。 (*anata no otōsan wa isha desu*)

9 There are at least five words: 父 (*chichi*), お父さん (*otōsan*), 父親 (*chichioya*), 親父 (*oyaji*), and パパ (*papa*).

10 First meaning: somebody else's elder sister / Second meaning: one's own elder sister / Third meaning: used to call a young girl whose name we don't know

Lesson 22

1 側に = beside. It is an adverb of place / まだ = still, yet. It is an adverb of time.

2 The last *i* is replaced with *ku*.

3 すごい = すごく (*sugoku* → amazingly), 低い = 低く (*hikuku* → low), 熱い = 熱く (*atsuku*, hotly)

4 The last *na* is replaced with *ni*.

5 貧乏な = 貧乏に (*binbō-ni*, poorly), 複雑な = 複雑に (*fukuzatsu-ni*, intricately), 必要な = 必要に (*hitsuyō-ni*, necessarily)

6 This exam is very difficult.

7 a) ちょっと雨が降る。 (*chotto ame ga furu*) b) 少し雨が降る。 (*sukoshi ame ga furu*)

8 To write kanji in small characters

9 a) 早い = quick (in time), soon b) 速い = fast (in speed)

10 a) Japanese liquor distilled from rice (*sake*)
   b) any kind of alcoholic drink / It is most commonly used in the b) sense.

Lesson 23

1 English, of course

2 It is a characteristic of Japanese society: before a setback or an enemy, the natural thing is keeping a poker face and not showing the rival one's own feelings. Moreover, the Japanese have great respect for other people and they would never insult anybody in public.

3 馬鹿者 (*bakamono*) / 馬鹿野郎 (*bakayarō*) / 馬鹿にする (*baka ni suru*) / 馬鹿を言う (*baka o iu*) / 馬鹿馬鹿しい (*bakabakashii*)

4 Rubbish, junk, scum

5 In Osaka, *aho* is a rather non-offensive, even friendly, word, whereas *baka* is extremely offensive. In Tokyo we find exactly the opposite, *baka* is friendly and *aho* is offensive.

6 ちくしょう (*chikushō*)

7   They are usually written in katakana, because katakana causes a much more shocking visual effect than kanji or hiragana. And a swearword should shock the reader.

8   うるさい！ (*urusai!*)

9   It is the word ブス (*busu*), literally "ugly," but it is actually a very insulting word.

10   Damn teacher: クソ先生 (*kuso-sensei*) / バカ先生 (*baka-sensei*)
     Fucking computer: クソコンピューター (*kuso-konpyūtā*) / バカコンピューター (*baka-konpyūtā*)

Lesson 24

1   The –*te* form is basic to form many grammatical expressions, the gerund and the *kudasai* request form among them. The –*te* form is essential in Japanese and it should be completely mastered.

2   飛ぶ = 飛んで (*tonde*) / 見る = 見て (*mite*) / 座る = 座って (*suwatte*)

3   寝る = 寝ている (*nete iru*, to be sleeping) / 転ぶ = 転んでいる (*koronde iru*, to be falling) / 笑う = 笑っている (*waratte iru*, to be laughing)

4   Past gerund = 寝ていた (*nete ita*, was sleeping) / 転んでいた (*koronde ita*, was falling) / 笑っていた (*waratte ita*, was laughing) / Negative gerund = 寝ていない (*nete inai*, not to be sleeping) / 転んでいない (*koronde inai*, not to be falling) / 笑っていない (*waratte inai*, not to be laughing)

5   彼らは遊んでいる。(*karera wa asonde iru*)

6   With the –*te* form + *kudasai*

7   りんごを食べてください。(*ringo o tabete kudasai*)

8   Present: 発生する (*hassei suru*, occur) / past: 発生した (*hassei shita*, occurred) / negative: 発生しない (*hassei shinai*, doesn't occur) / past negative: 発生しなかった (*hassei shinakatta*, didn't occur)

9   The *i* in the verb *iru* is removed. Example: 動いている (*ugoite iru*, to be moving) → 動いてる (*ugoiteru*) / 書いていた (*kaite ita*, was writing) → 書いてた (*kaiteta*).

10   Very often, the word *kudasai* is removed to suggest a much more familiar and informal sense. Ex.: 書いてください (*kaite kudasai*, write, please) → 書いて (*kaite*, write).

Lesson 25

1   A counter is a suffix placed after a numeral. We use it to indicate number, to say "how many" things there are.

2   It depends on the physical characteristics of the noun we want to count. Depending on the form, the material it is made from, the kind of thing it is, we will choose one counter or another.

3   1 = 一枚 (*ichimai*) / 2 = 二枚 (*nimai*) / 3 = 三枚 (*sanmai*) / 4 = 四枚 (*yonmai*) / 5 = 五枚 (*gomai*) / 6 = 六枚 (*rokumai*) / 7 = 七枚 (*nanamai*) / 8 = 八枚 (*hachimai*) / 9 = 九枚 (*kyūmai*) / 10 = 十枚 (*jūmai*). We use it to count flat things, such as pieces of paper, blankets, CDs...

4   1 = 一本 (*ippon*) / 2 = 二本 (*nihon*) / 3 = 三本 (*sanbon*) / 4 = 四本 (*yonhon*) / 5 = 五本 (*gohon*) / 6 = 六本 (*roppon*) / 7 = 七本 (*nanahon*) / 8 = 八本 (*happon*) / 9 = 九本 (*kyūhon*) / 10 = 十本 (*juppon.*) We use it to count long, slender things, such as trees, ballpoint pens, fingers... We also use it with video or audio tapes, or telephone calls.

5　Books = 冊 (*satsu*) / oranges = 個 (*ko*)

6　There are six cars on the road.

7　ねこを五匹ください。(*neko o gohiki kudasai*)

8　One person = 一人 (*hitori*, irregular reading) / two people = 二人 (*futari*, irregular reading) / three people = 三人 (*sannin*, regular reading) From *futari* on, they are all regular, with the exception of "four people," which is *yonin* and not *yonnin*.

9　We use it to count cups (coffee, tea...), glasses (milk, water, whisky, wine...), and spoonfuls.

10　*Hachijō* are "eight tatami." A tatami is more or less 1.6 m². Therefore, eight tatami x 1.6 = approximately 12.8 m².

Lesson 26

1　Body: 体 (*karada*) / 頭 (*atama*, head) / 顔 (*kao*, face) / おなか (*onaka*, stomach) / 腕 (*ude*, arm) / 手 (*te*, hand) / 首 (*kubi*, neck) / 胸 (*mune*, breast) / 足 (*ashi*, leg, foot) / 髪の毛 (*kaminoke*, hair) / 背中 (*senaka*, back)

2　Face = 顔 (*kao*) / hand = 手 (*te*) // Face: 口 (*kuchi*, mouth) / 耳 (*mimi*, ear) / 目 (*me*, eye) / 鼻 (*hana*, nose) / 舌 (*shita*, tongue) / ひげ (*hige*, beard) / and 歯 (*ha*, tooth) // Hand: 指 (*yubi*, finger) / 手の平 (*tenohira*, palm) / and 爪 (*tsume*, nail)

3　Brain = 頭脳 (*zunō*) / lungs = 肺臓 (*haizō*) / stomach = 胃 (*i*)

4　あなたの目はきれいです。(*anata no me wa kirei desu*)

5　His arms are strong.

6　背中が痛いです。(*senaka ga itai desu*)

7　My shoulder hurts me. / My shoulders hurt me.

8　The words 心 (*kokoro*) and 心臓 (*shinzō*) While *shinzō* has a purely physical meaning (it refers to the actual organ which pumps the blood in our body, that is, the heart), *kokoro* has a spiritual meaning. *Kokoro* refers to the soul, the mind, what makes us human, it refers to the center of things...

9　There are literally thousands; there are as many words as parts in our body, no matter how small or insignificant.

10　O-shiri = ケツ (*ketsu*, bum) / mune = オッパイ (*oppai*, boobs)

Lesson 27

1　こんばんは。(*konban wa*, Good evening)

2　お休みなさい。(*o-yasumi nasai*, Good night)

3　Farewell: 行ってきます。(*itte kimasu*, I'm leaving) /
Mother's answer: 行ってらっしゃい。(*itte rasshai*, See you later)

4　いらっしゃいませ。(*irasshaimase*, welcome, can I help you?) (It is very often said at the top of their voices!)

5　おめでとうございます。(*omedetō gozaimasu*, Congratulations)

6　つまらない物ですけれど、どうぞ。(*tsumaranai mono desu keredo, dōzo...*, It's something insignificant, but please take it)

7　お大事に (*o-daiji ni*, Get well soon)

8　22-year-old man to his friends = 腹が減った (*hara ga hetta*) / to his boss (but in a quite informal situation): お腹がすいた (*onaka ga suita*) / 5-year-old child = お腹がペコペコ (*onaka ga peko peko*)

9 あけましておめでとうございます。今年もよろしくお願いします。(*Akemashite omedetō gozaimasu. Kotoshi mo yoroshiku o-negai shimasu*)

10 1 お疲れさま。(*otsukare sama*) Thanks for your effort. / Good job...
2 ご苦労さま。(*gokurō sama*) Thanks for your trouble. / You did a good job

Lesson 28

1 *Naru* has no exact translation in English, although its use is very similar to that of "become."
Present: なる (*naru*) / past: なった (*natta*) / negative: ならない (*naranai*) / past negative: ならなかった (*naranakatta*)

2 やさしくなる (*yasashikunaru*, to become easy) / 便利になる (*benri ni naru*, to become convenient) / 学生になる (*gakusei ni naru*, to become a student)

3 "i" adjectives = we replace the last *i* with *ku* and add *naru* / "na" adjectives = we replace the last *na* with *ni* and add *naru* / nouns = we add *ni* + *naru*

4 He goes to see a film.

5 彼は小説を書きに来る。(*kare wa shōsetsu o kaki ni kuru*)

6 *Ageru* = to give / *morau* = to receive. Both *morau* and *kureru* mean "to receive," but *kureru* is used when the receiver is "I" or someone close to "I," such as a good friend or a relative of "I."

7 Frank gave Michiko a book. (*ageta* is the past form of the verb *ageru*)

8 スミスさんはブラウンさんに書類をもらう。(*Sumisu-san wa Buraun-san ni shorui o morau.*) *Morau* is the best verb in this case. However, we could use *kureru* if Mr. Smith were someone very close to "I."

9 I teach Japanese to the pupils.

10 牛乳を飲んでくれ。(*gyūnyū o nonde kure*)

Lesson 29

1 *Gitaigo* are words that imitate a physical condition or a state of mind.

2 *Gion* are sound-imitating words, similar to our onomatopoeias.

3 *Shikushiku*: (to weep) silently / *hotto*: to feel relieved / *guruguru*: to go round and round / *pakupaku*: (to eat) with relish

4 To laugh boisterously: げらげら (*geragera*) / to be exhausted: くたくた (*kutakuta*) / to glitter, dazzling: (1) ぴかぴか (*pikapika*) (2) きらきら (*kirakira*)

5 He speaks Japanese fluently.

6 Pikachu's flash is dazzling.

7 No, they are words all adults and children know and frequently use, both in spoken and written Japanese. Knowing at least the most basic ones is essential.

8 びっくりする (*bikkuri suru*)

9 *Gion* and *gitaigo* are some of the few words in Japanese that aren't written in a set kana or kanji. Depending on the author, they are written either in hiragana or in katakana (there are very few *gitaigo* and *gion* written in kanji.) Where manga is concerned, we often find them written in katakana, but there can be exceptions.

10 Dog: わんわん (*wan wan*) / Frog: げろげろ (*gero gero*)

Lesson 30

1 No. In real life using the imperative is considered bad manners and very rude. The *–te* form + *kudasai* (Lesson 24) is used much more often.

2 There is the "straightforward" imperative, the "gentle" imperative (*–nasai*) and the *–tamae* imperative. The "straightforward" imperative is rough and used only by men. The "gentle" imperative is mainly used by women when they want to give an order. Otherwise, it is also used by an adult with a child, or by a superior with a subordinate (although this last case is not that usual). The *–tamae* imperative is quite uncommon. It is used by a superior when talking to a subordinate.

3 *Miru* = 見ろ (*miro*) / *kiku* = 聞け (*kike*) / *noru* = 乗れ (*nore*) / *arau* = 洗え (*arae*)

4 *Miru* = 見なさい (*minasai*) / *kiku* = 聞きなさい (*kikinasai*) / *noru* = 乗りなさい (*norinasai*) / *arau* = 洗いなさい (*arainasai*)

5 *Miru* = 見たまえ (*mitamae*) / *kiku* = 聞きたまえ (*kikitamae*) / *noru* = 乗りたまえ (*noritamae*) / *arau* = 洗いたまえ (*araitamae*)

6 Because it is too rough and vulgar. A woman uses the *–nasai* form to give orders, in situations where she is very close to the person she is talking to.

7 Read the Japanese language course.

8 新聞を買え。(*shinbun o kae*)

9 いすに座りなさい。(*isu ni suwarinasai*)

10 The *–tamae* form is used when the speaker is or feels superior to his or her interlocutor. It is a seldom used form.

A Brief Note on Kanji

James W. Heisig

Kanji represent the only writing system that dates from the ancient world. Egyptian hieroglyph, Mesopotamian cuneiform writing, and Indus characters, also dating back to the beginnings of civilization, have since disappeared from use. The origins of kanji are lost in the mists of time, but the primitive forms of kanji found on bone fragments and turtle shells in China date back to a time between 4800 and 4200 BCE. Later inscriptions on bronze, dating from the Shang period (1523–1028 BCE), are often more complex than the earlier bone and shell fragments, leading some scholars to think that they may actually be older. In any case, both these forms of writing are more pictographic than present-day kanji, but as they came into wider and wider use as a means of writing the spoken language, their form became more abstract and simplified. As these abbreviated shapes increased in number, periodical revisions simplified the form still further and gradually brought the whole system under the control of guiding principles.

MEANING	ORACLE BONES	BRONZES	TODAY
eye			目
ear			耳
deer			鹿

Kanji are commonly referred to as ideographs. Unlike phonetic alphabets, individual symbols do not indicate pronunciation but represent a specific meaning, concrete or abstract, which can then be combined with other characters to form more complex meanings or ideas. Since kanji began in China, the sounds assigned to these ideographs reflected the spoken languages of China. As kanji spread to other countries and other language groups—Korea, Malaysia, Vietnam, and finally Japan—their pronunciation and usage changed accordingly.

When kanji were first introduced into Japan in the late fifth century CE, there was no existing system of writing for the Japanese language, only a language with a different structure and different sounds. In the process of adjusting kanji to Japanese, two things happened. First, kanji had to be chosen to represent the sounds of the language. This was done by approximating these sounds to already existing pronunciations of the kanji .

Second, Japanese sounds were used to form new words, not previously existing in Japanese.

In other words, it was not a mere phonetic system that was being introduced, but a means to express complex ideas that spoken Japanese had no equivalents for, ideas that in many cases required a written language to standardize. In time, the purely phonetic kanji were simplified into syllabaries that functioned more or less like Western alphabets to reproduce all the sounds of the spoken language. Today there are two such syllabaries in use, hiragana and katakana, which contain 46 characters each. Kanji assigned to re-present indigenous Japanese words kept a "Japanese reading" (kun'yomi), while kanji belonging to Chinese terms not previously existing in Japanese survived with "Chinese readings" (the most common of which are the on'yomi).

The most complete list of kanji that exists counts some 80,000 distinct characters, but they have never all been used in any given period. In the case of Japan, a list of 1,945 characters have been nominated as "daily-use kanji" in 1981, and these are the kanji that are taught to all children in the schools and have produced virtually total literacy in what is certainly the most complex writing system in the world today.

SOUND AND MEANING IN KANJI

The easiest way to understand how sound and meaning are carried by kanji in con-temporary Japanese is by way of an example. The Chinese city of Shanghai writes its name with two kanji 上海, meaning literally "on the sea."

The first character 上, for "on" or "above" is drawn with a horizontal baseline and a 卜 above it. The oldest bone inscriptions wrote the upper part with a shorter horizontal line: 二, about by the eigth century BCE the upper stroke had become vertical, giving us ⊥. Later revisions of kanji changed it to what we have today. (As you might expect, something similar happened with the character that means "under." It evolved from ⊥ and 丅 to get to its present form 下.) Chinese pronounces the character 上 shang.

The second character, 海, means «sea» and it is made up of three parts. To the left you see 氵, the three drops of water, indicating that it has something to do with water. The upper right two-stroke combination 𠂉 is an abbreviated form of 屮 which is one of the many forms for grass and anything that flourishes luxuriously like grass. Below it is a slightly simplified form of 母, the pictograph of two breasts, meaning "mother." Together, the right side is an image of a woman with her hair up. It has had a wide range of meanings: always, often, luxuriant growth, trifling, dark. Today it means sim-ply "each." Putting these two sides together, the "water" was seen to combine with an image of "dark, wide, and deep" to create an image of the sea. It is pronounced hai.

So 上海 is pronounced shanghai in Chinese and it means "on the sea." The writing and meaning were taken over by the Japanese. Obviously, since they received their kanji from China long after the major changes in form had been made, it would not have made sense for them to ignore the etymology and start shifting the elements around or introducing new ones. Japanese pronunciation is another matter. In the case of the city of Shanghai, they actually keep something close to the Chinese, but this is a very rare exception. On their own, these characters head off in a completely different direction. Let us look at just the first of the two characters of Shanghai.

Whereas 上 has only one reading in Chinese, *shang*, in Japanese it has at least ten recognized pronunciations, six of which all school children have to learn:

- two standard Chinese *(on)* readings: *jō* and *shō*
- four standard Japanese *(kun)* readings: *kami, ue, a[garu], no[boru]*, (and three more, if you include variations on these last two)
- four rare Japanese readings: *hotori, kuwa[eru], tate[matsuru]*, and *tatto[bu]*

Which reading is used in which situation? It all depends on the context. You have to look at what comes before or after (sometime both before and after) the simple character 上 to know how to pronounce it. Thus, if you see 上位 you should know it is read *jōi;* and that 上人 is read *shōnin*. The second character gives away the meaning of the term and hence the pronunciation memorized for that meaning jumps to mind. And if you see 上がる you know that it is read *a* from the hiragana *garu* that inflect it; or, similarly, that 上る is read *noboru*. Standing all on its own, you would have to look at the context of the phrase and decide if the proper reading for 上 is *kami* or *ue*.

This may seem like too much for a single mind to manage, but in fact we have something similar in English, even if on a much more modest scale. Take the following shape: "2". You look at it and immediately know what it means and how to pronounce it. But in fact there is no connection between the pronunciation and the written form. If you saw the letter in the middle of a Vietnamese novel, you would still know what it means, but you would no longer know how to pronounce it.

But wait—it isn't always pronounced "two" even in English. Adjust the context of surrounding symbols and you end up with four additional and quite distinct readings: 12, 20, 2nd, and 1/2. What your mind does when it adjusts the reading to the context is roughly what the Japanese-reading mind does when it locates a kanji in its context and decides on how to read it.

STUDYING KANJI

The big question is, of course, how to train one's mind to read and write Japanese. There are those who simplify matters by deciding that there is no need for those educated outside of the Japanese school system to bother learning how to *write* the language. If you can read, you will remember how to write a few hundred kanji along the way and you can leave the rest to computers to handle for you. Or so the argument goes. It has the full support of most Japanese who have never met a Western-educated individual who can write kanji with the same fluency as they and have somehow decided that, without the benefit of an education in writing that begins at the pre-school level and goes all the way up to the last year of high school, there is no way they ever could. This is not only the case for ordinary readers of Japanese but also for the great mass of scholars of Japanese scholarship in the West. Hiragana and katakana, and perhaps a third-grade level of writing—but more than that is unreasonable to expect.

If you accept the argument, you are solidly in the majority camp. You would also be as wrong as they are. To begin with, there is no reason you cannot learn to write kanji as fluently as you read them, and in a fraction of the time it takes to do it through the Japanese school system. What is more, without the ability to write, you are forever crippled, or at least limited to walking with the crutch of an electronic dictionary or computer. Finally, by learning to write you have helped to internationalize the fullness of the Japanese language beyond the present-day limits. All of this is common sense to the Korean and Chinese who come to Japan to learn the language. The reason Westerners tend to dismiss it is their fear of not being able to learn to write, or at least not without devoting long years to the task. As I said, this fear is unfounded.

The key to learning to write is to forget the way the Japanese learn and pay attention instead to the way the Chinese learn Japanese, and then adapt it to the West. Consider the following diagram.

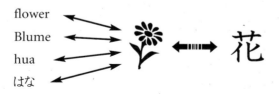

For the English speaker, the word *flower* is linked with the memory or visual perception of an actual flower, ❀. This link goes both ways, so that thinking about or seeing a ❀ the word *flower* comes to mind at once, just as speaking or reading the word *flower* calls up an image, however vague, of a ❀. The same is true for the German, Chinese, or Japanese speaker, each of whom associates the ❀ with the equivalent term in their own language: *Blume, hua,* はな. The phonetic symbols for that that word—in the examples here, the alphabet, and the Japanese kana—have no necessary connection with the actual ❀ itself. They are linguistic conventions that differ from language to language.

The kanji on the far right, in contrast, has no phonetic value, as the words on the right do; nor has it any pictographic link to the actual ❀. It is ideographic, that is, it represents the pure meaning or idea of the flower without specifying any sound or image. For one who knows the meaning of the kanji, there is a link to the actual ❀, just as the actual 🌺 (or even a mere idea of it) is linked to the memory of the written kanji 花.

When the Japanese study kanji, they have only one step to take: はな → 花. When the Chinese study Japanese, they, too, have only one step to take, and it goes in the opposite direction: 花 → はな. But when someone who comes from a Western language learns kanji, both steps have to be taken: *flower* → はな ➡ 花. The problem is, these two steps are completely different and have nothing in common such that the learning of one might aid the learning of the other. Nevertheless, the traditional way of studying kanji is to try to take them both at the same time. One ends up walking in one direction with one leg and another direction with the other. Little wonder that progress is so painful and so slow.

The conclusion should be obvious: *If you want to learn to read and write all the general-use kanji, you should study them separately.*

Which one do you start with, the reading or the writing? You might be surprised, but the answer is—the writing. There are two reasons. First, by doing so you end up in basically the same position as the Chinese coming to the study of Japanese kanji: you know what they mean and how to write them, but you still have to learn how to pronounce them. Second, the writing is a rational system that can be learned by principles, whereas the reading requires a great deal of brute memory.

Kanji? Rational? Actually, yes. As mentioned at the beginning, the evolution of kanji over nearly seven millennia has not taken place haphazardly. Writing is, after all, a highly rational activity, and the refinement of a writing system naturally tends towards simplification and consistency. Without knowing a good number of kanji, it is hard to explain this in the concrete, but suffice it to say that with only a couple of exceptions, the present list of general-use kanji *obey rational principles completely*. What this means is that they are based on a limited number of pieces joined by a limited number of rules.

This brings us to a second conclusion: *The most efficient way for an adult to learn a rational system of writing is to learn the underlying principles, which can then be applied to blocks of information.* Or, put the other way around: *The most inefficient way for an adult to learn them is by repetition, the way Japanese school children, lacking the powers of abstraction, begin learning them.*

Once the meaning and writing of kanji have been learned, it is possible to introduce a limited number of principles for reading, which again help to learn blocks of information at one time, rather than have to study the kanji one by one. And, as you might expect, the best order for learning to write kanji is very different from the best order for learning to read them. All of this is spelled out in more detail in a series of books I wrote some years ago under the general title *Remembering the Kanji.*[1]

The 160 samples of kanji that appear in the "Kanji Dictionary" that follows is intended only to serve as a reference index for the lessons that make up this book. A sample of possible readings and examples are provided, along with the stroke order for writing the kanji.

James W. Heisig

Permanent Fellow of the Nanzan Institute for Religion and Culture, Nagoya, Japan

---

[1] *Remembering the Kanji I: A Complete Course on How Not to Forget the Meaning and Writing of Japanese Characters* (Tokyo: Japan Publications Trading Co., 4th edition, 2001); *Remembering the Kanji II: A Systematic Guide to Reading Japanese Characters* (Tokyo: Japan Publications Trading Co., 1987); and, with Tanya Sienko, *Remembering the Kanji III: Writing and Reading Japanese Characters for Upper-Level Proficiency* (Tokyo: Japan Publications Trading Co., Ltd., 1994).

Appendix: Kanji glossary

We already explained in Lesson 3 what kanji are and what we use them for. Reviewing that lesson before carrying on with this appendix is highly recommended. Kanji are characters originally imported from Chinese, used to write Japanese, which always come in a sentence with hiragana characters (Lesson 1), and, sometimes, katakana characters (Lesson 2) as well. The "cohabitation" in Japanese of the three ways of writing (hiragana, katakana, and kanji) is truly curious, as you can see in the following example:

私の名前はマリアです。

Watashi no namae wa maria desu (My name is Maria.)

The words *watashi*(私) and *namae*(名前) are written in kanji, the proper name *Maria* (マリア), being a non-Japanese name, is written in katakana, and, finally, the particle *wa* (は) and the verb *desu* (です) are written in hiragana.

Learning kanji is one of the most difficult parts of the study of the Japanese language, due to its complexity both when writing and reading it. At the same time, it is essential to learn the language correctly, because all Japanese texts use kanji.

We thought including a short appendix with the writing of the 160 most basic kanji was necessary. It is an extremely reduced list compared to the official list of common-use kanji (*Jōyō kanji*), which consists of 1,945 characters.

The kanji offered here have been chosen on the basis of the frequency of appearance and their actual usefulness in the study of the Japanese language. They are ordered so that there is a greater association between characters with complementary meanings and characters with similar forms.

We have tried to select a series of compound words, as examples of the usage of the kanji introduced here, which might be useful in the learning of the Japanese language.

The entry structure is the following:

1	2	5
3	6	
4	7	
		8

1   Entry number in this appendix.
2   Number of strokes which form the character (s = strokes.)
3   Kanji box.
4   In capital letters, character's *on'yomi* reading. In lower case letters, character's *kun'yomi* (see Lesson 3 for more references on these concepts).
5   Kanji's main meaning.
6   Kanji's writing and stroke order.
7   Compound words with this kanji.
8   Kanji included in this appendix which could be mistaken for the kanji in question due to their similarity (between brackets, reference number of the kanji open to confusion).

Stroke order

Kanji are always written in a specific way, and they always follow a particular stroke order. To help you learn these kanji, we have included each kanji's stroke order. We will now briefly mention the basic rules when writing kanji, according to their importance:

a)   Kanji are written from top to bottom (see kanji 3 and 155 for clear references).

b)   Kanji are written from left to right (see kanji 8, 95, and 133).

c)   Horizontal strokes come first (see kanji 49, 66, and 138).

d)   The center comes first (see kanji 19, 50, and 157).

e)   The outside comes first (see kanji 16, 17, and 152).

f)   Strokes which bend toward the left come before strokes which bend to the right (see kanji 15, 21 and 36).

g)   The stroke that divides the kanji from top to bottom comes last (see kanji 25, 64, and 93).

h)   The stroke that divides the kanji from left to right comes last (see kanji 34, 35, and 84).

List of the 160 kanji offered in this appendix.

1 一	2 二	3 三	4 四	5 五	6 六	7 七	8 八	9 九	10 十
11 百	12 千	13 万	14 円	15 人	16 日	17 月	18 火	19 水	20 木
21 金	22 土	23 口	24 目	25 手	26 足	27 心	28 耳	29 東	30 西
31 南	32 北	33 男	34 女	35 子	36 父	37 母	38 弟	39 兄	40 姉
41 妹	42 山	43 川	44 田	45 石	46 朝	47 昼	48 夜	49 大	50 小
51 多	52 少	53 分	54 年	55 前	56 後	57 今	58 午	59 時	60 上
61 下	62 右	63 左	64 中	65 方	66 元	67 気	68 文	69 出	70 入
71 白	72 赤	73 青	74 本	75 店	76 学	77 校	78 先	79 生	80 会
81 社	82 私	83 高	84 安	85 太	86 春	87 夏	88 秋	89 冬	90 半
91 間	92 道	93 車	94 自	95 動	96 近	97 遠	98 暑	99 寒	100 行
101 来	102 名	103 友	104 新	105 古	106 強	107 弱	108 力	109 立	110 若
111 広	112 悪	113 重	114 早	115 持	116 待	117 買	118 売	119 開	120 閉
121 始	122 終	123 帰	124 休	125 体	126 言	127 話	128 聞	129 書	130 読
131 見	132 思	133 作	134 教	135 習	136 使	137 知	138 雨	139 病	140 仕
141 事	142 者	143 地	144 所	145 外	146 好	147 変	148 着	149 物	150 食
151 飲	152 国	153 語	154 空	155 花	156 字	157 楽	158 電	159 明	160 家

1	1s	ONE

⼀

ICHI hito	一 *ichi* **one** 一月 *ichigatsu* **January** 一つ *hitotsu* **one** 一人 *hitori* **one person** 一日 *tsuitachi* **1st (of the month)**

2	2s	TWO

⼆

NI futa	二 *ni* **two** 二月 *nigatsu* **February** 二日 *futsuka* **2nd (of the month)** 二つ *futatsu* **two** 二人 *futari* **two people**　　　　三 (3)

3	3s	THREE

三

SAN mi	三 *san* **three** 三月 *sangatsu* **March** 三日 *mikka* **3rd (of the month)** 三脚 *sankyaku* **tripod** 三つ *mittsu* **three**　　　　二 (2)

4	5s	FOUR

四

SHI yon	四 *shi / yon* **four** 四月 *shigatsu* **April** 四季 *shiki* **the four seasons** 四人 *yonin* **four people** 四つ *yottsu* **four**　　　　西 (30)

5	4s	FIVE

五

GO itsu	五 *go* **five** 五感 *gokan* **the five senses** 五月 *gogatsu* **May** 五百 *gohyaku* **500** 五日 *itsuka* **5th (of the month)**

6	4s	SIX

六　ヽ 　一 　六 　六

ROKU

mu

六 *roku* **six**
六月 *rokugatsu* **June**
第六感 *dairokkan* **sixth sense**
六つ *muttsu* **six**
六日 *muika* **6th (of the month)**

7	2s	SEVEN

七　一 　七

SHICHI

nana

七 *shichi / nana* **seven**
七人 *nananin* **seven people**
七月 *shichigatsu* **July**
七つ *nanatsu* **seven**
七日 *nanoka* **7th (of the month)**

8	2s	EIGHT

八　ノ 　八

HACHI

ya

八 *hachi* **eight**
八月 *hachigatsu* **August**
八つ *yattsu* **eight**
八日 *yōka* **8th (of the month)**
八百屋 *yaoya* **greengrocer**

9	2s	NINE

九　ノ 　九

KYŪ
KU
kokono

九 *kyū / ku* **nine**
九州 *Kyūshū* **island of Kyushu**
九月 *kugatsu* **September**
九つ *kokonotsu* **nine**
九日 *kokonoka* **9th (of the month)**

10	2s	TEN

十　一 　十

JŪ

tō

十 *jū* **ten**
十月 *jūgatsu* **October**
十分 *jūbun* **enough**
十字架 *jūjika* **cross, crucifix**
十日 *tōka* **10th (of the month)**

11	6s	HUNDRED

百　一　フ　ア　万　百　百

HYAKU

百 *hyaku* **hundred**
百円 *hyakuen* **one hundred yen**
百科事典 *hyakka jiten* **encyclopedia**
百姓 *hyakushō* **farmer**
八百屋 *yaoya* **greengrocer**

12	3s	THOUSAND

千　ノ　二　千

SEN

千 *sen* **1,000**
五千 *gosen* **5,000**
千円 *sen en* **1,000 yen**

13	3s	TEN THOUSAND

万　一　フ　万

MAN
BAN

一万 *ichiman* **10,000**
万年 *man nen* **10,000 years**
万一 *man ichi* **just in case**
万引き *manbiki* **shoplifting**
万歳 *banzai* **hooray!**

14	4s	YEN, CIRCLE

円　丨　冂　冂　円

EN
maru

円 *en* **yen, circle**
円高 *endaka* **high yen rate**
円周 *enshū* **circumference**
円満 *enman* **perfect, harmonious**
円い *marui* **round**

15	2s	PERSON

人　ノ　人

JIN
NIN
hito

人 *hito* **person**
人間 *ningen* **person, human**
日本人 *nihonjin* **Japanese person**
人気 *ninki* **popular**
人工 *jinkō* **artificial**

16	4s	SUN, DAY

日　　｜　冂　日　日

NICHI JITSU hi ka	日 *hi* **sun** 日本 *nihon* **Japan** 二日 *futsuka* **2nd (of the month)** 休日 *kyūjitsu* **holiday** 日曜日 *nichiyōbi* **Sunday**　　　　　　目 (24)、耳 (28)

17	4s	MOON, MONTH

月　　丿　几　月　月

GETSU GATSU tsuki	月 *tsuki* **moon** 満月 *mangetsu* **full moon** 月曜日 *getsuyōbi* **Monday** 月給 *gekkyū* **monthly salary** 十二月 *jūnigatsu* **December**　　　　日 (16)

18	4s	FIRE

火　　丶　丷　ソ　火

KA hi	火 *hi* **fire** 花火 *hanabi* **fireworks** 火星 *kasei* **Mars** 火事 *kaji* **a fire** 火曜日 *kayōbi* **Tuesday**　　　　方 (65)

19	4s	WATER

水　　亅　水　水　水

SUI mizu	水 *mizu* **water** 水着 *mizugi* **swimming costume** 水道 *suidō* **waterworks** 水曜日 *suiyōbi* **Wednesday** 海水 *kaisui* **sea water**　　　　小 (50)

20	4s	TREE, WOOD

木　　一　十　才　木

MOKU ki	木 *ki* **wood** 植木 *ueki* **pot plant** 木材 *mokuzai* **wood** 木造 *mokuzō* **wooden** 木曜日 *mokuyōbi* **Thursday**　　　未 (70)、休 (124)

21	8s	METAL, GOLD, MONEY
金	ノ 入 人 全 全 全 金 金	
KIN kane	お金 *okane* **money** 金持ち *kanemochi* **rich** 金属 *kinzoku* **metal** 純金 *junkin* **pure gold** 金曜日 *kinyōbi* **Friday**	

22	3s	EARTH
土	一 十 土	
DO tsuchi	土 *tsuchi* **earth** 国土 *kokudo* **territory** 土砂 *dosha* **earth and sand** 土器 *doki* **earthenware** 土曜日 *doyōbi* **Saturday** 上 (60)	

23	3s	MOUTH, ENTRANCE
口	丨 冂 口	
KŌ kuchi	口 *kuchi* **mouth** 入口 *iriguchi* **entrance** 火口 *kakō* **crater** 人口 *jinkō* **population** 口座 *kōza* **bank account**	

24	5s	EYE
目	丨 冂 月 月 目	
MOKU me	目 *me* **eye** 目指す *mezasu* **aim at** 一番目 *ichibanme* **the first** 注目 *chūmoku* **attention** 目的 *mokuteki* **goal** 日 (16)、自 (94)	

25	4s	HAND
手	ノ 二 三 手	
SHU te	手 *te* **hand** 手首 *tekubi* **wrist** 相手 *aite* **opponent** 拍手 *hakushu* **hand clapping** 歌手 *kashu* **singer** 千 (12)	

26	7s	FOOT, TO BE ENOUGH

足　丶 丨 口 口 尸 尸 尸 足

SOKU
ashi
ta(riru)

足 *ashi* **foot**
手足 *teashi* **hands and feet**
足跡 *ashiato* **footprint**
足りる *tariru* **to be enough**
遠足 *ensoku* **excursion**

27	4s	HEART, SOUL

心　丶 心 心 心

SHIN
kokoro

心 *kokoro* **heart, spirit, soul**
心理 *shinri* **psychology**
関心 *kanshin* **interest**
中心 *chūshin* **center**
心電図 *shindenzu* **electrocardiogram**

28	6s	EAR

耳　一 丆 下 下 耳 耳

JI
mimi

耳 *mimi* **ear**
左耳 *hidarimimi* **left ear**
早耳 *hayamimi* **quick-eared**
内耳 *naiji* **internal ear**
耳目 *jimoku* **eyes and ears**

目 (24)、日 (16)

29	8s	EAST

東　一 丆 厂 冂 百 百 車 東 東

TŌ
higashi

東 *higashi* **east**
東口 *higashiguchi* **east exit**
東洋 *tōyō* **the East**
東南 *tōnan* **south-east**
東京 *tōkyō* **Tokyo**

30	6s	WEST

西　一 丆 冂 丙 西 西

SEI
SAI
nishi

西 *nishi* **west**
西口 *nishiguchi* **west exit**
西欧 *seiō* **Western Europe**
北西 *hokusei* **north-west**
関西 *kansai* **Kansai area**

四 (4)

31	9s	SOUTH
南	一 十 ナ 厂 肉 南 南 南 南	

NAN minami	南 *minami* **south** 南口 *minamiguchi* **south exit** 南風 *minamikaze* **south wind** 南米 *nanbei* **South America** 東南 *tōnan* **south-east**

32	5s	NORTH
北	一 十 キ 北 北	

HOKU kita	北 *kita* **north** 北口 *kitaguchi* **north exit** 北東 *hokutō* **north-east** 北極 *hokkyoku* **North Pole** 北海道 *hokkaidō* **island of Hokkaido**

33	7s	MAN
男	丨 冂 冂 田 田 甲 男	

DAN otoko	男 *otoko* **man** 男前 *otokomae* **handsome man** 男性 *dansei* **man, male** 男子 *danshi* **young man** 男女 *danjo* **man and woman**

34	3s	WOMAN
女	く 女 女	

JO onna	女 *onna* **woman** 女らしい *onnarashii* **effeminate** 女性 *josei* **woman, female** 少女 *shōjo* **young woman** 女優 *joyū* **actress**

35	3s	CHILD
子	７ 了 子	

SHI ko	子 *ko* **child** 子供 *kodomo* **child** 息子 *musuko* **son** 弟子 *deshi* **disciple** 女子 *joshi* **girl**

字 (156)、学 (76)

36	4s	FATHER

父　ノ　ハ　グ　父

FU chichi tō	父 *chichi* **father** 父親 *chichioya* **father** お父さん *otōsan* **father** 父母 *fubo* **father and mother** 祖父 *sofu* **grandfather** 　　文 (68)

37	5s	MOTHER

母　ㄴ　ㄩ　ㄐ　ㄐ　母

BO haha kā	母 *haha* **mother** 母親 *hahaoya* **mother** お母さん *okāsan* **mother** 祖母 *sobo* **grandmother** 母国 *bokoku* **native country**

38	7s	YOUNGER BROTHER

弟　丶　ゝ　ソ　ヴ　ヴ　弟　弟

TEI DAI otōto	弟 *otōto* **younger brother** 兄弟 *kyōdai* **brothers** 子弟 *shitei* **son** 義弟 *gitei* **stepbrother** 師弟 *shitei* **teacher and disciple**

39	5s	ELDER BROTHER

兄　丶　ㄇ　ㅁ　ㅁ　兄

KEI KYŌ ani nii	兄 *ani* **elder brother** 兄貴 *aniki* **elder brother** お兄さん *oniisan* **elder brother** 兄弟 *kyōdai* **brothers** 長兄 *chōkei* **eldest brother** 　　見 (131)

40	8s	ELDER SISTER

姉　く　夕　女　女'　ㄠ　ㄠ　姉　姉

SHI ane nee	姉 *ane* **elder sister** お姉さん *oneesan* **elder sister** 姉妹 *shimai* **elder sister** 姉妹都市 *shimai toshi* **sister cities** 義姉 *gishi* **stepsister** 　　妹 (41)、始 (121)

41	8s	YOUNGER SISTER

妹　　く　夕　女　圹　奻　妌　妹　妹

MAI	妹 *imōto*　**younger sister**
imōto	妹娘 *imōtomusume*　**younger daughter**
	弟妹 *teimai*　**younger brothers and sisters**
	姉妹 *shimai*　**sisters**
	義妹 *gimai*　**stepsister**

姉 (40)、始 (121)

42	3s	MOUNTAIN

山　　丨　山　山

SAN	山 *yama*　**mountain**
yama	山脈 *sanmyaku*　**mountain range**
	登山 *tozan*　**mountain climbing**
	火山 *kazan*　**volcano**
	富士山 *fujisan*　**Mt. Fuji**

出 (69)

43	3s	RIVER

川　　丿　川　川

SEN	川 *kawa*　**river**
kawa	川上 *kawakami*　**upper river**
	小川 *ogawa*　**stream**
	河川 *kasen*　**rivers**
	山川 *sansen*　**rivers and mountains**

44	5s	RICE FIELD

田　　丨　冂　冂　甲　田

DEN	田 *ta*　**rice field**
ta	田んぼ *tanbo*　**rice field**
	乾田 *kanden*　**dry rice field**
	油田 *yuden*　**oil field**
	炭田 *tanden*　**coalfield**

男 (33)、思 (132)

45	5s	STONE

石　　一　厂　石　石　石

SEKI	石 *ishi*　**stone**
ishi	石油 *sekiyu*　**oil**
	宝石 *hōseki*　**precious stone**
	石炭 *sekitan*　**coal**
	石像 *sekizō*　**stone statue**

右 (62)、若 (110)

46	12s	MORNING
朝	一 十 十 古 古 吉 吉 卓 朝 月 v.17	
CHŌ asa	朝 *asa* **morning** 朝日 *asahi* **rising sun** 朝食 *chōshoku* **breakfast** 朝刊 *chōkan* **morning edition** 早朝 *sōchō* **early**	

47	9s	NOON
昼	一 コ 尸 尺 尺 尽 昼 昼 昼	
CHŪ hiru	昼 *hiru* **noon** 昼寝 *hirune* **afternoon nap** 昼間 *hiruma* **in the daytime** 昼食 *chūshoku* **lunch** 昼夜 *chūya* **night and day**	

48	8s	NIGHT
夜	亠 广 广 疒 夜 夜 夜	
YA yoru yo	夜 *yoru* **night** 夜中 *yonaka* **midnight** 夜空 *yozora* **night sky** 夜間 *yakan* **at night** 徹夜 *tetsuya* **sit up all night**	

49	3s	BIG, UNIVERSITY
大	一 ナ 大	
DAI TAI oo(kii)	大きい *ookii* **big** 大型 *oogata* **large** 大事 *daiji* **important** 大会 *taikai* **meeting** 大学 *daigaku* **university**　　　太 (85)	

50	3s	SMALL
小	亅 小 小	
SHŌ chii(sai) ko	小さい *chiisai* **small** 小鳥 *kotori* **small bird** 小学校 *shogakkō* **primary school** 最小 *saishō* **the least** 小説 *shōsetsu* **novel**　　　少 (52)、水 (19)	

51	6s	MANY, MUCH

多　　ノ　ク　タ　タ　多　多

TA oo(i)	多い *ooi* **many, much** 多目 *oome* **in large quantity** 多数 *tasū* **great number** 多量 *taryō* **large quantity** 多分 *tabun* **maybe**　　名 (102)

52	4s	FEW, LITTLE

少　　亅　小　小　少

SHŌ suku(nai) suko(shi)	少ない *sukunai* **few, little** 少し *sukoshi* **a few, a little** 少年 *shōnen* **boy, young man** 少量 *shōryō* **small quantity** 減少 *genshō* **a decrease**　　小 (50)

53	4s	TO DIVIDE, TO UNDERSTAND, MINUTE

分　　ノ　八　分　分

BUN FUN wa(karu) wa(keru)	分かる *wakaru* **understand** 分ける *wakeru* **divide** 気分 *kibun* **mood, state of mind** 半分 *hanbun* **half** 二分 *nifun* **two minutes**　　今 (57)

54	6s	YEAR

年　　ノ　ヒ　ヒ　午　生　年

NEN toshi	年 *nen* **year** 年金 *nenkin* **annuity** 中年 *chūnen* **middle-aged** 定年 *teinen* **retirement** 今年 *kotoshi* **this year**　　午 (58)

55	9s	IN FRONT OF, BEFORE

前　　丶　丷　丷　广　产　肖　肖　前　前

ZEN mae	前 *mae* **in front of, before** 名前 *namae* **name** 人前 *hitomae* **before others** 前線 *zensen* **a front** 前進 *zenshin* **advance**

56	9s	AFTER, BEHIND
後	ノ　ク　彳　彳　犭　犭　犭　後　後	

GO KŌ ushi(ro) ato	後ろ *ushiro* **behind** 後 *ato* **after** 背後 *haigo* **the back** 最後 *saigo* **last** 後期 *kōki* **the latter period**

57	4s	NOW
今	ノ　人　今　今	

KON ima	今 *ima* **now** 今頃 *imagoro* **at this time** 今週 *konshū* **this week** 今月 *kongetsu* **this month** 今回 *konkai* **this time**

会 (80)、分 (53)

58	4s	NOON
午	ノ　ト　卜　午	

GO	午前 *gozen* **morning** 午後 *gogo* **afternoon** 正午 *shōgo* **noon**

年 (54)

59	10s	TIME
時	丨　冂　冃　日　日ˉ　日⁺　日±　昨　時　時	

JI toki	時 *toki* **hour, time** 時々 *tokidoki* **sometimes** 時間 *jikan* **time** 五時 *goji* **five o'clock** 時代 *jidai* **age, era**

待 (116)、持 (115)

60	3s	UP, TO GO UP
上	丨　卜　上	

JŌ ue a(garu) nobo(ru)	上 *ue* **up** 上がる *agaru* **go up, lift** 上る *noboru* **go up, climb** 屋上 *okujō* **roof** 以上 *ijō* **more than**

土 (22)

61	3s	UNDER, TO GO DOWN
下	一 丁 下	

KA, GE shita sa(garu) kuda(ru)	下 *shita* **under** 下がる *sagaru* **go down, drop** 下る *kudaru* **do gown, descend** 地下鉄 *chikatetsu* **subway** 下品 *gehin* **vulgar**

62	5s	RIGHT
右	ノ ナ 大 右 右	

U YŪ migi	右 *migi* **right** 右手 *migite* **right hand** 右折 *usetsu* **right turn** 右翼 *uyoku* **right wing** 左右 *sayū* **left and right** 石 (45)、若 (110)

63	5s	LEFT
左	一 ナ 𠂇 左 左	

SA hidari	左 *hidari* **left** 左手 *hidarite* **left hand** 左折 *sasetsu* **left turn** 左翼 *sayoku* **left wing** 左方 *sahō* **left side** 右 (62)

64	4s	CENTER, INSIDE
中	丶 冂 口 中	

CHŪ naka	中 *naka* **center, inside** 中身 *nakami* **contents** 中東 *chūtō* **Middle East** 中世 *chūsei* **Middle Age** 中国 *chūgoku* **China**

65	4s	DIRECTION, PERSON, WAY OF
方	丶 亠 方 方	

HŌ kata	方 *hō* **direction** 方法 *hōhō* **way** 方面 *hōmen* **direction** 話し方 *hanashikata* **way of talking** 方 *kata* **person (formal)** 万 (13)

66	4s	ORIGIN

元　一　二　テ　元

GEN moto	元は *moto wa* **originally** 地元 *jimoto* **place of birth** 元気 *genki* **healthy, vigorous** 元価 *genka* **cost price** 紀元 *kigen* **Anno Domini**

67	6s	SPIRIT, GAS

気　ノ　ハ　上　气　気　気

KI	元気 *genki* **healthy, vigorous** 勇気 *yūki* **courage** 天気 *tenki* **weather** 気温 *kion* **atmospheric temperature** 気体 *kitai* **gas, steam**

68	4s	LETTER, WRITING

文　丶　亠　ナ　文

BUN MO	文学 *bungaku* **literature** 文章 *bunshō* **sentence** 作文 *sakubun* **composition** 文法 *bunpō* **grammar** 文字 *moji* **letter, character**　　　父 (36)

69	5s	TO GO OUT, TO TAKE OUT

出　丨　屮　中　出　出

SHUTSU de(ru) da(su)	出る *deru* **go out** 出口 *deguchi* **exit** 出す *dasu* **take out, give** 輸出 *yushutsu* **export** 出発 *shuppatsu* **departure**　　　山 (42)

70	2s	TO GO IN, TO PUT IN

入　ノ　入

NYŪ hai(ru) i(reru)	入る *hairu* **go in** 入れる *ireru* **put in** 入口 *iriguchi* **entrance** 輸入 *yunyū* **import** 入学 *nyūgaku* **enter a school**　　　人 (15)

71	5s	WHITE
白	ノ イ 白 白 白	

HAKU shiro(i)	白い *shiroi* **white** 白黒 *shirokuro* **black and white** 白紙 *hakushi* **white sheet of paper** 自白 *jihaku* **confession** 空白 *kūhaku* **void** 百 (11)、日 (16)

72	7s	RED
赤	一 十 土 亍 赤 赤 赤	

SEKI aka(i)	赤い *akai* **red** 赤字 *akaji* **red figures** 赤ん坊 *akanbō* **baby** 赤道 *sekidō* **equator** 赤十字 *sekijūji* **Red Cross**

73	8s	BLUE, GREEN
青	一 十 キ 主 青 青 青 青	

SEI ao(i)	青い *aoi* **blue** 青空 *aozora* **blue sky** 青信号 *aoshingō* **green light on** 青年 *seinen* **young person** 青春 *seishun* **youth**

74	5s	BASIS, BOOK
本	一 十 才 木 本	

HON	本 *hon* **book** 絵本 *ehon* **picture book** 基本 *kihon* **basis** 本当 *hontō* **true** 日本 *nihon (nippon)* **Japan** 木 (20)、体 (125)

75	8s	SHOP
店	` 亠 广 广 庄 庄 店 店	

TEN mise	店 *mise* **shop** 店員 *ten'in* **shop assistant** 書店 *shoten* **bookshop** 支店 *shiten* **branch** 喫茶店 *kissaten* **coffee shop**

76	8s	TO LEARN, SCHOOL

学　　丶　丶丶　ソ　ツ　ツ　学　学　学

GAKU mana(bu)	学ぶ *manabu* **learn** 学校 *gakkō* **school** 大学 *daigaku* **university** 学生 *gakusei* **student** 医学 *igaku* **medicine**　　　字 (156)、子 (35)

77	10s	SCHOOL

校　一　十　才　木　木'　杧　杧　柊　柊　校

KŌ	学校 *gakkō* **school** 中学校 *chūgakkō* **secondary school** 校長 *kōchō* **school principal** 登校 *tōkō* **go to school** 校舎 *kōsha* **school building**

78	6s	AHEAD, BEFORE

先　ノ　ᅳ　牛　生　先　先

SEN saki	先 *saki* **ahead, tip** 指先 *yubisaki* **finger tip** 先生 *sensei* **teacher** 先月 *sengetsu* **last month** 先行 *senkō* **go ahead of**　　　生 (79)

79	5s	LIFE, TO BE BORN, STUDENT

生　ノ　ᅳ　牛　牛　生

SEI i(kiru) u(mareru) nama	生 *nama* **raw** 生まれる *umareru* **to be born** 生きる *ikiru* **to live** 学生 *gakusei* **student** 人生 *jinsei* **life**　　　先 (78)

80	6s	TO MEET, SOCIETY

会　ノ　入　八　会　会　会

KAI a(u)	会う *au* **meet** 出会い *deai* **meeting** 会社 *kaisha* **company** 会話 *kaiwa* **conversation** 会員 *kaiin* **member**　　　今 (57)

81	7s	COMPANY, SOCIETY

社　` ﾗ ｨ ﾈ ﾈ 礻 社 社

SHA
JA

会社 *kaisha* **company**
社会 *shakai* **society**
社長 *shachō* **president of a company**
出版社 *shuppansha* **publishing company**
神社 *jinja* **Shinto shrine**

82	7s	I, PRIVATE

私　´ ⼆ 千 禾 禾 私 私

SHI
watashi

私 *watashi* **I**
私立 *shiritsu* **private**
公私 *kōshi* **public and private**
私学 *shigaku* **private school**
私語 *shigo* **whisper**

秋 (88)

83	10s	HIGH, EXPENSIVE

高　' ⼀ ⼆ 古 古 户 高 高 高 高

KŌ
taka(i)

高い *takai* **high, expensive**
高校 *kōkō* **high school**
高速 *kōsoku* **high speed**
最高 *saikō* **the highest**
高価 *kōka* **expensive**

84	6s	CHEAP, SAFE

安　' ⼚ ⼧ 宁 安 安

AN
yasu(i)

安い *yasui* **cheap**
安全 *anzen* **safety**
安定 *antei* **stability**
安心 *anshin* **feel easy**
安易 *an'i* **easy, simple**

女 (34)

85	4s	FAT, THICK

太　⼀ ナ 大 太

TAI
futo(i)
futo(ru)

太い *futoi* **fat, thick**
太る *futoru* **put on weight**
太字 *futoji* **bold type**
太陽 *taiyō* **the sun (star)**
太平洋 *taiheiyō* **Pacific Ocean**

大 (49)

86	9s	SPRING

春 　一 二 三 丰 夫 未 春 春 春

SHUN
haru

春 *haru* **spring**
春風 *harukaze* **spring wind**
青春 *seishun* **youth**
春分 *shunbun* **vernal equinox**
売春 *baishun* **prostitution**

87	10s	SUMMER

夏 　一 一 厂 亣 百 百 百 頁 夏 夏

KA
natsu

夏 *natsu* **summer**
夏休み *natsuyasumi* **summer holidays**
真夏 *manatsu* **midsummer**
夏季 *kaki* **summer**
初夏 *shoka* **early summer**

88	9s	FALL

秋 　ノ 二 千 手 禾 禾 禾ノ 秒 秋

SHŪ
aki

秋 *aki* **fall**
秋風 *akikaze* **autumnal wind**
秋分 *shūbun* **autumnal equinox**
今秋 *konshū* **this fall**
晩秋 *banshū* **late fall**

私 (82)

89	5s	WINTER

冬 　ノ ク タ 冬 冬

TŌ
fuyu

冬 *fuyu* **winter**
冬休み *fuyuyasumi* **winter holidays**
真冬 *mafuyu* **midwinter**
初冬 *shotō* **early winter**
冬眠 *tōmin* **hibernation**

終 (122)

90	5s	HALF

半 　丶 丶ノ 丷 丷一 半

HAN
naka(ba)

半ば *nakaba* **half**
半分 *hanbun* **half**
半径 *hankei* **radius (of a circle)**
前半 *zenhan* **first half**
半島 *hantō* **peninsula**

91	12s	INTERVAL, BETWEEN

間 　丨 冂 冂 戸 戸 門 門 門 間 日 v.16

KAN aida, ma	間 *aida* **between, interval** 間に合う *maniau* **be in time** 仲間 *nakama* **companion** 時間 *jikan* **time** 空間 *kūkan* **space** 　　　　聞 (128)、開 (119)

92	12s	ROAD

道 　丶 丷 丷 䒑 首 首 道 道 目 v.24

DŌ michi	道 *michi* **way, road** 道路 *dōro* **road** 鉄道 *tetsudō* **railway** 武道 *budō* **martial arts** 書道 *shodō* **calligraphy**

93	7s	CAR, CART

車 　一 厂 厈 戸 百 亘 車

SHA kuruma	車 *kuruma* **car, cart** 車椅子 *kurumaisu* **wheelchair** 自動車 *jidōsha* **car** 電車 *densha* **train** 風車 *fūsha* **windmill**

94	6s	ONESELF

自 　丿 亻 冂 白 自 自

JI SHI mizuka(ra)	自ら *mizukara* **oneself** 自分 *jibun* **oneself** 自転車 *jitensha* **bicycle** 自由 *jiyū* **freedom** 自然 *shizen* **nature** 　　　目 (24)、日 (16)

95	11s	TO MOVE

動 　丿 二 千 舌 舌 舌 重 重 重 動

DŌ ugo(ku)	動く *ugoku* **move** 動物 *dōbutsu* **animal** 運動 *undō* **exercise** 活動 *katsudō* **activity** 感動 *kandō* **emotion** 　　　重 (113)

96	7s	NEAR, RECENT

近 ノ ナ 广 斤 斤 近 近

KIN chika(i)	近い *chikai* **near** 近頃 *chikagoro* **lately** 近道 *chikamichi* **shortcut** 近所 *kinjo* **neighborhood** 近眼 *kingan* **short-sightedness**

97	13s	FAR

遠 一 土 キ 吉 吉 吉 声 专 袁 遠

EN too(i)	遠い *tooi* **far** 遠足 *ensoku* **excursion** 永遠 *eien* **eternity** 遠景 *enkei* **distant view** 遠視 *enshi* **long-sightedness**

98	12s	HOT

暑 丶 冂 冂 日 旦 早 星 昇 暑 日 v.16

SHO atsu(i)	暑い *atsui* **hot** 蒸し暑い *mushiatsui* **sultry** 残暑 *zansho* **lingering summer heat** 暑気 *shoki* **hot weather** 暑中 *shochū* **midsummer** 者 (142)

99	12s	COLD

寒 宀 宀 宀 审 宯 宯 寒 寒 宀 v.84

KAN samu(i)	寒い *samui* **cold** 寒空 *samuzora* **cold weather** 寒帯 *kantai* **cold front** 寒気 *kanki* **cold weather** 寒波 *kanpa* **cold wave** 家 (160)

100	6s	TO GO, TO HOLD

行 丶 彳 彳 彳 行 行

KŌ GYŌ i(ku) okona(u)	行く *iku* **go** 行う *okonau* **hold, celebrate** 旅行 *ryokō* **trip** 歩行 *hokō* **walk** 行列 *gyōretsu* **parade**

101	7s	TO COME

来　一　﹁　冖　亚　平　来　来

RAI ku(ru)	来る *kuru* **come** 来年 *rainen* **next year** 到来 *tōrai* **come, arrive** 由来 *yurai* **origin** 将来 *shōrai* **future**

102	6s	NAME

名　ノ　ク　タ　タ　名　名

MEI na	名前 *namae* **name** 仮名 *kana* **kana (Japanese syllabaries)** 有名 *yūmei* **famous** 指名 *shimei* **nomination** 名刺 *meishi* **business card**　　　多 (51)

103	4s	FRIEND

友　一　ナ　方　友

YŪ tomo	友達 *tomodachi* **friend** 友人 *yūjin* **friend** 親友 *shinyū* **close friend** 友情 *yūjō* **friendship** 友軍 *yūgun* **allied army**

104	13s	NEW

新　亠　亠　宀　立　立　辛　辛　亲　新　斤 v.96

SHIN atara(shii)	新しい *atarashii* **new** 新聞 *shinbun* **newspaper** 最新 *saishin* **the newest** 新鮮 *shinsen* **cool** 革新 *kakushin* **reformation**

105	5s	OLD, ANCIENT

古　一　十　十　古　古

KO furu(i)	古い *furui* **old** 古本 *furuhon* **second hand book** 古風 *kofū* **old-fashioned** 古代 *kodai* **ancient times** 中古 *chūko* **second hand**

106	11s	STRONG

強　コ コ 弓 弓 弓 弓 弓 弓 弓 強 強 強

KYŌ tsuyo(i)	強い *tsuyoi* **strong** 力強い *chikarazuyoi* **strong, powerful** 勉強 *benkyō* **study** 強国 *kyōkoku* **strong nation** 最強 *saikyō* **the strongest**

107	10s	WEAK

弱　コ コ 弓 弓 弓 弓 弓 弱 弱 弱

JAKU yowa(i)	弱い *yowai* **weak** 弱火 *yowabi* **low flame** 弱点 *jakuten* **weak point** 病弱 *byōjaku* **sickly** 衰弱 *suijaku* **grow weak**

108	2s	POWER

力　フ 力

RYOKU chikara	力 *chikara* **power** 体力 *tairyoku* **physical strength** 能力 *nōryoku* **capacity** 暴力 *bōryoku* **violence** 圧力 *atsuryoku* **pressure**

109	5s	TO STAND UP, TO ESTABLISH

立　丶 一 十 六 立

RITSU ta(tsu)	立つ *tatsu* **stand up** 目立つ *medatsu* **be striking, stand out** 独立 *dokuritsu* **independence** 市立 *shiritsu* **municipal** 立派 *rippa* **excellent, extraordinary**

110	8s	YOUNG

若　一 十 艹 艹 芋 芊 若 若

JAKU waka(i)	若い *wakai* **young** 若者 *wakamono* **young, youth** 若夫婦 *wakafūfu* **young couple** 若年 *jakunen* **youth** 若輩 *jakuhai* **the young**　　石 (45)、右 (62)

111	5s	WIDE

広 ` 亠 广 広 広

KŌ
hiro(i)

広い *hiroi* **wide**
背広 *sebiro* **suit**
広大 *kōdai* **wide, huge**
広域 *kōiki* **wide territory**
広告 *kōkoku* **advertisement**

112	11s	BAD

悪 一 厂 戸 币 币 币 亜 亜 悪 悪

AKU
waru(i)

悪い *warui* **bad**
悪口 *waruguchi* **speak ill of someone**
最悪 *saiaku* **the worst**
悪質 *akushitsu* **bad, mean**
悪魔 *akuma* **devil**

113	9s	HEAVY, TO DOUBLE

重 ノ 一 亠 斤 台 旨 faire 重 重

JŪ
CHŌ
omo(i)

重い *omoi* **heavy**
重量 *jūryō* **weight**
貴重 *kichō* **valuable, precious**
重要 *jūyō* **important**
重傷 *jūshō* **serious injury** 動 (95)

114	6s	EARLY, FAST

早 丶 冂 冂 日 旦 早

SŌ
haya(i)

早い *hayai* **early**
早起き *hayaoki* **wake up early**
早口 *hayakuchi* **tongue twister**
早朝 *sōchō* **early in the morning**
早産 *sōzan* **premature birth**

115	9s	TO HOLD, TO OWN

持 一 十 扌 扩 扩 拌 挂 持 持

JI
mo(tsu)

持つ *motsu* **hold, own**
金持ち *kanemochi* **rich**
気持ち *kimochi* **feeling**
支持 *shiji* **support**
所持 *shoji* **own** 待 (116)、時 (59)

116	9s	TO WAIT

待　ノ　ク　イ　彳　彳　彳　彳　待　待

TAI ma(tsu)	待つ *matsu* **wait** 信号待ち *shingōmachi* **wait at the traffic light** 接待 *settai* **reception, welcome** 招待 *shōtai* **invitation** 期待 *kitai* **hope, expectation**　　持 (115)、時 (59)

117	12s	TO BUY

買　丶　冂　冂　罒　罒　冒　買　買　目 v.24

BAI ka(u)	買う *kau* **buy** 買物 *kaimono* **shopping** 買い手 *kaite* **client** 売買 *baibai* **business** 購買 *kōbai* **purchase**　　見 (131)

118	7s	TO SELL

売　一　十　士　士　声　声　売

BAI u(ru)	売る *uru* **sell** 売店 *baiten* **stall** 商売 *shōbai* **business** 販売 *hanbai* **sale** 売春 *baishun* **prostitution**　　読 (130)

119	12s	TO OPEN, DEVELOP

開　門　門　門　開　開　　　　門 v.91

KAI hira(ku) a(keru)	開ける *akeru* **open** 開く *hiraku* **open, develop** 開発 *kaihatsu* **develop** 開会 *kaikai* **open a meeting** 展開 *tenkai* **development**　　間 (91)、閉 (120)

120	11s	TO CLOSE

閉　門　門　閉　閉　　　　　門 v.91

HEI shi(meru) to(jiru)	閉める *shimeru* **close** 閉じる *tojiru* **close, finish** 閉店 *heiten* **close up shop** 閉鎖 *heisa* **closing** 閉会 *heikai* **end a meeting**　　間 (91)、開 (119)

121	8s	TO START

始 く 女 女 女 女 女 始 始

SHI
haji(meru)

始める *hajimeru* **start**
始終 *shijū* **from the beginning to the end**
始業式 *shigyōshiki* **opening ceremony**
開始 *kaishi* **start**
始動 *shidō* **start (a motor)**

妹 (41)、姉 (40)

122	11s	TO FINISH

終 く 幺 幺 糸 糸 糸 糸 紋 終 終

SHŪ
owa(ru)

終わる *owaru* **finish**
終始 *shūshi* **from beginning to end**
終了 *shūryō* **finish**
終点 *shūten* **terminus**
終結 *shūketsu* **conclusion**

冬 (89)

123	10s	TO RETURN

帰 ｜ リ リ 「 ｢ヨ ｢ヨ ｢尸 尸 帰 帰

KI
kae(ru)

帰る *kaeru* **return**
帰り道 *kaerimichi* **the way back**
帰国 *kikoku* **return to one's country**
帰宅 *kitaku* **go back home**
帰路 *kiro* **the way back**

124	6s	TO REST

休 ノ イ 仁 什 付 休

KYŪ
yasu(mu)

休む *yasumu* **rest**
夏休み *natsuyasumi* **summer holidays**
休憩 *kyūkei* **a break**
休講 *kyūkō* **cancelled class**
休日 *kyūjitsu* **holiday**

体 (125)、木 (20)

125	7s	BODY

体 ノ イ 仁 什 付 休 体

TAI
karada

体 *karada* **body**
肉体 *nikutai* **body, flesh**
体操 *taisō* **gymnastics**
固体 *kotai* **solid**
体験 *taiken* **experience**

休 (124)、本 (74)

126	7s	TO SAY

言 丶 亠 亖 言 言 言 言

GEN
GON
i(u)
koto

言う *iu* **say**
言葉 *kotoba* **word**
発言 *hatsugen* **speak, utter**
方言 *hōgen* **dialect**
無言 *mugon* **silence**

話 (127)、読 (130)

127	13s	TO TALK

話 言 訁 訐 訐 話 話 言 v.126

WA
hana(su)
hanashi

話す *hanasu* **talk**
話 *hanashi* **conversation, topic**
会話 *kaiwa* **conversation**
電話 *denwa* **telephone**
話題 *wadai* **topic**

言 (126)、読 (130)

128	14s	TO HEAR

聞 門 門 門 門 門 聞 聞 門 v.91

BUN
ki(ku)

聞く *kiku* **hear**
聞き取り *kikitori* **hearing**
見聞 *kenbun* **experience, observation**
伝聞 *denbun* **hearsay**
新聞 *shinbun* **newspaper**

間 (91)、開 (119)

129	10s	TO WRITE

書 フ コ ヨ ヨ 聿 聿 書 書 書 書

SHO
ka(ku)

書く *kaku* **write**
葉書 *hagaki* **postcard**
書道 *shodō* **calligraphy**
書類 *shorui* **document**
辞書 *jisho* **dictionary**

130	14s	TO READ

読 言 言 訁 訐 誜 誜 読 読 言 v.126

DOKU
yo(mu)

読む *yomu* **read**
音読み *on'yomi* **on'yomi reading**
訓読み *kun'yomi* **kun'yomi reading**
読者 *dokusha* **reader**
読書 *dokusho* **read a book**

売 (118)、話 (127)

131	7s	TO SEE

見　| 一 冂 冂 月 目 貝 見

KEN mi(ru)	見る *miru* **see, look** 見本 *mihon* **sample** 花見 *hanami* **cherry blossom viewing** 意見 *iken* **opinion** 発見 *hakken* **discover**	目 (24)、買 (117)

132	9s	TO THINK

思　| 丨 冂 冂 用 田 甲 思 思 思

SHI omo(u)	思う *omou* **think** 思い出す *omoidasu* **remember** 思考 *shikō* **thought** 意思 *ishi* **will** 思案 *shian* **consider, ponder**	田 (44)、男 (33)

133	7s	TO MAKE

作　| ノ 亻 亻 仁 作 作 作

SAKU SA tsuku(ru)	作る *tsukuru* **make** 製作 *seisaku* **manufacture, produce** 作品 *sakuhin* **work (literary, pictorial)** 作戦 *sakusen* **strategy** 作業 *sagyō* **work, operations**	使 (136)

134	11s	TO TEACH, RELIGION

教　| 一十 土 尹 耂 考 孝 孝 孝 教 教

KYŌ oshi(eru)	教える *oshieru* **teach** 教育 *kyōiku* **education** 教室 *kyōshitsu* **classroom** 宗教 *shūkyō* **religion** 仏教 *bukkyō* **Buddhism**

135	11s	TO LEARN, HABIT

習　| 一ヲ 刁 习 刁 羽 羽 羽 習 習 習

SHŪ nara(u)	習う *narau* **learn** 学習 *gakushū* **learning** 実習 *jisshū* **practice** 習慣 *shūkan* **habit** 悪習 *akushū* **vice, bad habit**

136	8s	TO USE, TO SEND

ノ イ 仁 仁 仨 伫 伊 使

SHI
tsuka(u)

使う *tsukau* **use**
使用 *shiyō* **use, employment**
行使 *kōshi* **use, employ**
天使 *tenshi* **angel**
使者 *shisha* **messenger**

作 (133)、仕 (140)

137	8s	TO KNOW

ノ ト ヒ 午 矢 矢 知 知

CHI
shi(ru)

知る *shiru* **know**
知識 *chishiki* **knowledge**
知恵 *chie* **wisdom**
知能 *chinō* **intelligence**
知人 *chijin* **acquaintance, friend**

138	8s	RAIN

一 厂 冂 币 雨 雨 雨 雨

U
ame
ama

雨 *ame* **rain**
大雨 *ooame* **heavy rain**
雨水 *amamizu* **rainwater**
雨雲 *amagumo* **rain cloud**
雨量 *uryō* **rainfall**

電 (158)

139	10s	ILLNESS

丶 亠 广 广 疒 疒 疒 病 病 病

BYŌ
yamai

病 *yamai* **illness**
病気 *byōki* **illness**
病人 *byōnin* **patient**
病院 *byōin* **hospital**
難病 *nanbyō* **incurable disease**

140	5s	TO SERVE, TO DO

ノ イ 仁 什 仕

SHI

仕事 *shigoto* **job**
仕上げ *shiage* **finishing touches**
仕方 *shikata* **way of doing**

使 (136)

141	8s	MATTER, THING (ABSTRACT)
事		一 一 一 写 写 写 事

JI koto	事 *koto* **thing (abstract)** 仕事 *shigoto* **job** 記事 *kiji* **article** 事件 *jiken* **incident** 用事 *yōji* **things to do**

142	8s	PERSON
者		一 十 土 耂 耂 者 者 者

SHA mono	若者 *wakamono* **young person** 怠け者 *namakemono* **idle person** 学者 *gakusha* **scholar** 医者 *isha* **doctor** 芸者 *geisha* **geisha** 暑 (98)

143	6s	EARTH, PLACE
地		一 十 土 圠 坳 地

CHI JI	地図 *chizu* **map** 地理 *chiri* **geography** 地球 *chikyū* **the Earth** 地面 *jimen* **surface** 地震 *jishin* **earthquake**

144	8s	PLACE, SPOT
所		一 三 三 戸 戸 所 所 所

SHO JO tokoro	所 *tokoro* **place, spot** 台所 *daidokoro* **kitchen** 場所 *basho* **place** 住所 *jūsho* **address** 便所 *benjo* **toilet**

145	5s	OUTSIDE
外		ノ ク タ 列 外

GAI GE soto	外 *soto* **outside** 外人 *gaijin* **foreigner** 案外 *angai* **unexpected** 外出 *gaishutsu* **go out** 外科 *geka* **surgery** 名 (102)、多 (51)

146	6s	TO LIKE
好		く 女 女 女 好 好

KŌ su(ki)	好き *suki* **like** 好況 *kōkyō* **prosperity** 好都合 *kōtsugō* **favorable** 好意 *kōi* **kindness** 好物 *kōbutsu* **favorite dish** <div align="right">姉 (40)、始 (121)</div>

147	9s	STRANGE, TO CHANGE
変		` 亠 广 方 亦 亦 亦 変 変

HEN ka(waru)	変わる *kawaru* **change** 変 *hen* **weird, strange** 変化 *henka* **change, transformation** 大変 *taihen* **tough, difficult** 変態 *hentai* **abnormal, pervert**

148	12s	TO WEAR, TO ARRIVE
着		` ` 丷 丷 羊 羊 羊 着 目 v.24

CHAKU ki(ru) tsu(ku)	着る *kiru* **wear** 着く *tsuku* **arrive** 着物 *kimono* **kimono** 到着 *tōchaku* **arrival** 着席 *chakuseki* **sit**

149	8s	THING
物		ノ ト 牛 牛 牛 牜 物 物

BUTSU MOTSU mono	物 *mono* **thing (physical)** 物語 *monogatari* **story, tale** 建物 *tatemono* **building** 植物 *shokubutsu* **plant** 荷物 *nimotsu* **luggage**

150	9s	TO EAT
食		ノ 入 入 今 今 今 食 食 食

SHOKU ta(beru)	食べる *taberu* **eat** 食べ物 *tabemono* **food** 食堂 *shokudō* **dining room, restaurant** 食事 *shokuji* **meal** 和食 *washoku* **Japanese food** <div align="right">飲 (151)</div>

151	12s	TO DRINK
飲	丿 𠆢 今 今 今 𩙿 𩙿 𩙿 飣 飲	

IN
no(mu)

飲む *nomu* **drink**
飲み物 *nomimono* **a drink**
飲酒 *inshu* **drink alcohol**
飲料 *inryō* **a drink**
飲食 *inshoku* **eat and drink**

食 (150)

152	8s	COUNTRY
国	丨 冂 冂 尸 用 国 国 国	

KOKU
kuni

国 *kuni* **country**
雪国 *yukiguni* **snow country, Hokkaido**
国民 *kokumin* **citizens**
国際 *kokusai* **international**
外国 *gaikoku* **foreign country**

153	14s	LANGUAGE, WORD, TO TELL
語	言 言 訂 語 語 語 語 語 言	v.126

GO
kata(ru)

語る *kataru* **tell**
物語 *monogatari* **story, tale**
日本語 *nihongo* **Japanese language**
英語 *eigo* **English language**
単語 *tango* **word**

話 (127)、読 (130)

154	8s	SKY, VOID, AIR
空	` 宀 宀 穴 空 空 空	

KŪ
sora
kara
a(ku)

空 *sora* **sky**
空手 *karate* **karate**
空き缶 *akikan* **empty can**
空気 *kūki* **atmosphere**
空港 *kūkō* **airport**

155	7s	FLOWER
花	一 十 艹 艻 花 花	

KA
hana

花 *hana* **flower**
花火 *hanabi* **fireworks**
生け花 *ikebana* **floral arrangement**
開花 *kaika* **bloom**
花弁 *kaben* **petal**

156	6s	CHARACTER

字　　　丶　丷　宀　宀　宁　字

JI

字 *ji* **character, letter**
文字 *moji* **character, letter**
漢字 *kanji* **kanji**
数字 *sūji* **number**
太字 *futoji* **bold type**

学 (76)、子 (35)

157	13s	MERRY, PLEASANT, MUSIC

楽　　　丶　丨　白　白　白　泊　泊　泪　楽

GAKU RAKU tano(shii)

楽しい *tanoshii* **pleasant**
音楽 *ongaku* **music**
楽器 *gakki* **musical instrument**
楽 *raku* **easy, simple**
極楽 *gokuraku* **paradise**

158	13s	ELECTRICITY

電　　雨　雨　雨　雨　雪　電　　雨 v.138

DEN

電気 *denki* **electricity**
電話 *denwa* **telephone**
電車 *densha* **train**
電子 *denshi* **electron**
電球 *denkyū* **light bulb**

雨 (138)

159	8s	CLEAR, BRIGHT

明　　丨　冂　日　日　旫　明　明　明

MEI aka(rui)

明るい *akarui* **clear**
説明 *setsumei* **explain**
不明 *fumei* **unknown**
文明 *bunmei* **civilization**
透明 *tōmei* **transparent**

日 (16)、月 (17)

160	10s	HOUSE

家　　丶　丷　宀　宀　宁　宇　家　家　家　家

KA ie

家 *ie* **house**
家族 *kazoku* **family**
家事 *kaji* **house duties**
画家 *gaka* **artist**
漫画家 *mangaka* **comic artist**

字 (156)

Vocabulary of the 30 lessons

A

abunai (iAdj.) L13	危ない	あぶない	dangerous
ageru (V) L16,19,28	あげる	あげる	to give
ago (N) L26	あご	あご	chin
ahō (N) L23	阿呆	あほう	fool, silly
aho-na (nAdj.) L1	アホな	あほな	stupid
ai (N) L16	愛	あい	love
aite (N) L13	相手	あいて	opponent, rival
aitsu (PN) L21	あいつ	あいつ	that guy
akai (iAdj.) L13	赤い	あかい	red
akarui (iAdj.) L13	明るい	あかるい	clear
akemashite omedetō (Ph) L27	明けましておめでとう	あけましておめでとう	Happy New Year
aki (N) L4	秋	あき	autumn
amaru (V) L13	余る	あまる	to be left
ame (N) L10	雨	あめ	rain
anata (PN) L4	あなた	あなた	you
anatagata (PN) L7	あなた方	あなたがた	you (plural)
anatatachi (PN) L7	あなた達	あなたたち	you (plural)
ane (N) L21	姉	あね	elder sister
ani (N) L21	兄	あに	elder brother
anime (N) L9	アニメ	あにめ	anime
anna (PN) L7	あんな	あんな	that kind of
ano (PN) L3	あの	あの	that
anta (PN) L7	あんた	あんた	you (inf.)
antara (PN) L7	あんたら	あんたら	you (plural, inf.)
antatachi (PN) L7	あんた達	あんたたち	you (plural, inf.)
anzen-na (naAdj.) L14	安全な	あんぜんな	safe
aoi (iAdj.) L13	青い	あおい	blue
apaato (N) L25	アパート	あぱーと	appartment
arashi (N) L10	嵐	あらし	storm
arau (V) L30	洗う	あらう	to wash
arigatō (Ph) L1,27	ありがとう	ありがとう	thank you
aru (V) L5, 16,18	ある	ある	there is/are, to be (things)
arubaito (N) L2	アルバイト	あるばいと	part-time job
arukōru (N) L8	アルコール	あるこーる	alcohol
asa (N) L11	朝	あさ	morning
ase (N) L26	汗	あせ	sweat
ashi (N) L25,26	足	あし	leg, foot
ashimoto (N) L26	足元	あしもと	foot
ashita (Adv.) L11,17,22	明日	あした	tomorrow
asobu (V) L17, 19, 20	遊ぶ	あそぶ	to play, to enjoy oneself
asoko (PN) L9	あそこ	あそこ	there
asshi (PN) L7	あっし	あっし	I (older men)
atakushi (PN) L7	あたくし	あたくし	I (fem. formal)
atama (N) L7,26	頭	あたま	head
atarashii (iAdj.) L3,13, 22	新しい	あたらしい	new
atashi (PN) L7	あたし	あたし	I (fem.)
atashira (PN) L7	あたしら	あたしら	we (fem.)
atashitachi (PN) L7	あたし達	あたしたち	we (fem.)
atatakai (iAdj.) L10	暖かい	あたたかい	warm
atsui (iAdj.) L10	暑い	あつい	hot (weather)
atsui (iAdj.) L22	熱い	あつい	hot (a thing)

B

baka (N) L9,L23	馬鹿	ばか	fool, stupid
baka ni suru (Ph) L23	馬鹿にする	ばかにする	to make a fool of
baka o iu (Ph) L23	馬鹿を言う	ばかをいう	to say nonsense

bakabakashii (iAdj.) L23	馬鹿馬鹿しい	ばかばかしい	absurd, ludicrous
bakamono (N) L23	馬鹿者	ばかもの	fool, stupid
bakari (Adv.) L9	ばかり	ばかり	only
bakayarō (N) L23	馬鹿野郎	ばかやろう	fool, idiot
bakemono (N) L23	化け物	ばけもの	monster
banana (N) L11	バナナ	ばなな	banana
bara (N) L18	バラ	ばら	rose
bareebōru (N) L8	バレーボール	ばれーぼーる	volleyball
basu (N) L16	バス	ばす	bus
beddo (N) L8	ベッド	べっど	bed
benkyō (sV) L16,22,24	勉強	べんきょう	to study
benri-na (naAdj.) L22,28	便利な	べんりな	convenient
bideo (N) L16	ビデオ	びでお	video
biiru (N) L19	ビール	びーる	beer
bijin (N) L13	美人	びじん	beautiful woman
bikkuri (sV) L29	びっくり	びっくり	to surprise
binbō-na (naAdj.) L22	貧乏な	びんぼうな	poor
bisshori (Adv.) L29	びっしょり	びっしょり	to be soaked
boku (PN) L7	僕	ぼく	I (masc.)
bokura (PN) L7	僕ら	ぼくら	we (masc.)
bokutachi (PN) L7	僕達	ぼくたち	we (masc.)
bōru (N) L8	ボール	ぼーる	ball
bōrupen (N) L9	ボールペン	ぼーるぺん	ballpoint pen
buchō (N) L15	部長	ぶちょう	head of a department
bunbōgu-ya (N) L15	文房具屋	ぶんぼうぐや	stationery shop
bunpō (N) L9	文法	ぶんぽう	grammar
burōdouee (T) L8	ブロードウエー	ぶろーどうえー	Broadway
busu (N) L23	ブス	ぶす	ugly, plain
buubuu (Adv.) L29	ぶうぶう	ぶうぶう	pig's grunting
byōin (N) L11	病院	びょういん	hospital

C

-chan (Ph) L15	ちゃん	ちゃん	suffix for children
chesu (N) L8	チェス	ちぇす	chess
chi (N) L11	血	ち	blood
chichi (N) L9, 21	父	ちち	father
chichioya (N) L21	父親	ちちおや	father
chigau (V) L7	違う	ちがう	to be wrong
chiisai (iAdj.) L13	小さい	ちいさい	small
chikara (N) L22	力	ちから	strength, power
chikushō (Ph) L23	畜生	ちくしょう	damn
chittomo (Adv.) L14	ちっとも	ちっとも	nothing, no one
chō (N) L26	腸	ちょう	intestines
chotto (Adv.) L22	ちょっと	ちょっと	a little, a bit
chūgoku (T) L17	中国	ちゅうごく	China

D

-dai (C) L11,25	台	だい	counter for machines
daigaku (N) L4	大学	だいがく	university
daijōbu-na (naAdj.) L14	大丈夫な	だいじょうぶな	to be well, to be safe
daikirai-na (naAdj.) L14	大嫌いな	だいきらいな	to hate
daiku (N) L14	大工	だいく	carpenter
dainō (N) L26	大脳	だいのう	brain
daiō (N) L3	大王	だいおう	great king
daisuki-na (naAdj.) L25	大好きな	だいすきな	to be very fond of
dake (Adv.) L1, 22	だけ	だけ	only
daku (V) L22,24	抱く	だく	hug
dare (IP) L7	誰	だれ	who?
de gozaimasu (V) L15	でございます	でございます	to be (formal)
deeto (N) L29	デート	でーと	date

dekiru (V) L10, 20	出来る	できる	to be able to/ to know
denki-ya (N) L15	電気屋	でんきや	electric appliance store
densha (N) L16	電車	でんしゃ	train
desu (V) L3,9	です	です	to be
dō itashimashite (Ph) L2,27	どういたしまして	どういたしまして	you're welcome
doji (N) L23	ドジ	どじ	stupid, blunder
dokidoki (Adv.) L29	どきどき	どきどき	to be nervous
doko (IP) L9	どこ	どこ	where?
doku (V) L23	退く	どく	to move aside
dōmyaku (N) L26	動脈	どうみゃく	artery
donna (IP) L9	どんな	どんな	what kind of?
donna ni (IP) L22	どんなに	どんなに	how?
doraibaa (N) L8	ドライバー	どらいばー	screwdriver
dore (IP) L9	どれ	どれ	which?
dōshita (IP) L10, 20	どうした	どうした	what's the matter?
doyōbi (N) L6	土曜日	どようび	Saturday
dōzo (Ph) L2	どうぞ	どうぞ	please, go ahead

E

eiga (N) L11,17,28	映画	えいが	film
eigo (N) L20	英語	えいご	English
en (N) L4,17	円	えん	yen (Japanese currency)
enpitsu (N) L11,25	鉛筆	えんぴつ	pencil
etsuraku (N) L11	悦楽	えつらく	pleasure

F

fan (N) L8	ファン	ふぁん	fan
fonto (N) L8	フォント	ふぉんと	font
fude (N) L9,16	筆	ふで	writing brush
fujisan (T) L3	富士山	ふじさん	Mount Fuji
fukuzatsu-na (naAdj.) 22	複雑な	ふくざつな	complicated
furigana (N) L1	振り仮名	ふりがな	furigana
furu (V) L10	降る	ふる	fall (rain, snow…)
furui (iAdj.) L13	古い	ふるい	old
futari (Nu) L25	二人	ふたり	two people
futatsu (Nu) L18,25	二つ	ふたつ	two
fuyu (N) L4	冬	ふゆ	winter

G

gaijin (N) L7,15	外人	がいじん	foreigner
gakkō (N) L2	学校	がっこう	school
gakuchō (N) L15	学長	がくちょう	school dean
gakusei (N) L4, 15	学生	がくせい	student
ganbaru (V) L24	頑張る	がんばる	to persist in, to hold out
ganbatte kudasai (Ph) L24	頑張って下さい	がんばってください	Stick to it! Come on!
garagara (Adv.) L29	がらがら	がらがら	(to open) a sliding door
genki-na (naAdj.) L14	元気な	げんきな	strong, lively
genshi bakudan (N) L12	原子爆弾	がんしばくだん	atomic bomb
geragera (Adv.) L29	げらげら	げらげら	(to laugh) boisterously
gerogero (Adv.) L29	げろげろ	げろげろ	frog's croaking
getsuyōbi (N) L6	月曜日	げつようび	Monday
gion (N) L29	擬音	ぎおん	sound-imitating word
gitaa (N) L11	ギター	ぎたー	guitar
gitaigo (N) L29	擬態語	ぎたいご	state-imitating word
go (N) L3	五	ご	5
gochisō sama (Ph) L27	ごちそう様	ごちそうさま	thank you for the meal
gogatsu (N) L6	五月	ごがつ	May
gohan (N) L11	ご飯	ごはん	rice
goi (N) L4	語彙	ごい	vocabulary
gokurō sama (Ph) L27	ご苦労様	ごくろうさま	good job
gomen kudasai (Ph) L27	ごめんください	ごめんください	is there anybody home?

gomen nasai (Ph) L4,27	ごめんなさい	ごめんなさい	excuse me
gomu (N) L16	ゴム	ごむ	eraser
goshujin (N) L21	ご主人	ごしゅじん	husband
guruguru (Adv.) L29	ぐるぐる	ぐるぐる	(to go) round and round
gutai (N) L22	具体	ぐたい	concrete
gutaiteki ni (Adv.) L22	具体的に	ぐたいてきに	concretely
gutto (Adv.) L29	ぐっと	ぐっと	at once, suddenly
gyūnyū (N) L28	牛乳	ぎゅうにゅう	milk
H			
ha (N) L26	歯	は	tooth
haadodisuku (N) L8	ハードディスク	はーどでぃすく	hard disk
hachi (Nu) L3	八	はち	8
hachigatsu (N) L6	八月	はちがつ	August
hae (N) L18	ハエ	はえ	fly
haha (N) L21	母	はは	mother
hahaoya (N) L21	母親	ははおや	mother
-hai (C) L25	杯	はい	counter for glasses, cups
hai (Ph) L2	はい	はい	yes
hairu (V) L8, 20	入る	はいる	to enter, get in
haizō (N) L26	肺臓	はいぞう	lungs
hajimaru (V) L20	始まる	はじまる	to start
hajimemashite (Ph) L4	はじめまして	はじめまして	pleased to meet you
hajimeru (V) L10	始める	はじめる	to start
hajimete (Adv.) L22	初めて	はじめて	for the first time
hakase (N) L4	博士	はかせ	doctor
haki (sV) L5	破棄	はき	to rescind (a contract)
hamukau (V) L11	歯向かう	はむかう	to lift one's hand
han (Adv.) L12	半	はん	half
hana (N) L14	花	はな	flower
hana (N) L4,26	鼻	はな	nose
hanasu (V) L8	離す	はなす	to separate
hannin (N) L16	犯人	はんにん	criminal
hansamu-na (naAdj.) L1	ハンサムな	はんさむな	handsome
hara ga hetta (Ph) L27	腹が減った	はらがへった	I'm hungry (masc. inf.)
hare (N) L10	晴れ	はれ	clear weather
haru (N) L4	春	はる	spring
hashi (N) L18	はし	はし	chopsticks
hashiru (V) L19	走る	はしる	to run
hassei (sV) L24	発生	はっせい	to occur
hayai (iAdj.) L13,22	速い	はやい	fast
hayai (iAdj.) L17,22	早い	はやい	fast, early
heisei (T) L6	平成	へいせい	Heisei Era (1989-?)
heso (N) L26	へそ	へそ	navel
hetakuso (N) L23	下手糞	へたくそ	clumsy, useless
heta-na (naAdj.) L14	下手な	へたな	clumsy
hi (N) L10	日	ひ	sun
hi (N) L3	火	ひ	fire
hibi (N) L11	日々	ひび	day by day
hidari (N) L4	左	ひだり	left
higai (N) L12	被害	ひがい	damage
higashi (N) L4	東	ひがし	east
hige (N) L26	ひげ	ひげ	beard
hiji (N) L26	ひじ	ひじ	elbow
-hiki (C) L11,25	匹	ひき	counter for animals
hikui (iAdj.) L13,22	低い	ひくい	low
hima-na (naAdj.) L14	暇な	ひまな	spare time
hinto (N) L8	ヒント	ひんと	hint
hiragana (N) L1,2	平仮名	ひらがな	hiragana

Vocabulary 255

hiroshima (T) L10	広島	ひろしま	Hiroshima
hiru (N) L11	昼	ひる	noon
hitai (N) L26	額	ひたい	forehead
hito (N) L3,9	人	ひと	person
hitori (Nu) L25	一人	ひとり	one person / alone
hitosashiyubi (N) L26	人差し指	ひとさしゆび	index finger
hitotsu (Nu) L25	一つ	ひとつ	one
hitsuyō-na (naAdj.) L22	必要な	ひつような	necessary
hiza (N) L26	ひざ	ひざ	knee
hokkaidō (T) l10	北海道	ほっかいどう	Hokkaidō
-hon (C) L11,13,25	本	ほん	counter for flat things
hon (N) L9	本	ほん	book
honshū (T) L10	本州	ほんしゅう	Honshū
hontō (Adv.) L18	本当	ほんとう	truth
hon-ya (N) L15	本屋	ほんや	bookstore
hoo (N) L26	ほお	ほお	cheek
hoshi (N) L10	星	ほし	star
hotto (Adv.) L29	ほっと	ほっと	to feel relieved
hyaku (Nu) L3	百	ひゃく	100
hyō (N) L10	雹	ひょう	hail

I

i (N) L26	胃	い	stomach
ichi (Nu) L3	一	いち	1
ichido ni (Ph) L25	一度に	いちどに	at once, in unison
ichigatsu (N) L6	一月	いちがつ	January
ichiichi (Adv.) L22	一々	いちいち	one by one
ii (iAdj.) L7,13	いい	いい	good, well
iie (Ph) L2	いいえ	いいえ	no
iku (V) L8,16	行く	いく	to go
ikura (IP) L4, 22	幾ら	いくら	how much is it?
ima (Adv.) L8,12, 20, 22	今	いま	now
imōto (N) L21	妹	いもうと	younger sister
imōtosan (N) L21	妹さん	いもうとさん	younger sister
inochi (N) L19	命	いのち	life
inu (N) L9	犬	いぬ	dog
ippai (Adv.) L17	いっぱい	いっぱい	a lot
iraira (Adv.) L29	いらいら	いらいら	to be irritated
irasshai (Ph) L27	いらっしゃい	いらっしゃい	come in
irasshaimase (Ph) L4,27	いらっしゃいませ	いらっしゃいませ	welcome, can I help you?
ireru (V) L8,25	入れる	いれる	to put in
iru (V) L16,18	いる	いる	there is/are, to be
isha (N) L21	医者	いしゃ	doctor
isogu (V) L19, 20	急ぐ	いそぐ	to hurry
isshoni (Adv.) L20	一緒に	いっしょに	together
isu (IP) L9,30	椅子	いす	chair
itadakimasu (Ph) L27	いただきます	いただきます	bon appetit
itai (iAdj.) L26	痛い	いたい	painful
itsu (Adv.) L22	いつ	いつ	when?
itte kimasu (Ph) L27	行ってきます	いってきます	I'm leaving
itte rasshai (Ph) L27	行ってらっしゃい	いってらっしゃい	see you soon
iu (V) L16,19	言う	いう	to say
iyakukin (N) L5	違約金	いやくきん	indemnity
iya-na (naAdj.) L7,14	嫌な	いやな	unpleasant
izaka-ya (N) L15	居酒屋	いざかや	bar, tavern

J

jettokōsutaa (N) L8	ジェットコースター	じぇっとこーすたー	roller coaster
ji (N) L16	字	じ	letter
jinzō (N) L26	腎臓	じんぞう	kidneys

jishin (N) L10	地震	じしん	earthquake
jitensha (N) L11,16	自転車	じてんしゃ	bicycle
jitto (Adv.) L29	じっと	じっと	to stare
-jō (C) L25	畳	じょう	counter for tatami
jōbu-na (naAdj.) L14	丈夫な	じょうぶな	healthy, vigorous
joshi (N) L16	助詞	じょし	particle
jōyō kanji (T) L3	常用漢字	じょうようかんじ	common-use kanji
jōzu-na (naAdj.) L14	上手な	じょうずな	skillful
jū (Nu) L3	十	じゅう	10
jūbun (Adv.) L22	十分	じゅうぶん	enough
jūdan (N) L26	銃弾	じゅうだん	bullet
jūgatsu (N) L6	十月	じゅうがつ	October
jūichigatsu (N) L6	十一月	じゅういちがつ	November
jūnigatsu (N) L6	十二月	じゅうにがつ	December

K

kaapetto (N) L8	カーペット	かーぺっと	carpet
kaban (N) L13	かばん	かばん	brief case
kabin (N) L18	花瓶	かびん	vase
kaeru (V) L16, 19, 20	帰る	かえる	to return
-kai (C) L25	階	かい	counter for building floors
kaijō (N) L24	会場	かいじょう	assembly hall
kakeru (V) L26	欠ける	かける	to come off, to be missing
kakkoii (iAdj.) L13	かっこいい	かっこいい	handsome
kakomu (V) L22	囲む	かこむ	to surround
kaku (V) L16, 19, 20	書く	かく	to write
kame (N) L18	亀	かめ	turtle
kamera (N) L11	カメラ	かめら	camera
kami (N) L11	紙	かみ	paper
kaminoke (N) L26	髪の毛	かみのけ	hair
kamo (G) L28	かも	かも	perhaps
kamo shirenai (G) L16	かもしれない	かもしれない	perhaps
kanai (N) L21	家内	かない	wife
kane (N) L3	金	かね	metal, money
kangeki (sV) L17	感激	かんげき	to impress, to move
kanji (N)L1,3	漢字	かんじ	kanji
kannō (N) L26	間脳	かんのう	diencephalon
kanojo (PN) L7	彼女	かのじょ	she / girlfriend
kanryō (sV) L11	完了	かんりょう	to finish
kantai (N) L5	艦隊	かんたい	fleet
kantan-na (naAdj.) L22	簡単な	かんたんな	easy, simple
kanzō (N) L26	肝臓	かんぞう	liver
kao (N) L7,9,26	顔	かお	face
kappa (N) L2	カッパ	かっぱ	cape, raincoat
kara (G) L20	から	から	from
karada (N) L26	体	からだ	body
karakara (Adv.) L29	からから	からから	to be dry
kare (PN) L7	彼	かれ	he / boyfriend
karee (N) L8	カレー	かれー	curry
karera (PN) L7	彼ら	かれら	they
kari ni (Adv.) L22	仮に	かりに	hypothetically
kasei (T) L3	火星	かせい	Mars
kasu (V) L16,19, 20	貸す	かす	to lend
kasumeru (V) L26	かすめる	かすめる	to graze
kata (N) L26	肩	かた	shoulder
katakana (N) L1,2	片仮名	かたかな	katakana
kau (V) L19, 20	買う	かう	to buy
kawa (N) L3	川	かわ	river
kayōbi (N) L6	火曜日	かようび	Tuesday

kaze (N) L10	風	かぜ	wind
kazoku (N) L10,21	家族	かぞく	family
keirin (N) L6	競輪	けいりん	bicycle race
keirinjō (N) L6	競輪場	けいりんじょう	cycling stadium
keiyaku (N) L5	契約	けいやく	contract
kekkan (N) L26	血管	けっかん	artery, vein
kekkon (sV) L16, 24	結婚	けっこん	to marry
ketsu (N) L26	ケツ	けつ	bottom (vulg.)
ki (N) L3,13	木	き	tree
ki o tsukete (Ph) L4,15	気をつけて	きをつけて	take care
kihon (N) L4	基本	きほん	basis, basic
kiiroi (iAdj.) L13	黄色い	きいろい	yellow
kiken-na (naAdj.) L14	危険な	きけんな	dangerous
kikōgun (N) L5	機甲軍	きこうぐん	armored division
kiku (V) L30	聞く	きく	to hear
kimi (PN) L7	君	きみ	you (sing.)
kimira (PN) L7	君ら	きみら	you (plural)
kimitachi (PN) L7	君達	きみたち	you (plural)
kimochiwarui (iAdj.) L23	気持ち悪い	きもちわるい	unpleasant
kinō (Adv.) L11, 22	昨日	きのう	yesterday
kinyōbi (N) L6	金曜日	きんようび	Friday
kirai-na (naAdj.) L14	嫌いな	きらいな	to dislike
kirakira (Adv.) L29	きらきら	きらきら	to glitter, dazzle
kirei-na (naAdj.) L14, 22	きれいな	きれいな	pretty, clean
kiri (N) L10	霧	きり	fog
kisama (PN) L7	貴様	きさま	you (threatening)
kisetsu (N) L10	季節	きせつ	season
kishokuwarui (iAdj.) L23	気色悪い	きしょくわるい	unpleasant
kiso (N) L9	基礎	きそ	basic
kissaten (N) L2	喫茶店	きっさてん	coffee shop
kita (N) L4	北	きた	north
kitte (N) L11	切手	きって	stamp
kitto (Adv.) L22	きっと	きっと	certainly
-ko (C) L25	個	こ	counter for small things
ko (N) L4	子	こ	child
kōbe (T) L10	神戸	こうべ	Kobe
kōchi (N) L9	コーチ	こーち	coach
kodomo (N) L25	子供	こども	child
kōhai (N) L15	後輩	こうはい	junior
kōhii (N) L11	コーヒー	こーひー	coffee
koitsu (PN) L7	こいつ	こいつ	this guy
koko (PN) L9	ここ	ここ	here
kokonotsu (N) L25	九つ	ここのつ	nine
kokoro (N) L26	心	こころ	soul, mind, spirit, essence
kokuban (N) L16	黒板	こくばん	blackboard
konban wa (Ph) L2,4,27	こんばんは	こんばんは	good evening
kondo (Adv.) L17	今度	こんど	next time
konnichi wa (Ph) L2,4,27	こんにちは	こんにちは	good day
kono (PN) L3	この	この	this
konpyūtaa (N) L2,23	コンピューター	こんぴゅーたー	computer
koppu (N) L18	コップ	こっぷ	glass
kore (PN) L4,9	これ	これ	this
korobu (V) L24	転ぶ	ころぶ	to fall
korosu (V) L11,28	殺す	ころす	to kill, murder
koto (PN) L9	事	こと	thing
kotoshi (Adv.) L27	今年	ことし	this year
kowai (iAdj.) L13	怖い	こわい	to be afraid
kowasu (V) L17	壊す	こわす	to break

単語集

koyubi (N) L26	小指	こゆび	little finger
kōza (N) L30	講座	こうざ	course
ku (Nu) L3	九	く	9
kubi (N) L26	首	くび	neck
kuchi (N) L4,26	口	くち	mouth
kuchihige (N) L26	口ひげ	くちひげ	moustache
kudamono-ya (N) L15	果物屋	くだものや	fruit shop
-kudasai (G) L24,25	下さい	ください	"please"
kugatsu (N) L6	九月	くがつ	September
kuma (N) L18	熊	くま	bear
kumo (N) L10	雲	くも	cloud
kumo (N) L18	クモ	くも	spider
kumori (N) L10	曇り	くもり	cloudy
-kun (Ph) L3,15	君	くん	suffix for young men
kun'yomi (N) L3	訓読み	くんよみ	Japanese reading for kanji
kurai (iAdj.) L13	暗い	くらい	dark
kurakku (N) L8	クラック	くらっく	crack
-kure (G) L28	くれ	くれ	"imperative"
kureru (V) L15,28	くれる	くれる	to receive
kuroi (iAdj.) L13	黒い	くろい	black
kuru (V) L16, 19, 20	来る	くる	to come
kuruma (N) L11,25,28	車	くるま	car
kurushii (iAdj.) L23	苦しい	くるしい	painful
kuso (N) L2, 23	糞	くそ	shit
kusokurae (Ph) L23	糞食らえ	くそくらえ	go to hell
kūso-na (naAdj.) L2	空疎	くうそ	empty, unsubstantial
kusottare (N) L23	くそったれ	くそったれ	swine, son of a bitch
kusuriyubi (N) L26	薬指	くすりゆび	ring finger
kutakuta (Adv.) L29	くたくた	くたくた	to be exhausted
kutsu-ya (N) L15	靴屋	くつや	shoe shop
kuzu (N) L23	屑	くず	rubbish, scum
kyō (Adv.) L11,22	今日	きょう	today
kyōshitsu (N) L11	教室	きょうしつ	classroom
kyōto (T) L10	京都	きょうと	Kyoto
kyū (Nu) L3	九	きゅう	9
kyūshū (T) L10	九州	きゅうしゅう	Kyushu

M

mada (Adv.) L22	未だ	まだ	(not) yet, still
made (G) L8	まで	まで	until
mae (Adv.) L12	前	まえ	in front of
mago (N) L21	孫	まご	grandchild
-mai (C) L11,25	枚	まい	counter for flat things
makeru (V) L19	負ける	まける	to lose
mama (N) L21	ママ	まま	mummy
man (Nu) L3	万	まん	10,000
manga (N) L9	漫画	まんが	manga, comic
manuke (N) L23	間抜け	まぬけ	stupid, fool
masaka (Ph) L16	まさか	まさか	Oh, no!
massaaji (N) L2	マッサージ	まっさーじ	massage
mata (Adv.) L4,23	また	また	later / again
mata ne (Ph) L4, 27	またね	またね	see you later
matsu (V) L15, 19, 20	待つ	まつ	to wait
matsuge (N) L26	まつげ	まつげ	eyelashes
mattaku (Adv.) L22	まったく	まったく	totally
mayuge (N) L26	眉毛	まゆげ	eyebrows
me (N) L4,26	目	め	eye
mechakucha (Adv.) L29	めちゃくちゃ	めちゃくちゃ	to be a mess
megami (N) L7	女神	めがみ	goddess

megane (N) L18	眼鏡	めがね	glasses
mei (N) L21	めい	めい	niece
meigosan (N) L21	めいごさん	めいごさん	niece
meiji (T) L6	明治	めいじ	Meiji Era (1868-1912)
meishi (N) L7,11	名詞	めいし	noun
meshi (N) L27	飯	めし	meal (inf.)
mesu (N) L11	雌	めす	female
metcha (Adv.) L17	めっちゃ	めっちゃ	very (inf.)
michi (N) L14,25	道	みち	road, way
michi (N) L22	未知	みち	unknown
migi (N) L4	右	みぎ	right
mimi (N) L4,26	耳	みみ	ear
minami (N) L4	南	みなみ	south
minna (N) L3,18	皆	みんな	all, everybody
miru (V) L24	見る	みる	to see, look
mitsukai (N) L11	御使い	みつかい	use
mittsu (Nu) L25	三つ	みっつ	three
mizu (N) L3,16	水	みず	water
mō (Adv.) L16,22	もう	もう	already
mo (G) L26	も	も	too
mokuhyō (N) L8	目標	もくひょう	aim
mokuyōbi (N) L6	木曜日	もくようび	Thursday
momiji (N) L10	紅葉	もみじ	autumn leaves
momo (N) L16,25	桃	もも	peach
morau (V) L28	もらう	もらう	to receive
mōshiwake nai (Ph) L27	申し訳ない	もうしわけない	excuse me (formal)
mōsu (V) L7	申す	もうす	to be called, to say
motto (Adv.) L22	もっと	もっと	more
mune (N) L26	胸	むね	breast
mushiatsui (iAdj.) L10	蒸し暑い	むしあつい	sultry
musuko (N) L21	息子	むすこ	son
musukosan (N) L21	息子さん	むすこさん	son
musume (N) L21	娘	むすめ	daughter
musumesan (N) L21	娘さん	むすめさん	daughter
muttsu (N) L25	六つ	むっつ	six
muzukashii (iAdj.) L13,22	難しい	むずかしい	difficult

N

nagoya (T) L10	名古屋	なごや	Nagoya
naka (N) L8,16	中	なか	center, inside
nakayubi (N) L26	中指	なかゆび	middle finger
namae (N) L4	名前	なまえ	name
namida (N) L11	涙	なみだ	tear
nana (Nu) L3	七	なな	7
nanatsu (Nu) L25	七つ	ななつ	seven
nani (IP) L3,8,22	何	なに	what?
nanimo (Adv.) L19	何も	なにも	nothing
nara (G) L16	なら	なら	(conditional)
naru (V) L7,28	なる	なる	to become
-nasai (G) L30	なさい	なさい	"gentle" imperative
natsu (N) L4	夏	なつ	summer
naze (IP) L7,25	何故	なぜ	why?
neko (N) L9	猫	ねこ	cat
nerai (N) L21	狙い	ねらい	target, to aim
nerau (V) L25	狙う	ならう	to aim, to go for
neru (V) L24	寝る	ねる	to sleep
ni (Nu) L3	二	に	2
nichi (N) L3	日	にち	day
nichiyōbi (N) L6	日曜日	にちようび	Sunday

nigatsu (N) L6	二月	にがつ	February
nigeba (N) L18	逃げ場	にげば	means of escape
nihon, nippon (T) L3	日本	にほん、にっぽん	Japan
nihongo (N) L3,17	日本語	にほんご	Japanese language
niku (N) L11,13	肉	にく	meat
niku-ya (N) L15	肉屋	にくや	butcher
-nin (C) L11,25	人	にん	counter for people
nioi (N) L8	臭い	におい	smell
niru (V) L18	似る	にる	to resemble
nishi (N) L4	西	にし	west
niwa (N) L11	庭	にわ	garden
nō (N) L26	脳	のう	brain
nodo (N) L26	のど	のど	throat
nodo ga karakara (Ph) L27	のどがカラカラ	のどがからから	to be thirsty (inf.)
nodo ga kawaita (Ph) L27	のどが渇いた	のどがかわいた	to be thirsty
nokonoko (Adv.) L29	のこのこ	のこのこ	brazenly
nokoru (V) L24	残る	のこる	to remain, to be left
nomu (V) L19, 20	飲む	のむ	to drink
noru (V) L30	乗る	のる	to ride
nuku (V) L22	抜く	ぬく	to outpass, to get ahead of
nyannyan (Adv.) L29	にゃんにゃん	にゃんにゃん	meow
nyūyōku (T) L2	ニューヨーク	にゅーよーく	New York

O

ō (N) L3	王	おう	king
oba (N) L21	おば	おば	aunt
obaasan (N) L21	お祖母さん	おばあさん	grandmother
obasan (N) L21	おばさん	おばさん	aunt
obentō-ya (N) L15	お弁当屋	おべんとうや	bentō store
ocha (N) L16	お茶	おちゃ	tea
ocha-ya (N) L15	お茶屋	おちゃや	tea shop
o-daiji ni (Ph) L17,27	お大事に	おだいじに	get well soon
ofukuro (N) L21	お袋	おふくろ	mother (masc. inf.)
ofuro (N) L10	お風呂	おふろ	bath
o-genki desu ka (Ph) L4,27	お元気ですか	おげんきですか	how are you?
ohayō gozaimasu (Ph) L2,4	おはようございます	おはようございます	good morning
o-hisashiburi desu (Ph)L27	お久しぶりです	おひさしぶりです	it's been a long time
oishii (iAdj.) L13	美味しい	おいしい	delicious
o-jama shimashita (Ph)L27	お邪魔しました	おじゃましました	sorry for the trouble
o-jama shimasu (Ph) L27	お邪魔します	おじゃまします	May I come in?
oji (N) L21	おじ	おじ	uncle
ōji (N) L4	王子	おうじ	prince
ojiisan (N) L21	お祖父さん	おじいさん	grandfather
ojisan (N) L21	おじさん	おじさん	uncle
okaasan (N) L21	お母さん	おかあさん	mother
o-kaeri nasai (Ph) L27	お帰りなさい	おかえりなさい	welcome
okane (N) L9	お金	おかね	money
okashi (N) L11	お菓子	おかし	sweet
okashii (iAdj.) L13	おかしい	おかしい	strange
okashi-ya (N) L15	お菓子屋	おかしや	bakery
o-ki o tsukete (Ph) L9	お気をつけて	おきをつけて	take care
okinawa (T) L10	沖縄	おきなわ	Okinawa
okiru (V) L19, 20	起きる	おきる	to wake up
okosan (N) L21	お子さん	おこさん	son / daughter
oku (V) L22	置く	おく	to leave, to put
okusan (N) L21	奥さん	おくさん	wife
o-kyaku-sama (N) L15	お客様	おきゃくさま	Mr. client
omae (PN) L7	お前	おまえ	you (sing. masc. inf.)
omaera (PN) L7	お前ら	おまえら	you (plural, masc. inf.)

omaetachi (PN) L7	お前達	おまえたち	you (plural, masc. inf.)
omagosan (N) L21	お孫さん	おまごさん	grandchild (form.)
o-matase shimashita (Ph)27	お待たせしました	おまたせしました	Sorry I kept you waiting
omedetō gozaimasu (Ph) L4	おめでとうございます	おめでとうございます	congratulations
omoi (iAdj.) L13	重い	おもい	heavy
omoshiroi (iAdj.) L3,13	面白い	おもしろい	interesting, amusing
omou (V) L13	思う	おもう	to think
onaka (N) L26	お腹	おなか	stomach
onaka ga peko peko (Ph)L27	お腹がペコペコ	おなかがぺこぺこ	I'm hungry (childish)
onaka ga suita (Ph) L27	お腹がすいた	おなかがすいた	I'm hungry
ondo (N) L10	温度	おんど	temperature
oneesan (N) L21	お姉さん	おねえさん	elder sister / girl
o-negai shimasu (Ph) L4	お願いします	おねがいします	please
oniisan (N) L21	お兄さん	おにいさん	elder brother
onna (N) L3	女	おんな	woman
on'yomi (N) L3	音読み	おんよみ	Chinese reading for kanji
ookii (iAdj.) L13, 22	大きい	おおきい	big
oppai (N) L26	オッパイ	おっぱい	boobs, breast (vulg.)
oranda (N) L8	オランダ	おらんだ	Holland
ore (PN) L7	俺	おれ	I (masc. inf.)
oretachi (PN) L7	俺達	おれたち	we (masc. inf.)
oriru (V) L30	下りる	おりる	to descend
ōsaka (T) L10	大阪	おおさか	Osaka
o-sake (N) L22	お酒	おさけ	sake / liquor
oshieru (V) L19, 20	教える	おしえる	to teach
o-shiri (N) L26	お尻	おしり	bottom
o-shishō-sama (N) L19	お師匠様	おししょうさま	Mr. teacher
osoraku (Adv.) L11	おそらく	おそらく	perhaps
osu (N) L11	雄	おす	male
o-sushi (N) L17	お寿司	おすし	sushi
otoko (N) L3,18	男	おとこ	man
otōsan (N) L3,21	お父さん	おとうさん	father
otōto (N) L21	弟	おとうと	younger brother
otōtosan (N) L21	弟さん	おとうとさん	younger brother
o-tsukare sama (Ph) L27	お疲れ様	おつかれさま	good job
otto (N) L21	夫	おっと	husband
owaru (V) L25	終わる	おわる	to finish, end
oyaji (N) L21	親父	おやじ	father (masc.)
o-yasumi nasai (Ph) L4,27	お休みなさい	おやすみなさい	good night
oyayubi (N) L26	親指	おやゆび	thumb

P

paatii (N) L11	パーティー	ぱーてぃー	party
pakupaku (Adv.) L29	ぱくぱく	ぱくぱく	(to eat) with relish
pan (N) L2,11, 19	パン	ぱん	bread
papa (N) L21	パパ	ぱぱ	daddy
pechapai (N) L28	ペチャパイ	ぺちゃぱい	flat breasts
pekopeko (Adv.) L29	ぺこぺこ	ぺこぺこ	to be hungry
pen (N) L16	ペン	ぺん	ballpoint pen
perapera (Adv.) L29	ぺらぺら	ぺらぺら	(to talk) fluently
pikapika (Adv.) L29	ぴかぴか	ぴかぴか	to shine, glitter
poketto (N) L8	ポケット	ぽけっと	pocket
puretaporute (N) L2	プレタポルテ	ぷれたぽるて	prêt-à-porter

R

raamen-ya (N) L15	ラーメン屋	らーめんや	*ramen* shop
raketto (N) L2	ラケット	らけっと	racket
remon (N) L9	レモン	れもん	lemon
renzu (N) L8	レンズ	れんず	lens
resutoran (N) L11	レストラン	れすとらん	restaurant

ringo (N) L9,16,24,25	りんご	りんご	apple
roku (Nu) L3	六	ろく	6
rokugatsu (N) L6	六月	ろくがつ	June
rōmaji (N) L1	ローマ字	ろーまじ	Western characters
ryōri (N) L22	料理	りょうり	food, cuisine
S			
saabisu (N) L8	サービス	さーびす	service
sachū (N) L26	左中	さちゅう	center-left part
saifu (N) L18	財布	さいふ	wallet
saisho (Adv.) L10	最初	さいしょ	the first
sakana (N) L11	魚	さかな	fish
sakana-ya (N) L15	魚屋	さかなや	fish shop
saka-ya (N) L15	酒屋	さかや	sake store
sake (N) L11,22	酒	さけ	sake / liquor
sakura (N) L10,18	桜	さくら	cherry tree
-sama (Ph) L3,15	様	さま	suffix for names
same (N) L18	サメ	さめ	shark
samui (iAdj.) L10	寒い	さむい	cold
-san (Ph) L15	さん	さん	suffix for names
san (Nu) L3	三	さん	3
sangatsu (N) L6	三月	さんがつ	March
sapporo (T) L10	札幌	さっぽろ	Sapporo
sasu (V) L12	指す	さす	to point, mark
satō (N) L25	砂糖	さとう	sugar
-satsu (C) L11,25	冊	さつ	counter for books
sawaru (V) L28	触る	さわる	to touch
sayōnara (Ph) L2,27	さようなら	さようなら	good bye
seikazoku kyōkai (Ph) L17	聖家族教会	せいかぞくきょうかい	The Sagrada Familia
seishoku kikan (N) L26	生殖器官	せいしょくきかん	reproductive organs
seito (N) L28	生徒	せいと	pupil
sekai (N) L12	世界	せかい	world
sekkyoku (N) L22	積極	せっきょく	positive
sekkyokuteki (Adv.) L22	積極的	せっきょくてき	positively
sen (Nu) L3,17	千	せん	1,000
senaka (N) L26	背中	せなか	back
senpai (N) L15	先輩	せんぱい	senior
sensei (N) L4,15	先生	せんせい	teacher
sentaa (sV) L8	センター	せんたー	to center
shachō (N) L15	社長	しゃちょう	boss
shashin (N) L9	写真	しゃしん	photograph
shi (Nu) L3	四	し	4
shibashiba (Adv.) L22	しばしば	しばしば	often
shichi (Nu) L3	七	しち	7
shichigatsu (N) L6	七月	しちがつ	July
shigatsu (N) L6	四月	しがつ	April
shigoto (N) L9	仕事	しごと	job
shiken (N) L14,22	試験	しけん	exam
shikkari (Adv.) L29	しっかり	しっかり	decidedly, firmly
shikoku (T) L10	四国	しこく	Shikoku
shikushiku (Adv.) L29	しくしく	しくしく	(to cry) silently
shinbun (N) L3,11	新聞	しんぶん	newspaper
shinjirarenai (Ph) L23	信じられない	しんじられない	I can't believe it
shinsetsu-na (naAdj.) L14	親切な	しんせつな	kind
shinu (V) L3,17,19,20	死ぬ	しぬ	to die
shinzō (N) L11,26	心臓	しんぞう	heart
shiriizu (N) L6	シリーズ	しりーず	series
shiroi (iAdj.) L13	白い	しろい	white
shiru (V) L19	知る	しる	to know

shita (N) L26	舌	した	tongue
shita (N) L4	下	した	underneath
shita ni (Adv.) L22	下に	したに	under
shitsumon (sV) L24	質問	しつもん	to ask
shitsurei shimasu (Ph) L27	失礼します	しつれいします	excuse me
shizumaru (V) L10	静まる	しずまる	to calm down
shizuka-na (naAdj.) L14	静かな	しずかな	quiet
shōko (N) L24	証拠	しょうこ	proof
shōnō (N) L26	小脳	しょうのう	cerebellum
shorui (N) L28	書類	しょるい	document
shōsetsu (N) L28	小説	しょうせつ	novel
shōwa (T) L6	昭和	しょうわ	Shōwa Era (1926-1989)
shujin (N) L21	主人	しゅじん	husband
shūjoshi (N) L17	終助詞	しゅうじょし	end-of-sentence particle
shuppatsu (sV) L2	出発	しゅっぱつ	to leave
shuriken (N) L16	手裏剣	しゅりけん	shuriken, ninja weapon
sō desu (Ph) L2	そうです	そうです	that's right
soba ni (Adv.) L22	側に	そばに	beside
sobo (N) L21	祖母	そぼ	grandmother
sofu (N) L21	祖父	そふ	grandfather
soko (PN) L9	そこ	そこ	there
sono (PN) L3	その	その	that
sora (N) L13	空	そら	sky
sore (PN) L9	それ	それ	that
sōri daijin (N) L9	総理大臣	そうりだいじん	Prime Minister
sorou (V) L10	揃う	そろう	to gather
soshite (G) L19,25	そして	そして	then
sugi (Adv.) L12	過ぎ	すぎ	to pass
sugoi (iAdj.) L22	凄い	すごい	fantastic, great
suika (N) L18	すいか	すいか	watermelon
suiyōbi (N) L6	水曜日	すいようび	Wednesday
sūji (N) L5	数字	すうじ	numeral
suki-na (naAdj.) L14	好きな	すきな	to like
sukkiri (Adv.) L29	すっきり	すっきり	refreshed, relieved
sukoshi (Adv.) L22	少し	すこし	a little
sumimasen (Ph) L2,12,27	すみません	すみません	sorry, excuse me
supagetti (N) L8	スパゲッティ	すぱげってぃ	spaghetti
sūpu (N) L11	スープ	すーぷ	soup
surippa (N) L8	スリッパ	すりっぱ	slipper
suru (V) L8, 19, 20	する	する	to do
sushi-ya (N) L15	寿司屋	すしや	sushi shop
sutajiamu (N) L8	スタジアム	すたじあむ	stadium
suu (V) L7	吸う	すう	to smoke
suwaru (V) L24,30	座る	すわる	to sit
suzu (N) L18	鈴	すず	bell
suzushii (iAdj.) L10	涼しい	すずしい	cool

T

ta (N) L3	田	た	rice field
tabako (N) L7,11	たばこ	たばこ	tobacco
taberu (V) L10,16, 19	食べる	たべる	to eat
tada (Adv.) L28	ただ	ただ	only
tadaima (Ph) L27	ただいま	ただいま	I'm home
tadashii (iAdj.) L9	正しい	ただしい	correct, right
tai (T) L17	タイ	たい	Thailand
taifū (N) L10	台風	たいふう	typhoon
taihen (Adv.) L22	大変	たいへん	very
taihen-na (naAdj.) L14	大変な	たいへんな	difficult, complicated
taimu rimitto (N) L12	タイムリミット	たいむりみっと	time limit

taisetsu-na (naAdj.) L14	大切な	たいせつな	important
taishō (T) L6	大正	たいしょう	Taishō Era (1912-1926)
takai (iAdj.) L13	高い	たかい	expensive / high
tako (N) L23	タコ	たこ	pervert / octopus
takusan (Adv.) L22	沢山	たくさん	much, many
tama (N) L3	玉	たま	ball, sphere
-tamae (G) L30	たまえ	たまえ	–tamae imperative
tane (N) L16	種	たね	seed
tataku (V) L22	叩く	たたく	to hit
tatami (N) L25	畳	たたみ	tatami
tatemono (N) L11	建物	たてもの	building
te (N) L4,8,25,26	手	て	hand, arm
teeburu (N) L9, 22	テーブル	てーぶる	table
tegami (N) L11	手紙	てがみ	letter
teikoku (N) L5	帝国	ていこく	empire
teki (N) L22	敵	てき	enemy
-teki ni (G) L22	的に	てきに	suffix to form adv.
tekubi (N) L26	手首	てくび	wrist
temee (PN) L7	てめえ	てめえ	you (threatening)
tenohira (N) L26	手の平	てのひら	palm
terebi (N) L9,22	テレビ	てれび	television
tobu (V) L24	飛ぶ	とぶ	to fly
toire (N) L11	トイレ	といれ	toilet
tokidoki (Adv.) L22	時々	ときどき	sometimes
tōkyō (T) L6	東京	とうきょう	Tokyo
too (Nu) L25	十	とお	ten
tora (N) L18	虎	とら	tiger
tori (N) L9	鳥	とり	bird
toshi (N) L10	年	とし	year
toshokan (N) L16	図書館	としょかん	library
tōzoku (N) L24	盗賊	とうぞく	thief
-tsu (C) L25	つ	つ	universal counter
tsuaa (N) L8	ツアー	つあー	tour
tsuchi (N) L3	土	つち	earth
tsukareru (V) L17	疲れる	つかれる	to be tired
tsukeru (V) L21	付ける	つける	to put
tsuki (N) L3,10	月	つき	moon
tsukue (N) L18	机	つくえ	desk
tsuma (N) L21	妻	つま	wife
tsume (N) L26	爪	つめ	nail
tsuyoi (iAdj.) L22,26	強い	つよい	strong
tsuyu (N) L10	梅雨	つゆ	wet season

U

uchi (N) L11,17	家	うち	house
uchū (N) L3	宇宙	うちゅう	space
ude (N) L26	腕	うで	arm
udon-ya (N) L15	うどん屋	うどんや	udon noodle shop
ue (N) L4	上	うえ	above
ue ni (Adv.) L22	上に	うえに	above
ugoku (V) L24,25	動く	うごく	to move
ukeru (V) L12	受ける	うける	to receive
uketoru (V) L5	受け取る	うけとる	to accept
unten (sV) L24	運転	うんてん	to drive
urusai (iAdj.) L23	うるさい	うるさい	noisy
urusai (Ph) L23	うるさい	うるさい	shut up
ushiro ni (Adv.) l22	後ろに	うしろに	behind
uta (N) L9,11,17	歌	うた	song

utau (V) L17	歌う	うたう	to sing
utsukushii (iAdj.) L13	美しい	うつくしい	beautiful
uun (Ph) L10	ううん	ううん	no

w

wain (N) L28	ワイン	わいん	wine
wakareru (V) L7	別れる	わかれる	to separate, to cut
wakarimasen (Ph) L2	わかりません	わかりません	I don't understand
wakaru (V) L19	分かる	わかる	to be nervous, excited
wakuwaku (Adv.) L29	わくわく	わくわく	to be nervous, excited
wanwan (Adv.) L29	わんわん	わんわん	bow-wow
warau (V) L24	笑う	わらう	to laugh
warui (iAdj.) L13	悪い	わるい	bad
washi (PN) L1	わし	わし	I (elder men)
watakushi (PN) L7	私	わたくし	I (very formal)
watakushidomo (PN) L7	私ども	わたくしども	we (very formal)
watakushitachi (PN) L7	私達	わたくしたち	we (formal)
watashi (PN) L4	私	わたし	I
watashitachi (PN) L7	私達	わたしたち	we

Y

yama (N) L3	山	やま	mountain
yaoya (N) L15	八百屋	やおや	greengrocer
yaru (V) L12	やる	やる	to do
yasashii (iAdj.) L13,17,28	易しい	やさしい	easy
yasui (iAdj.) L13	安い	やすい	cheap
yasumi (N) L11	休み	やすみ	break
yatsu (N) L11	奴	やつ	guy
yatta (Ph) L4	やった	やった	Yes! I made it!
yattsu (Nu) L25	八つ	やっつ	eight
yōbi (N) L6	曜日	ようび	day of the week
yobu (V) L15	呼ぶ	よぶ	to call
yokan (N) L14	予感	よかん	premonition
yokohama (T) L10	横浜	よこはま	Yokohama
yoku (Adv.) L3, 22	良く	よく	much, well, often
yomu (V) L3	読む	よむ	to read
yon (Nu) L3	四	よん	4
yononaka (N) L9	世の中	よのなか	in the world
yori (G) L1	より	より	more than
yorokonde (Adv.) L22	喜んで	よろこんで	gladly
yoroshiku onegai shimasu (Ph) L27	宜しくお願いします	よろしくおねがいします	please/pleased to meet you
yoru (N) L11	夜	よる	night
yottsu (Nu) L25	四つ	よっつ	four
you (V) L20	酔う	よう	to feel dizzy
yubi (N) L26	指	ゆび	finger
yubisaki (N) L26	指先	ゆびさき	fingertip
yūgata (N) L11	夕方	ゆうがた	evening
yuki (N) L10	雪	ゆき	snow
yukkuri (Adv.) L22	ゆっくり	ゆっくり	slowly
yūmei-na (naAdj.) L14	有名な	ゆうめいな	famous

z

zannen-na (naAdj.) L14	残念な	ざんねんな	what a pity
zasshi (N) L11	雑誌	ざっし	magazine
zenbu (Adv.) L28	全部	ぜんぶ	all
zenpen (N) L29	前編	ぜんぺん	first part
zunō (N) L26	頭脳	ずのう	brain
zutsu (G) L25	ずつ	ずつ	one each

N: Noun
PN: Pronoun
G: Word with a grammatical function
naAdj.: "na" adjective
Ph: Phrase
sV: *suru* Verb. Noun which becomes a verb when adding *suru*
T: Toponym
iAdj.: "i" adjective
V: Verb
IP: Interrogative pronoun
C: Counter
Nu: Number
Inf.: Infinitive
Vulg: Vulgarism
Masc.: Masculine
Fem.: Feminine

Acknowledgements

This section is devoted to all those who have made this project possible. Thank you very much!

Special thanks go to:

My publishers, Japan Publications Trading, Co., Ltd. (Japan / USA) and Norma Editorial (Spain), for believing in this project and giving it an opportunity in the competitive publishing world.

Thanks to:

Albert Torres i Graell / Àngel Ferrer / Hiromi Komeyoshi / Ignasi Riera / James W. Heisig / Mary Molina / Minoru Shiraishi / Nacho Carmona / Olinda Cordukes / Osamu Kamada / Óscar Valiente / Shigeko Suzuki / Yasuyuki Takahashi / Yunosuke Murakami / To everybody who wrote to me all through this time, offering help, suggestions, and, above all, much support: thanks!

Thank you to dreamers.com for kindly lodging my web pages in their server:
www.dreamers.com

Nipoweb, page on Japanese language and culture, it is this book's "mother page." Here you can find many projects related to Japan and to "Japanese in MangaLand." (mainly in Spanish, though)
www.nipoweb.com/eng

Index